Consuming Anxieties

TRANSITS
LITERATURE, THOUGHT & CULTURE, 1650–1850

Series editors:
Miriam Wallace, New College of Florida
Mona Narain, Texas Christian University

A landmark series in long-eighteenth-century studies, *Transits* publishes monographs and edited volumes that are timely, transformative in their approach, and global in their engagement with arts, literature, culture, and history. Books in the series have engaged with visual arts, environment, politics, material culture, travel, theater and performance, embodiment, connections between the natural sciences and medical humanities, writing and book history, sexuality, gender, disability, race, and colonialism from Britain and Europe to the Americas, the Far East, the Middle/Near East, Africa, and Oceania. Works that make provocative connections across time, space, geography, or intellectual history, or that develop new modes of critical imagining are particularly welcome.

Recent titles in the series:

Consuming Anxieties: Alcohol, Tobacco, and Trade in British Satire, 1660–1751
Dayne C. Riley

The Part and the Whole in Early American Literature, Print Culture, and Art
Matthew Pethers and Daniel Diez Couch, eds.

Teaching the Eighteenth Century Now: Pedagogy as Ethical Engagement
Kate Parker and Miriam L. Wallace, eds.

Women and Music in the Age of Austen
Linda Zionkowski with Miriam F. Hart, eds.

Louis Sébastien Mercier: Revolution and Reform in Eighteenth-Century Paris
Michael J. Mulryan

Alimentary Orientalism: Britain's Literary Imagination and the Edible East
Yin Yuan

Thomas Holcroft's Revolutionary Drama: Reception and Afterlives
Amy Garnai

Families of the Heart: Surrogate Relations in the Eighteenth-Century British Novel
Ann Campbell

For more information about the series, please visit www.bucknelluniversitypress.org.

Consuming Anxieties

ALCOHOL,
TOBACCO,
AND TRADE
IN BRITISH SATIRE,
1660–1751

DAYNE C. RILEY

LEWISBURG, PENNSYLVANIA

Library of Congress Cataloging-in-Publication Data

Names: Riley, Dayne C., author.
Title: Consuming anxieties : alcohol, tobacco, and trade in British satire, 1660–1751 / Dayne C. Riley.
Description: Lewisburg, Pennsylvania : Bucknell University Press, 2024. | Series: Transits: literature, thought & culture, 1650–1850 | Includes bibliographical references and index.
Identifiers: LCCN 2023047876 | ISBN 9781684485314 (paperback) | ISBN 9781684485321 (hardcover) | ISBN 9781684485338 (epub) | ISBN 9781684485345 (pdf)
Subjects: LCSH: English literature—17th century—History and criticism. | English literature—18th century—History and criticism. | Drinking of alcoholic beverages in literature. | Tobacco in literature. | Satire, English—History and criticism. | Literature and society—Great Britain—History—17th century. | Literature and society—Great Britain—History—18th century. | National characteristics, British, in literature. | LCGFT: Literary criticism.
Classification: LCC PR438.D75 R55 2024 | DDC 820.9/3564—dc23/eng/20240202
LC record available at https://lccn.loc.gov/2023047876

A British Cataloging-in-Publication record for this book is available from the British Library.

Copyright © 2024 by Dayne C. Riley

All rights reserved

No part of this book may be reproduced or utilized in any form or by any means, electronic or mechanical, or by any information storage and retrieval system, without written permission from the publisher. Please contact Bucknell University Press, Hildreth-Mirza Hall, Bucknell University, Lewisburg, PA 17837–2005. The only exception to this prohibition is "fair use" as defined by U.S. copyright law.

References to internet websites (URLs) were accurate at the time of writing. Neither the author nor Bucknell University Press is responsible for URLs that may have expired or changed since the manuscript was prepared.

♾ The paper used in this publication meets the requirements of the American National Standard for Information Sciences—Permanence of Paper for Printed Library Materials, ANSI Z39.48-1992.

bucknelluniversitypress.org

Distributed worldwide by Rutgers University Press

For Lori and the dogs

CONTENTS

List of Illustrations ix

Introduction 1

1 "The Vice of the Time": Wine, Libertinism, and Commerce in the Age of Charles II 12

2 Bottling Up Your Anger: Alehouse and Tavern Satire in Stuart England 36

3 Sot-Weed or Indian Weed? Pipe Tobacco and Satire, 1689–1709 65

4 "The Ceremony of the Snuff-Box": Snuff in British Satirical Essays and Poems, 1709–1732 109

5 English Satirical Writing in the Age of Mother Gin, 1723–1751 137

Epilogue: The Smoke of War and the Imperial Thirst 177

Acknowledgments 181

Notes 183

Bibliography 195

Index 203

ILLUSTRATIONS

Figure 3.1 Clay tobacco pipe, London, England, ca. 1640–1670 — 103

Figure 3.2 Clay pipe, late seventeenth century, recovered from a pond at the Rich Neck Plantation site — 104

Figure 4.1 Snuffbox, ca. 1720–1740 — 112

Figure 5.1 William Hogarth, *Beer Street*, 1751 — 171

Figure 5.2 William Hogarth, *Gin Lane*, 1751 — 172

Consuming Anxieties

INTRODUCTION

IN A 1699 PAMPHLET PUBLISHED by the Society for the Reformation of Manners, the anonymous author blames alcohol as a primary cause of England's indecency and degradation. The pamphlet, entitled *An Essay to Suppress Prophaness and Immorality, Pay the Nations Debts, Support the Government, and Maintain the Poor*, notes William III's commitment to combating immoral behavior, but it argues that until the practice of drinking (and at the end of the essay, tobacco smoking) is curbed, England will see no true moral improvement.[1] As the title makes clear, the essay seeks not only to offer a solution to moral issues but also to help England economically, bolster William's rule, and assist the lower class. To deal with these issues, the essayist advises Parliament to make the selling of alcohol prohibitively expensive through heavy taxation, thereby forcing the average English citizen to abstain without imposing more directly restrictive policies on alcohol.

The Society for the Reformation of Manners, a group of closely connected, voluntary organizations bent on stemming licentious behavior, began operating in the first years of William and Mary's reign. While a reader familiar with modern prohibition rhetoric may assume that the Society would oppose any heavy drinking, the organizations actually took a relatively relaxed position on those willing to brew or distill alcohol for their own private consumption: "if any, or all men were Necessitous by their having to drink stronger, Let them Brew and welcome. I am fully perswaded, they will soon be weary of giving their Drink away" (4). While the essayist certainly does not wish to encourage citizens to take up distilling, they are certain that the financial cost of and labor involved in production will deter most people from sharing their drinks with others. They also insist that the Society does not preach complete abstinence, but rather seeks to limit working-class access to intoxicating beverages that lead the average worker to loss of wages and financial ruin. The essay also seeks to counter economic arguments in favor of alcohol production by showing how heavy drinking affects English morality. For instance, the writer acknowledges that the current taxes on alcohol production contribute greatly to the "King's coffers," but also highlights the moral implications of a country grown rich from a practice that leads many families to financial ruin. Alcohol consumption, they argue, is driven by sinful desires. The pamphleteer notes, "if in Drinking nothing but the Appetite was indulged, Men would soon be weary of it. But under the Notion of Conversation, Idle and Profane Talk, Cursing, and Swearing, (which they call Pleasant Company) betrays them into loss of Time, Health, Wealth, Body, and I doubt, too many Souls into the Bargain" (4). Here, the natural desire to fulfill an appetite is connected with various forms of idleness, while the wealth accrued by the alehouse and tavern owners leads to other sinful behavior, pride and luxuriousness.

Although tobacco is only discussed briefly at the end of the essay, the pamphleteer pairs it with alcohol consumption as twin evils. They complain that Europeans "swallowed [the Native American] Custom of Smoking" and "added Drinking thereto," deriding the product for its origins in Indigenous religious rites (5). Writing that the Native peoples "Worship [the Devil] with Fire and Smoak out of their Mouths," the pamphleteer portrays Native American religious practices through a racist, Christian lens, reviling the plant as a savage, idolatrous tool. The writer then concludes the essay with a tale of a Turkish emperor who realizes that his soldiers have become weak. The mufti, the emperor's trusted advisor, attributes their physical change to tobacco consumption: "the Souldiers, who used to Eat Rice Bread and other wholesome Food, had of late lived upon fire and smoak, which could not long Nourish, but consume Nature" (5). The emperor outlaws tobacco in the camp, and when an adventurous merchant, who is described as "more Covetous than honest," attempts to smuggle in and sell tobacco, he is caught and burned at the stake, using his own illegal tobacco as fuel for the fire (6). This violent conclusion to the essay encapsulates its main thesis: English economic expansion must not come at the cost of the country's moral, physical, and spiritual health. For the writer of this pamphlet, alcohol and tobacco reflect the key tension between English financial successes and the country's moral identity.

Writers of the late seventeenth and early eighteenth centuries—a period of vast economic change—recognized the ability of alcohol and tobacco to affect culture and policy, and while these consumable substances seemed to promise a brighter financial future for England, overindulgence posed serious moral problems. Examining satirical texts from 1660–1751, this book evaluates the ways in which British writers exposed and combated their anxieties surrounding the changing nature of Britishness in terms of class distinctions, gender dynamics, and in the case of American tobacco cultivation, ideas of race. For the purposes of this book, I define anxiety as feelings of profound discomfort exhibited by British citizens, and especially satirists, toward their lack of agency and control over the many financial, moral, and social factors at work in alcohol and tobacco consumption.

INTRODUCTION

In their writing, satirists of the era represent material consumption both as the literal imbibing of individual British citizens and as the metaphorical imbibing of the same materials by the nation through domestic commerce and importation. In a century that witnessed both the satire-steeped court of Charles II and the golden age of British satire—the Augustan era (1702–1745) in which so many of the greatest poets and writers were self-described satirists—it may be unsurprising that writers of the satirical persuasion engaged meaningfully with the burgeoning economic world and with two of the primary consumables that fueled its expansion. Satire, however, is a very pragmatic art form, a genre fixated on ridiculing society in a way that pushes people to question their actions and motives even as it recognizes harsh truths. Satirists of the period understood the importance of alcohol and tobacco to British global supremacy, even as they sought to critique trade and its ability to shape the world.

Because writers of this era viewed alcohol and tobacco abuse as irrational—a foolish obsession, a moral weakness, and a sin to which anyone was susceptible—satirists examining these items mocked substance abuse while also paying special attention to the practical and fiscal effects of such behavior. Most of the writers discussed in this book examine alcohol and tobacco in accordance with their ability to drain British wealth. Satirists championed Britain's economic strength on the world stage while also questioning alcohol and tobacco products' ability to impact an individual citizen's private finances.

Those satirists who sought to defend specific forms of alcohol and tobacco as central to British commerce and global trade highlighted the problematic behaviors and moral failings associated with other types of consumable items. These writers oftentimes targeted the politicians, public figures, and pamphleteers making war on the respective writer's product of choice; in these cases, satirists tended to argue that opposition to these goods weakened England, working against the financial (and in some instances physical) health of the nation. Like their ideological opponents, these writers sought to frame the alcohol and tobacco question as one of British agency: Would policy or taxation deprive British citizens of the very items they viewed as necessities?

The moral and practical problems these satirists raised were largely due to the developing consumer economy, a key facet of the larger financial, commercial, and social changes occurring during the seventeenth and eighteenth centuries. During this period, international trade became increasingly complex. At the same time, Britain developed more complicated financial systems, such as the sinking fund for reducing the national debt, stock trading and investment, and the Bank of England, and the aristocracy felt its power slowly diminish with the rise of these financial systems. Luxury items and their accompanying customs and excise taxes became more entrenched and crucial contributors to the Crown's revenue, and the government developed its bureaucratic branches like the Excise Office to collect these monies efficiently. The importance of early economic writers, such as Daniel Defoe, Bernard Mandeville, John Graunt, and Henry Fielding, cannot be understated when considering commercial activity's effect on consumable items and on literature. Still primarily working within the confines of mercantilism, the main economic theory in Europe since the Renaissance, these writers oftentimes stretch the limits of this older model of economic thought. While writing prior to Adam Smith's influential free market capitalist treatise, *The Wealth of Nations* (1776), these thinkers present decidedly nontraditional views that, while still rooted in mercantilism, illuminate Europe's path toward capitalism, a system in which continuous consumption is desirable for the financial success of the nation. Tracing the changes from the reign of James I through the administrations of Sir Robert Walpole administration and his successors illuminates how alcohol and tobacco existed within the broader economic trends in Britain, while also showing the reactionary views of satirists who see the problematic nature of overindulgence.

To understand how and why satirists of this period examined alcohol and tobacco so closely, it is imperative to recognize the differences in early modern views of overindulgence. While writers of the seventeenth and eighteenth centuries recognized the ability of alcohol and tobacco to affect the body and behavior, the culture in which they lived still understood most health issues from a Galenic perspective. Discussing early eighteenth-century views of habitual drinking, Roy Porter writes,

> Eighteenth century medicine still largely subscribed to what Temkin has called the "physiological" theory of disease, a legacy of classical humoralism, viewing disease essentially as "dis-ease," a morbid imbalance in the individual constitution, attributable to inattention to regimen, diet, and the other nonnaturals. Regimen required moderation in food and drink. Within this diagnostic framework, drunkenness was an excess, and was often associated with extremes of the passions. Sickness was its immediate consequence and the vices of excess would in due course assert mastery and become habitual.[2]

As Porter illustrates, overindulgence, a lack of moderation, caused the imbalance of Galenic humors in the body, which could spiral out into long-term, overly passionate behavior. While from a modern perspective, the disease of addiction leads to excess, an early modern view would have been that the initial excess itself led to imbalanced passions and behavior, and, sadly, more substance abuse. These views are especially problematic, given that the seventeenth-century European did not recognize that certain people are more susceptible and vulnerable to addictions, ideas that are just now becoming mainstream in modern society. In this period, an overindulgence in alcohol and tobacco was almost solely a moral matter, and rather than recognizing the nicotine-addicted, the problem drinker, or the alcoholic, they would view these people as being in thrall to immoral behavior, be it gluttony, idleness, lust, and luxurious pride. The Londoner visiting a tavern and becoming appalled at the man at the neighboring table, for example, would have viewed the drunk as sinfully proud of his drinking, and he would have believed that the man was actively choosing to ignore rationality of the mind in favor of bodily, animalistic pleasures. As in the Society pamphlet quoted above, the European smoker is also gluttonous, swallowing and consuming smoke in a greedy, hungry way.

The issue of the moral culpability of the drunkard, however, began to be readdressed in the second half of the eighteenth century. Harry G. Levine, one of the first historians to discuss the roots of the modern concept of the disease model of addiction, argues that this "new view of addiction had to be developed by individuals who were free from certain traditional assumptions about human behavior—who tended to see deviance in general, and drunkenness in particular, as problematic and unnatural."[3] While Levine dates this "discovery of addiction"—the realization that alcoholism and addiction is a disease rather than an active choice—to nineteenth-century America, Roy Porter, Jessica Warner, James Nicholls, and Jonathan White have all argued persuasively that the trend began earlier, developing during and in reaction to the Gin Craze, the period from roughly 1725–1751 during which the middle and upper classes responded with moral panic to the lower orders drinking gin to excess.[4] Porter and Nicholls point to the medical discourse around increased gin consumption as one area around which the disease model of addiction crystalized. Discussing the "medicalization" of alcohol in the eighteenth century as a key sign of this change in thinking, Nicholls writes, "the key features of the modern 'disease model' of addiction were being developed in Britain throughout the eighteenth century, and had become fairly well established by the 1770s. It was these developments that would lay the ground for some of the most critical aspects of the nineteenth-century drink question: debates over the treatment of habitual drunkards, their moral responsibility, and the role of the State in protecting them from their own destructive desires" (59).

Likewise, White argues that it is near the end of the Gin Craze that moral and literary writers began articulating the idea of addiction. According to White, this concept "emerged at midcentury, fulfilling a specific need in British capitalist society. Writers who positively identified themselves with commercial accumulation as a universally improving force and who wished to extend its benefits across humanity, had to explain why so many laboring people in cities preferred the dubious pleasures of compulsive drinking to those of thrifty accumulation and judicious expenditure" (63). As White makes clear, the desire for consumable items and the impact that such desires have on personal finance helped to reshape the discourse of moral culpability regarding those who overindulge.

Up until the Gin Craze, there was a relatively relaxed view of alcohol abuse; while overindulgence was discussed as an ethical issue and a social problem, there were no major movements toward total abstention, even within religiously grounded texts such as the Society pamphlet above. It was not until the nineteenth century that moralists advocated absolute temperance. In pre-Industrial Britain, alcohol abuse was broadly acceptable among the middle and upper classes. Discussing the moral panic of the Gin Craze, Warner notes that "At no time did reformers seek to rid their society of alcohol. And with only a few exceptions, they condoned fairly heavy drinking among the middle and upper classes" (493). Warner continues, noting that what reformers could "not condone was the downward mobility of spirits in the form of gin, in large part because the nation's elite associated the beverage with new and dangerous forms of disinhibition among the capital's poorer population" (493–494). The upper classes especially were bothered by what Warner calls the "disinhibition" of the laborers; the poor should not, the aristocracy believed, be capable of indulging in the drunken behaviors of their betters. For them to do so threatened social chaos.

Because of their inability to conceptualize alcohol and tobacco use through the lens of addiction, seventeenth- and eighteenth-century writers tended to use the discourse of morality to make sense of such behavior. They presented alcoholism as a "species of gluttony," mocking the drinker as animalistic and indulging in irrational thought (*The Politics of Alcohol*, 68). Pipe tobacco and nasal snuff were also associated with gluttony, but as discussed in chapter 3, they were also linked with lust and idleness due in part to racially bigoted associations with tobacco's Native American origins. Due to their perceived luxury status, these products were viewed as proof of vanity and pride. Of course, coffee, chocolate, and tea were also considered luxurious. Tea, for instance, was not only very expensive throughout this period but it necessitated its own paraphernalia; Markman Ellis, Richard Coulton, and Matthew Mauger have pointed out the associations between King Charles II's wife, Catherine of Braganza, and tea, noting that it was popularly believed that Catherine enjoyed both its exotic nature and the substantial and ornate paraphernalia needed to enjoy the beverage.[5] These products were often ridiculed by literary satirists. An obvious example can be found in Alexander Pope's *The Rape of the Lock*, which mocks both tea and coffee not only for their luxurious nature but by connecting their pharmacological effects to unchaste female thought.[6] Relatively new to the English palate, however, tea, coffee, and chocolate were not the chief trade items that late seventeenth- and early eighteenth-century satirists targeted in their writing. Because alcohol and tobacco abuse were closely associated with personal moral weakness, it is unsurprising that these intoxicants were more often ridiculed; alcohol and tobacco, after all, had long been the butt of English satire. However, there is another important dimension to alcohol and tobacco's aptness for satirical attention: the ubiquity of material objects related to their production, distribution, taxation, and consumption in the everyday lives of Britons.

The materiality of alcohol and tobacco had a strong grip on the British psyche. The ways in which they were shipped, the containers in which they were sold, and the vessels in which they were held and consumed were recognizable across the social spectrum. Ale and beer, though seen as part of the diet of the average lower- and middle-class worker, were as much the mug in which they were drunk and the tun in which they were shipped as the beverage itself. Further, given the increasingly large-scale brewing that developed in the late seventeenth century, these traditional beverages were becoming more associated with urban environments, rather than the domestic sphere of ale brewing, and thus associated more closely with commerce. Wine, often criticized during the period due to its (mostly) imported status, was viewed in an even more problematic light as it become increasingly available to the wealthier members of the middle class; indeed, emptied wine bottles spoke to the draining of bourgeois power. Even pipe tobacco, seen as a staple item by the early eighteenth century, was smoked in public spaces in easily broken and replaceable clay pipes; these same pipes were often supplied by the very alehouses and taverns in which it was enjoyed. Likewise, nasal snuff, which exploded in popularity in Britain in the first decade of the eighteenth century, offered the user the opportunity to spend money on expensive imported snuff, as well as highly ornate snuffboxes that could be shown off to those around them, and unlike tea, coffee, and chocolate, snuff and its bodily effects were easily observed by nonusers. To the seventeenth- and eighteenth-century British citizen, then, the consumption of alcohol and tobacco constituted something more than the substance itself; it was also the consumption of the materials enabling its shipping and usage (the objects left behind afterward).

The social rituals with which one engaged when enjoying alcohol and tobacco in a group setting also informed their materiality. While people certainly enjoyed these substances privately, alcohol and tobacco were social lubricants, an aspect of their nature that satirists ridiculed. As with the act of taking meals, the social rituals of drinking, smoking, and snuffing were "signifiers of group culture and identity."[7] Further, the group environment in which alcohol was drunk and tobacco used were spaces in which commerce was a primary backdrop. Not only were taverns, alehouses, and inns business establishments, but they were also the sites in which trade and business were conducted between sips and puffs of smoke. These material and social aspects of alcohol and tobacco, ubiquitous in the daily lives of Britons, offered clear signifiers by which satirists could articulate their anxieties toward luxury and consumerism. Additionally, as Maxine Berg argues, the "material reality" of British goods must not be lost amid the discussion of the burgeoning consumer culture. As Berg points out, the eighteenth century saw expanded global trade that brought a greater access to the "newly discovered luxuries of Asia and the Americas" and created a market for British imitations;[8] indeed, as we shall see with snuff powder, the ability to claim the foreignness of the tobacco product, even falsely, could inflate its value.

The material realities of consumer goods had their impact on cultural tastes as well. Cultural consumption, the ways in which British citizens developed consumerist attitudes toward art, music, and literature, constitutes a significant dimension of this book. For many writers pushing back against the types of alcoholic beverages and tobacco products enjoyed by the lower orders, "high" literary forms seemed to offer satirists the ability to bar their targets from the conversation. As Ann Bermingham argues, emulation—the consumerist impulse to surpass others in knowledge of culture or in ownership of cultural artifacts—is not a "top-down model" by which the aristocracy creates the culture, which then trickles down to those below;[9] citing examples such as the impact of milkmaid's milking bonnets on upper-class French straw *bergère* hats, Bermingham argues that many "cultural forms seem to flow in the reverse direction," moving from the lower orders to the elite (12). As Bermingham highlights, lower cultural forms often are enjoyed by the affluent.

One such example discussed in this book is John Gay's *The Beggar's Opera* (1728), which uses the "low" form of the ballad to satirize the "high" (but relatively new) form of the opera, though of course Gay's play seems to mock both. Discussing materiality and borrowing of the text, John Brewer writes,

> Works like *The Beggar's Opera* reinforced the sense that the cheap pamphlet and the highly paid castrato were somehow connected; the ballad opera made this new, heterogeneous world of high, low and commercial art coherent. *The Beggar's Opera*'s use of topical materials and of literature and music from high and low life was a response to an extraordinary cultural expansion, to the growth of new kinds of audience and to the development of hybrid cultural forms. Artists were using new sorts of material to reach and to shape a new audience.[10]

Despite Scriblerian complaints of Grub Street hack writing, supposedly low culture provides important insights into satirical discussions of alcohol and tobacco and the consumer economy developing in London. In exploring satires that feature alcohol and tobacco, this book brings together literary and extraliterary texts (including poems, plays, ballad operas, pamphlets, essays, and philosophical and economic treatises), canonical and noncanonical texts, to investigate how British citizens—male and female, and from different social classes—responded to these consumable items, and by examining satires across all levels of society, not only can we glean a more nuanced understanding of the give-and-take between these genres, but we can also gain a more holistic view of how British citizens interpreted policy, consumer trends, and the birth of luxury.

INTRODUCTION

This book consists of five chapters, each of which is organized around an alcoholic beverage or a tobacco product. Because the popularity of these luxury items fluctuated and overlapped, and because the commercial market, laws, means of taxation, and overarching economic systems and polices were constantly changing, this book necessarily covers a fairly broad range of years; however, since these different commodities are traced according to their varying levels of popularity, the chapters are arranged largely chronologically. I begin with the Restoration of Charles II in 1660, considering how the king's fiscal policies and use of taxes shaped libertine writers. I then look at the ways in which the wars of William III and Queen Anne affected taxation and the treatment of those goods by both canonical and noncanonical writers. Starting in the late 1720s, satirical responses to alcohol reveal Walpole's attempts to use both domestic products and imported commodities to maintain power. The book ends in 1751 with the conclusion of the Gin Craze, during which we see the Western world's first major governmental response to rampant alcohol abuse, a significant indicator of Britain's evolution as a consumer culture. Ultimately, this book aims to shed new light on the ways in which libertine poems and plays, anonymously published satirical verse, writers of ballad operas, and canonical satirists such as John Gay, Alexander Pope, and Jonathan Swift interact with consumable luxury items and their effects on the British body and consciousness, individually and nationally.

Chapter 1, "'The Vice of the Time': Wine, Libertinism, and Commerce in the Age of Charles II," examines the treatment of wine, England's chief import during the Restoration period, by libertine poets and playwrights. In the Earl of Rochester's poetry, William Wycherley's *The Gentleman Dancing-Master* (1672), Edward Ravenscroft's *The Careless Lovers* (1673), George Etherege's *The Man of Mode* (1676), and Aphra Behn's *The Rover, Part I* (1677), tensions develop between celebrations of Cavalier and libertine desires for alcohol and the problem of overconsumption. By celebrating wine, an expensive, imported beverage, these satirical writers interested in alcohol as a marker of upper-class male privilege and debauchery highlight the fiscal importance of alcohol, albeit indirectly. These writers also tend to elide wine's import status both to support Charles II's fiscal policies and to emphasize the libertine's aristocratic distinctions. These writers' representations of wine highlight male behaviors they see as problematic, with some seeking to disconnect the imported luxury from foreign foppery, others working to distinguish upper-class modes of drinking habits from those of the lower orders, and, in the case of Behn, investigating the role of wine in libertine sexual violence.

Chapter 2, "Bottling Up Your Anger: Alehouse and Tavern Satire in Stuart England," concerns treatments of ale, beer, and wine written by noncanonical satirical poets focusing on the more middle-class environments of the alehouse and tavern. Throughout the late seventeenth and early eighteenth centuries, the trade and commerce of alcohol went through major shifts in conjunction with the development of excise taxation and the increase of middle-class consumerism. During this time, wines such as claret, port, canary, and German Rhenish were more frequently purchased by the middle classes, who were gaining financial and political power. The common view of wine as a chiefly aristocratic beverage was coming to an end. Despite this increase in affordable luxuries for the middle class and the broader economic developments of late seventeenth and early eighteenth centuries, Britain still followed the mercantilist theory, relying on many of the same fundamental economic models that had existed in Europe since the Renaissance. Satirical treatments of wine and its domestically produced counterparts, ale and beer, illuminate ways in which writers push back against foreign wines. Using mercantilist thought in their writing, these poets—including John Earle, Charles Darby, Richard Ames, Ned Ward, and several anonymous poets—investigate more directly issues of daily domestic commerce and of complex international trade, exposing their anxieties regarding the effects of trade on middle-class English identity.

Chapter 3, "Sot-Weed or Indian Weed? Pipe Tobacco and Satire, 1689–1709," discusses texts by Aphra Behn, Ned Ward, Lawrence Spooner, and Ebenezer Cooke, considering how these writers treat pipe tobacco as an essential product to British colonial society while also fearing its Native American origins. I look briefly at Behn's *Oroonoko*, considering her treatment of the plant in her prose work in comparison with her final posthumously published play *The Widow Ranter* (1689); in her tragicomic play, Behn purposely elides tobacco's Indigenous background, while also using the product to poke fun at the figure of the aristocratic English trader within a colonial space marked by proto-capitalistic self-enterprise. I then turn to the satirical writings of Ned Ward and Lawrence Spooner, both of whom highlight tobacco's connection to Native culture in an attempt to curb English smoking. These writers represent tobacco smokers as gluttonous, idle, and lustful, positing that despite the cash crop's economic benefits, English citizens become more savage through the act of smoking. Finally, in his best-known work *The Sot-Weed Factor* (1708), Ebenezer Cooke, like Behn, satirizes both the figure of the English trader and the Anglo-American colonists through his treatment of tobacco and the tobacco trade.

Chapter 4, "'The Ceremony of the Snuff-Box': Snuff in British Satirical Essays and Poems, 1709–1732," focuses on the rising popularity of nasal tobacco, snuff, in Britain during the early eighteenth century. Sir Richard Steele's periodical essays in *The Tatler* and *The Spectator* often represent snuff as a disruptor of proper polite conversation, a motif picked up and developed by Alexander Pope in *The Rape of the Lock*. Pope represents snuff, a commodity that has received little scholarly attention, as a luxury invading English society and upper-class masculinity. I then consider the grotesque and scatological uses of snuff that appear in British writings of the 1720s and 1730s, discussing an anonymously published satirical essay, *Whipping Tom* (1722), before turning to Jonathan Swift's famous poem *The Lady's Dressing Room* (1732), as well as a reaction poem by an anonymous female poet, *The Gentleman's Study* (1732). In these texts, satirists criticize the long-term bodily effects of snuff, employing extreme hyperbole and prefiguring many of the reactions to gin that would occur during the Gin Craze.

The final chapter, "English Satirical Writing in the Age of Mother Gin, 1723–1751," examines eighteenth-century economic and literary reactions to the Gin Craze, the period in which lower-class gin consumption was a major social fear of the middle and upper classes. In his treatises, Bernard Mandeville criticizes the effects of gin on the English body (both the individual and the nation at large), representing gin as a kind of disruptive, lower-class luxury. Considering the context of mercantilism, gin's growing popularity, and contemporary reactions to the beverage, Mandeville's treatment of gin exposes an important cultural narrative running throughout the Gin Craze. In *The Beggar's Opera* (1728), John Gay not only gives voice to Mandeville's narrative of gin as lower-class luxury, but also plays with and posits differing views of the beverage; layering these competing views on top of each other, Gay uses gin to comment on the growing capitalistic mindset of Britain and to satirize the Walpolean ethos. After discussing Gay, I then move to three satirical pieces by noncanonical writers who question and mock many of the anti-gin sentiments at work in England. I argue that these writers counter many narratives used in anti-gin legislation and pamphlets, considering gin's importance to lower- and middle-class workers. The chapter ends with a brief look at Henry Fielding's 1751 treatise *An Inquiry into the Late Increase in Robbers*, a text that would signal the end of the Gin Craze—a period of social change that gestures toward modernity.

Examining these satirical pieces provides a more nuanced understanding of the way writers of the seventeenth and eighteenth centuries reacted to a changing world. While proto-capitalistic financial systems promised greater prosperity, skeptical writers sought to investigate how such promises may fall flat and, indeed, create bigger problems of themselves. Through these consumable items, satirists of the period represented their anxieties regarding where a consumer economy might take them even as they sought to grasp what such an economy was. The representations of alcohol and tobacco products then offer a glimpse into the skeptical British mind as it sought to understand a world in which economic power might trump morality.

1

"THE VICE OF THE TIME"

Wine, Libertinism, and Commerce in the Age of Charles II

IN 1660, CHARLES II MADE HIS triumphant return to England, and as John Evelyn notes in his diary, fountains ran red with wine, celebrating the Restoration of the monarchy.¹ Almost a full year later, on April 23, 1661, Charles II had his official coronation. Samuel Pepys, rising at four in the morning to get a good viewpoint, was greatly pleased with the splendor of the day. He describes the feast that took place after the official coronation as a "rare sight" and witnessed the ceremonial entry of Charles's champion, Sir Edward Dymock, who rode up "all in armor on horseback, with his Speare and targett carried before him," as a herald proclaimed that "if any dare deny Ch. Steward to be lawful King of England, here was a Champion that would fight with him."² Dymock ceremonially flung down his gauntlet, and then Charles drank to Dymock before giving him the golden cup, from which the champion himself drank before the end of the ceremony.

The rest of Pepys's day consisted of a flurry of drinking. When attending a post-coronation party in Axe Yard with his wife and Mrs. Frankelyn, Pepys describes several bonfire parties, noting that "many great gallants, men and women" were drinking together (87). These complete strangers "laid hold of us and would have us drink the King's health upon our knee . . . which we all did, they drinking to us one after another—which we thought a strange Frolique. But these gallants continued thus a great while, and I wondered to see how the ladies did tiple" (87). Pepys notes two elements that struck him as particularly unusual: that the gallants drank the health not only to Charles but also to nonaristocratic citizens and that "the ladies"—most likely not just his wife and her companion but the many women at the crowd—drank a great deal. Pepys's usage of the word "frolique," which could mean both general "fun, merriment, sportive mirth" or "a scene or occasion of gaiety or mirth; a merry-making; a party," is especially interesting because he draws attention to the "strangeness" of these two social choices, drinking the health of complete strangers and drinking with women.³ Pepys then "sent

[his] wife and her bedfellow to bed" (87), rather than allow her to continue in their revelry. Later, when toasting with the royal wine collector, he and his compatriots drink *only* to the king's health. As Pepys's journal entry attests, alcohol in the seventeenth century was considered the province of men, while the ways in which it was consumed spoke to social hierarchies and class dynamics.

The drinking of wine, a traditional way of honoring the monarchy, especially during and after the English Civil Wars, was a major component of Royalist culture. Wine also became, unsurprisingly, a major aspect of Restoration libertine culture, treated as a consumable material, a signifier of wealth and status, a symbol of pride at the Restoration of monarchal power, and a source of liquid inspiration. Charles's return was supposed to represent the triumph of the aristocracy, the return of seized lands and monies, and the disbanding of the taxation on alcohol. None of these fantasies, however, would become reality, despite the triumphant, grandiose spectacles of Charles's return and coronation. The Restoration government would continue the heavy taxation of imported wines, the primary luxury item bought from other countries, even as it increased markedly England's presence in the global market.

As we shall see, these lucrative customs duties on wine, and the government revenue that they generated, would play a significant role in the treatment of it and other alcoholic beverages in writings by libertine and courtly writers celebrating the monarchy. Alcohol, including wine, ale, and beer, was one of the most important commercial products for both internal and international trade, and for playwrights of the 1670s, it became a medium for investigating specific anxieties about trade, principally related to class and gender dynamics. Discussing John Dryden and Aphra Behn, Susan J. Owen writes, "Tory dramatists want to make light of concerns about French wine, just as Charles II, for political reasons, wanted to make light of Parliament's concerns about French imports."[4] As I argue in this chapter, these writers oftentimes seem to be actively avoiding the discussion of French wines as an import. For satirical writers such as the Earl of Rochester, William Wycherley, Edward Ravenscroft, George Etherege, and Aphra Behn, the exploits of libertine heroes reflected on both the hedonistic activities of Charles's court and on a taxation policy that centered alcohol as a linchpin of national finance. The poetry of Rochester, Wycherley's *The Gentleman Dancing-Master* (1672), Ravenscroft's *The Careless Lovers* (1673), Etherege's *The Man of Mode* (1676), and Behn's *The Rover, Part I* (1677) all expose a commerce-centered attitude toward wine and libertinism and, in particular, treat alcohol as a social marker that is directly related to commercial activity. When considered chronologically, these plays reflect in their depiction of wine an increasing awareness of the role of global commerce. These dramatists consider wine as a commercial substance—a consumable product greatly affected by popular taste and trends that plays a crucial role in international trade and global interactivity. To examine the historical and economic role of wine during Charles II's reign is thus to offer new insight into the dramatic output of the 1670s. Wine in these plays consistently serves as a cultural metaphor that would have been obvious to contemporary viewers but is largely invisible to modern audiences. These aristocratic beverages, and their myriad treatments in these texts, provide unique insight into the ways in which satirical dramatists understood, reinforced, mocked, and critiqued dynamics of class, gender, wealth, and taste.

ALCOHOL AND COMMERCE FROM THE INTERREGNUM THROUGH THE RESTORATION

Despite the famous characterization of Charles II as the Merry Monarch, the king put forth a proclamation specifically condemning the sin of drunkenness the very day after his return to England, May 30, 1660. This proclamation targeted those "who spend their time in Taverns, Tipling-houses, and Debauches," especially those who did so owing to their supposed "affection" for their king by "drinking [his] Health."[5] In his wording, Charles is deliberate in the public nature of this debauchery, providing the specific locations of drinking in which this licentiousness occurs. Discussing this proclamation and its connection to the history of toasting the king, James Nicholls suggests that it is the oaths, not the locations and public drunkenness, with which Charles is most concerned; I would argue, however, that his references specifically to these locations expose Charles's vilification of the public nature of the drunken declarations, especially given the type of drinking establishments referenced.[6] Here, it is important to differentiate between the drinking establishments listed and how class dynamics fit into their respective clientele. Alehouses, or "Tipling-houses" as they are called by Charles, served almost exclusively beer and ale, and were more often frequented by the lower orders and middling sorts. Inns, however, tended to provide lodging and food in addition to ale, beer, and sometimes wine; the lower class would likely have been here as well, but these establishments were also very attractive to traveling business people who would be able to find food and rest. While taverns often served food as well, these places tended to attract wealthier middle-class and upper-class patrons, serving as a meeting place for these groups to discuss matters of business; rather than serving many different types of beverages, taverns almost exclusively served wine. While Charles's proclamation seems, then, to call attention to the entire social strata of England, it is also important to recognize that he is primarily focused on these public spaces rather than the courtly environment in which he, Rochester, and other libertines would enjoy themselves.

In his proclamation, Charles critiques the publicity of heavy intoxication most clearly in his discussion of toasts to his health. Many of his subjects seek to show their loyalty through the same type of drinking ritual enacted by the strangers Samuel Pepys met at the bonfire discussed above. This type of health drinking was nothing new; indeed, Rebecca Lemon argues that the obsessiveness of health drinking in the late sixteenth and early seventeenth centuries constituted a form of addiction.[7] In the 1720s, Daniel Defoe would reference the start of this fad in his pamphlet, *The Behaviour of Servants in England Inquired Into*. In his text, Defoe implies that honoring Charles through a toast quickly devolved into people viewing intoxication as a sign of loyalty, writing "he that had the Victory at the Glass, was the best Subject; Drunkenness grew a Test of Loyalty."[8]

Charles clearly saw the damage that this kind of public display could create for him, especially given the relationship between alcohol and the Cavalier. Depictions of Cavalier debauchery had been used effectively in the parliamentary propaganda of the 1640s. Discussing this trope, Jennifer L. Airey notes that in "many of the [propaganda] tracts, Cavalier fondness for drink leads to alcohol-induced property damage," including the rape of Roundhead women designed to punish parliamentary enemies.[9] In his proclamation, Charles writes that these men who seek to show their loyalty do more to "discredit Our Cause by the License of their Manners and Lives, than they could ever advance it by their Affection and Courage." In his evaluation, however, Charles makes a clever political move by attributing alcoholic vice—much of which would have been customarily connected to Royalist Cavaliers—to the "Vice of the Time," constructing this sin as a result of chaotic parliamentary rule. Charles implicitly shifts the blame to the parliamentarians, displacing blame for overindulgent acts of drink and the assaults and property damage to which it led. His central goal with the pamphlet, then, was to demonstrate to his subjects that social stability, as well as relative sobriety, would be a hallmark of his reign, even as he and his court would establish a far different reputation.

Despite the traditional connections between royalism and overindulgence, Charles did not open the floodgates to alcohol when he was restored as monarch. In fact, patterns of alcohol consumption did not drastically change under parliamentary rule. Although the restrictions of the puritanical Commonwealth parliament have been well noted, they were not as fierce on alcohol as one may assume.[10] Many inn and alehouse closures had more to do with the presence of Royalist propaganda than a ban on alcohol.[11] As Charles Ludington notes, the parliamentarians were "no strangers to alcohol."[12] Beer, a major part of the English diet, was commonly brewed on most country estates, including Oliver Cromwell's.[13] Thus, the major division between the parliamentarians and the royalists manifested in the types of alcohol they commonly drank. While royalists favored the more highly intoxicating wine, the parliamentarians were known for their love of ale and beer, beverages that were less intoxicating and that allowed drinkers to practice moderation more easily (*The Politics of Wine*, 16); given the English, and thus Protestant, origin of these beverages, most parliamentarians would also have preferred them to wines produced in Catholic countries such as France, Spain, Portugal, and Italy.

Furthermore, since the sixteenth century, wine had traditionally been taxed more heavily than other alcoholic beverages because most wine was imported, as wine was not commonly produced domestically in England from the medieval period through the late seventeenth century. While some English vintners made their own wine, the product, a vast majority of which was imported, constituted a luxury item, one long associated with the wealthy aristocracy who could afford it (*The Politics of Wine*, 16). Ultimately, then, the choice between wine or ale and beer can be read as a political act. Marika Keblusek notes, "Drinking wine as opposed to the common pint of beer emphasised the aristocratic, courtly status of the Cavalier. . . . In a society that was roughly divided into the camps of royalists and parliamentarians, one's choice of drink could, therefore, mark one's political affiliation."[14] Unlike the prohibitionists of the nineteenth century, the parliamentarians did not favor banning alcohol entirely. As a group, they were, however, disgusted by the drunkenness that the royalists promoted. As Keblusek points out, the Royalist cause was associated with drunken licentiousness and the gluttonous consumption that accompanied it, rather than casual drinking (60). This overindulgence was a major distinction between Royalism and Puritanism.

During the Interregnum, alcohol consumption continued unhindered because the Cromwellian government needed the revenue from the lucrative excise taxes placed on alcohol, and although Cromwell restricted the number of alehouses per parish, Gregory A. Austin notes that "Cromwell himself ridicule[d] the notion of promoting sobriety through prohibition" and that the Long Parliament taxed alcohol "purely for financial purposes" (234). In the case of wine, Ludington points out, "the financially indebted Commonwealth government was anxious to collect taxes on wines, and therefore did not want to stifle a trade that had already been diminished by the fighting of the 1640s" (19). Up until the 1640s, England's chief trade routes were between London and Antwerp; however, Cromwell imposed the Acts of Navigation in 1651 to undercut the trading power of the Dutch. This law required that only English ships, or ships from the trade goods' country of origin, could import goods into London, thus restricting Dutch trading business substantially. It is noteworthy that German wines received one of the few exemptions to this rule because of the substantial taxes they accrued (*The Politics of Wine*, 19). If the wine trade was not as extensive during the Interregnum as it had been before the Civil Wars, it was not for lack of trying. After assuming the throne, Charles did not reverse the taxes on imports, nor did he lift the excise taxes from domestic alcohols. Charles, whose reign was fraught with a lack of monetary funds, levied higher taxes on alcohol than had previously existed in England. During the first year of his reign, Charles continued to enforce the existing taxes on the brewing trade, initiated in 1643.[15] Charles actually increased duties "on imported wines, linens, wrought iron, silks, and tobacco, among other items."[16] Judith Hunter stresses the importance of alcohol to the finances of Charles II's court, pointing to two acts of parliament passed in November 1660 that

> were concerned only with various liquors, home-produced and imported, mainly alcoholic, but also the new non-alcoholic beverages, coffee, chocolate, tea and sherbet. . . . In the matter of providing revenue, excise duties became all-important. By the end of our period [1757] they provided some £3,660,000 per annum, more than half the revenue raised nationally by taxation. . . . Moreover, ninety per cent of the excise revenue came from the duties on beer and ale. In contrast to the pre-Civil War period when the King was expected to "live of his own" except in exceptional circumstances, from 1660 Parliament through taxes of various kinds provided the King with a regular income and extra grants for an increasing number of occasions.[17]

Although Charles left the national treasury over a million and a half pounds in debt after his death, these changes, along with continued taxation of alcohol and other goods, allowed him to finance much of the Crown's expenses (*Alcohol in Western Society*, 47). Thus, alcohol played a vital role in sustaining Charles's rule.

With the ascension of Charles II and the development of his libertine court came an increase in the versification and dramatization of drink, as well as extreme overindulgence. As a traditional drink of the aristocracy, wine featured as a key aspect of libertine court society and appeared frequently in the plays of the 1670s. Satirical writers interested in court and libertinism, including Rochester, Wycherley, Ravenscroft, Etherege, and Behn, share a focus on commerce, money, and trade, both domestic and international; they treat alcohol as a symbol of wealth and status, a substance signifying the privilege of the aristocracy. Simultaneously, they tend to elide the commercial roots of alcohol to bolster libertine masculinity and to show support for their king.

One of the main literary figures to shape the discussion of alcohol in the 1670s was the quintessential libertine, John Wilmot, the second earl of Rochester, who establishes throughout his poetry the idea of aristocratic, and specifically male, privilege. This assertion of privilege was a staple of the libertine coterie writing of the Restoration period.[18] The discussion of alcohol in his poetry is central to his bawdy, and often pornographic, writings, which treat liquor as an essential component of the libertine lifestyle. In "Regime de Vivre," Rochester describes his daily regime, which features heavy drinking and sex with prostitutes.[19] John D. Patterson notes that "wine and women" are often "equal and complementary pleasures" in Rochester's poems.[20] This poem in particular focuses on the constant gain and loss of these two primary enjoyments. However, despite the "equal and complementary" nature of these pleasures, Rochester tends to elide alcohol's status as a commercial substance that must be purchased and paid for, which is much different from his often economically focused treatment of prostitution.

"Regime de Vivre," which both revels in licentiousness and reflects deep self-loathing, is intensely interested in the passage of time and the loss of money. In the first eight lines, for instance, the speaker states,

> I Rise at Eleven, I Dine about Two,
> I get drunk before Seven, and the next thing I do;
> I send for my *Whore*, when for fear of a *Clap*,
> I Spend in her hand, and I spew in her *Lap*;
> There we quarrel, and scold, till I fall asleep,
> When the *Bitch*, growing bold, to my Pocket does creep;
> Then slyly she leaves me, and to revenge th' affront,
> At once she bereaves me of Money, and *Cunt*. (ll. 1–8)

After the loss of his prostitute and money and after having sex with his young male page (resulting from his lack of his female partner), the poem ends with this cycle beginning again the next day. The speaker is at once bragging about his debauched way of living and seemingly bothered by its repetitive nature. The time loop described is connected to the constant loss of money, given that, as the title suggests, this "rule of life" is the way the speaker's daily life is conducted. Each day, he awakes from a drunken stupor, eats, gets drunk, has sex with women, young boys, and men, and then starts the process over. Furthermore, given the transactional nature of his use of the prostitute and his page, we see that the speaker layers his understanding of human interactions with his understanding of wine: both function as extensions of his consumerism. Using up these resources, day after day, the speaker cannot break his cyclical need for commodities.

In this poem, both time and money seem to be endless, reflecting the privileged position of the male, upper-class rake. Considering Rochester's consistent financial troubles, this image of the rake's infinite prosperity purposely obfuscates the crushing debt, and very real threat of destitution, that the true libertine often faced; instead, the automatic replenishment of funds as shown in the poem focuses the reader's attention on the self-destructive cycle of fulfilling one's baser desires, only to find them regrown the next day. The image of the prostitute, whose hand "growing bold, to [his] pocket does creep," metonymically signifies the constant loss of money that results from his dissipated lifestyle; however, this image of money loss, which forces him to "bugger [his] page" after the "loss of [his] punk," is imagined as an inevitability. While his money will seemingly regenerate with the next day—presumably his financial situation would be taken care of by the manager of his estate—his daily funds are always stolen, forcing him to deal with this loss and alter his plans for fornication. Just as the speaker's funds are seemingly unlimited, wine, too, is stylized as an almost naturally occurring substance. The expensiveness of the drink is never addressed, suggesting that the destructive consumption of alcohol only causes the loss of money to the extent that it inflames the speaker's desire and incapacitates him to the point that he becomes an easy target for theft. Like many of the libertine poets, Rochester portrays alcohol as a necessity for the privileged, upper-class man, largely choosing to ignore its commercial aspects as a substance; at the same time, it functions as a driver of economic loss due to its intoxicating and habit-forming nature. Rochester draws a clear connection between the loss of money and the abuse of alcohol, implying that the libertine lifestyle is *not* necessarily enjoyable, and that it can only be managed by someone in a good financial position.

A CAGED CANARY: HIPPOLITA AND THE WINE TRADE IN *THE GENTLEMAN DANCING-MASTER*

Wycherley's *The Gentleman Dancing-Master* (1672) stands out as a very different play from his most popular, and much bawdier play, *The Country Wife* (1673).[21] While also featuring two libertine figures, Gerrard and Martin, Gerrard is far less sexually debauched than Harry Horner; indeed, this libertine hero more greatly resembles the latter play's Harcourt, who, like Gerrard, takes part in a ruse to rob a foppish gentleman of an advantageous marriage that, due to his lack of libertine masculinity, he does not greatly desire. However, another interesting distinction between this earlier play and his more famous plays, *The Country Wife* and *The Plain-Dealer* (1676), is the activeness of his heroine character, Hippolita. Unlike Alithea or Margarey Pinchwife in *The Country Wife* or Fidelia in *The Plain-Dealer*, Hippolita is highly active in seeking the man she desires. Despite being a young woman of fourteen, subject to the whims of her watchful aunt and overly proud father, she works hard to navigate her strange social situation to her advantage, duping her father into thinking that Gerrard is in fact her dancing master; further, she manipulates her Francophile cousin and betrothed, Monsieur de Paris, into helping maintain the ruse and securing Gerrard's romantic interest. Addressing gender dynamics in Restoration social comedies, J. Douglas Canfield posits that Hippolita and young women in her position "are forced to be resourceful, in this instance displaying her merchandize—her beauty, her wit, and her worth—right under a foolish father's nose."[22] Canfield's description of Hippolita "displaying her merchandize" is doubly important when considering her father Don Diego's personal history. Making his fortune as an Anglo-Spanish wine merchant, Don Diego—whose actual name is later revealed to be Mr. James Formal—seeks to raise his family's social status through his daughter's marriage. However, due to his merchant past, Don Diego unwittingly treats his daughter like a cask of his finest wine, a role Hippolita actually uses to her advantage in the seventeenth-century marriage market. Through Hippolita, the scenes featuring wine drinking, and the elaboration of Don Diego's family line, Wycherley shows the importance of alcohol indulgence to libertine masculinity, setting up the interclass dynamics of the play. Through these elements, Wycherley shows that the commercial thinking of the Formal family line assists his heroine in marriage to the gentleman Gerrard. Like Rochester, Wycherley sees the libertine as entitled to both wine and women due to his proper masculinity and his aristocratic position.

This investigation of libertine wine consumption occurs within the first few lines of the play as the fourteen-year-old Hippolita engages in horticultural wordplay. After having spent a year with her controlling aunt, Mrs. Caution, she complains to her maid, Prue: "To confine a Woman just in rambling Age! take away her liberty at the very time she shou'd use it! O barbarous Aunt! O unnatural Father! to shut up a poor Girl at fourteen, and hinder her budding; all things are ripen'd by the Sun; to shut up a poor Girl at fourteen!" (ll. 1–6).

Within this opening speech, Wycherley works to connect Hippolita's "budding" sexuality with the very "ripen'd" grapes through which her father has gained both his wealth and his supposed social identity as a Spanish gentleman. Don Diego's most practical design in keeping Hippolita outside the social world of London is, of course, to maintain her profitability on the competitive marriage market by ensuring her continued virginity. He ages her before selling her off to an ideal buyer, treating her like the expensive, Spanish canary wines that helped him become rich. W. Gerald Marshall posits that Wycherley represents Don Diego's obsessively Spanish identity as a type of madness, arguing that he not only has an affinity for Spanish culture but actually treats the characters surrounding him as though they are Spanish as well, including his daughter who rejects the role.[23] It makes sense then that a person projecting Spanish culture onto his native England would apply this same madness to his own daughter; here, however, he projects not just this Spanish ancestry onto her but also the very canary wine he has traded to the English in the past. Seeking to sell his daughter off to her aristocratic cousin, Don Diego employs the same commercial mindset that has raised his family's social prospects.

This early connection of Hippolita to the commercial pursuit of wine is highlighted later during the act 1 discussion between Paris and Hippolita regarding Gerrard. Hippolita will cleverly present Gerrard as a dancing master to her own father in the second act, but in this scene we see her already beginning her trickery by fooling her betrothed as well. Paris does not pick up on Hippolita's clear romantic interest in Gerrard, as she asks her Francophile cousin about the eligible bachelor. Before assuring her foppish cousin that she despises Gerrard as "perfectly, even as much as I love you," she discusses how Gerrard came to be interested in her, despite her family's exhaustive efforts to restrict her social mobility (l. 168). She states, "You know my Chamber is backward, and has a door into the Gallery, which looks into the back-yard of a Tavern, whence Mr. *Gerrard* once spying me at the Window, has often since attempted to come in at that Window by the help of the Leads of a low Building adjoyning, and indeed 'twas as much as my Maid and I cou'd do to keep him out" (ll. 160–165).

After presenting Hippolita's clear frustrations with wasting her ripeness, Wycherley connects his heroine parataxically to wine by having Gerrard first notice Hippolita while enjoying a drink at the Ship Tavern. As indicated above by Canfield, Hippolita "merchandizes" herself by putting herself on display to the wine-loving Gerrard, presumably employing the Formal family business manner to pursue her future husband. Wycherley, then, presents his libertine hero as a lover and consumer of wine, and his desire for this alcohol is equated with his matrimonial and sexual pursuit of Hippolita. Indeed, as William R. Chadwick notes, the libertine Gerrard desires Hippolita for a sexual escapade he can later relive while drinking: "At the outset it is obvious that for Gerrard the affair is no more than an amusing escapade, one, moreover, that will make demands on his audacity and wit, and, if he is fortunate, conclude in a sexual conquest suitable for tavern gossip."[24] Gerrard's love of wine and Hippolita's role as an extension of the beverage are illustrated even further when he first attempts to elope with her. Near the end of act 3, Gerrard tells Hippolita his plan: "Well then, anon at nine of the Clock at night I'le try you; for I have already bespoke a Parson, and have taken up the three back Rooms of the Tavern, which front upon the Gallery-Window, that no body may see us escape; and I have appointed (precisely betwixt eight and nine of the Clock when it is dark) a Coach and Six to wait at the Tavern-door for us" (3.1.500–505). After connecting Hippolita to wine and presenting the libertine hero as a wine lover, Wycherley sets up the intended elopement—a plan that ultimately fails, leading to the comic ending of the play—within a tavern, thus connecting the couple's romantic interests with their future marriage and sex life.

Early in the play, Wycherley highlights the ingenuity of Hippolita's manipulation of her cousin, which Wycherley combines with his satirical treatment of Paris's French foppery. Paris's inability to drink like a proper Englishman highlights the importance of alcohol to libertine masculinity. During her conversation with Paris in act 1, scene 1, Hippolita pushes her betrothed to "railly him [Gerrard] soundly, do not spare him a jot," and repeats this purposely terrible advice to her cousin, pushing him to annoy Gerrard so the libertine will pursue her romantically out of spite (ll. 203–204). After having already pushed Paris to "railly" Gerrard twice, Hippolita tells him: "Ay, and railly him soundly; be sure you railly him soundly, and tell him, just thus—that the Lady he has so long courted, from the great Window of the *Ship*-Tavern, is to be your wife to morrow, unless he come at his wonted hour of six in the morning to her Window to forbid the Banes [wedding banns]" (ll. 209–213). This oft-repeated advice sinks in almost too well, and Wycherley showcases Paris's numerous attempts to "railly" Gerrard, satirizing the

Francophile's foolish talkativeness—a stereotypical dig at his adopted identity[25]—and his foppish intolerance of alcohol. Discussing the fop archetype of early modern comedy and satire, Susan Staves notes that the "avoidance of drunkenness" is a defining quality of foppery, at which the audience is "invited to laugh" for being "so-called effeminate."[26]

When Paris drinks with Gerrard and Martin in act 1, scene 2, he is clearly unable to keep up with the two libertines. In addition to his inability to drink with the two experienced libertines, Paris's discussion of alcohol reveals important elements of alcohol production and trade and their relation to class standing in the play. As the Paris drinks with Gerrard and Martin, he brags about his travels, often wandering into his French mode of speech. Responding to Paris's rejection of his own English identity after only three months abroad, Gerrard points out the fop's inability to drink, and he notes that his manner of speech makes him seem "so perfect a *French*-man, that the Drey-men [manual laborers] of your Fathers own Brew-house wou'd be ready to know thee in the head" (ll. 113–115). Clearly annoyed by the falsity of Paris's behavior and seeing his inability to fit proper English standards of masculinity, Gerrard specifically points to a traditional endeavor of the landed gentry: the brewing of ale and beer to monetize surplus grains and malts. Paris responds, "Vél, vél, my Father was a Merchant of his own of his own Beer, as the Noblessé of *France* of their own Wine: but I can forgive you that Raillery, that Bob, since you say I have the Eyré *Francéz*. But have I the Eyré *Francéz*?" (ll. 116–119). Sidestepping what is clearly meant to be a very personal insult, Paris instead realigns this traditional production of alcohol to his own Francophile standards, alluding to the French nobility's growing of wine grapes. Further, he complains about their excessive drinking, stating that "Tis ver [sic] veritable, Jarnié, what the *French* say of you *English*, you use the debauch so much . . . you are never enjoyeé" (ll. 1–2). Not only does he reject the English wine he is offered (l. 20), but he also continuously rejects his English identity in favor of a French one.

Beyond merely complaining about the frequent amount of drinking expected of him in England, Paris also exposes his extremely drunken state as he begins speaking in French more often. His French-style loquaciousness is increased due to his drunkenness, which leads him to mock his rival as he had been prodded to do by Hippolita. Paris has unwittingly become courier for Hippolita's indirect matrimonial pursuit of Gerrard. In this scene, Wycherley juxtaposes the upper-class fop with the genteel libertine, drawing attention to the latter's manliness. Paris's obsessively French speech and his fumbling attempts to demonstrate his worthiness of being a sexual and marital partner for Hippolita are made more noticeable due to his inability to drink, all of which highlight the English libertine Gerrard's appropriateness as a candidate for her affections and inheritance. Gerrard, a proper English gentleman whose alcohol tolerance fits the libertine standard, reads Hippolita's signals properly, proving his worth as a husband. For Wycherley, libertine masculinity and the women it attracts are directly linked to wine.

In act 5, scene 1, Wycherley connects Hippolita more fully to this commercial treatment of wine through Paris's tracing of her family history and by revealing Don Diego's lower- and middle-class background. Despite Don Diego's repeated rejection of his sister Mrs. Caution's belief that Gerrard is not a dancing master, it is not until his sister feigns trust in Gerrard that the contrarian Don Diego realizes the truth and admits he has been tricked. At this point, Paris—not yet grasping that he too is being manipulated by Hippolita—tries to convince his uncle of the innocent nature of what he sees as a "meer jest" (ll. 365). Defending his romantic rival, Paris tells his uncle that although he may have been presented as being nonaristocratic, Gerrard is in fact a gentleman. This reference to class pushes the proud Anglo-Spaniard to enhance his own familial line, leading Paris to correct him repeatedly and to reveal the lower-class status of Don Diego's ancestors. Rather than being a member of the nobility, Don Diego's great-great-grandfather was a pin maker. When his uncle starts to stammer a reply, Paris, likely growing annoyed, states that Don Diego's great-grandfather "was a Felt-maker, his Son a Wine-cooper, your Father a Vintner, and so you came to be a Canary-Merchant" (ll. 385–386). Paris's tracing of the Formal family line shows a clear progression toward not only greater affluence via mercantile wealth, but also a direct relation to wine. While his great-great-grandfather and great-grandfather likely had little to do with the wine trade, Don Diego's grandfather had the lower-class job of making wine barrels, and his father was either the owner of a tavern or inn specializing in wine or a moderately successful merchant.

While Paris does not at first ridicule his uncle when recounting his uncle's nonaristocratic lineage, he becomes (understandably) irritated at Don Diego's persistent lying, and Paris openly mocks the Formal family's long association with the wine trade. Following his nephew's description of his lineage, Don Diego once again attempts to establish his family's nobility, contending, "But we were still Gentlemen, for our Coat was as the Heralds say—was—" before his flummoxed reply is interrupted by his nephew (ll. 387–388). Paris, cutting in, reiterates his uncle's lack of gentility: "[Y]our sign was the Three Tuns, and the field Canary" (ll. 389–390). Here, Wycherley decorates the Formal family crest with the image of three wine barrels made for shipping, and the back of the crest he colors canary yellow, punning on the Spanish canary wine in which Don Diego specializes. Satirizing self-important members of the rising middle class, Wycherley shows that as Don Diego seeks to revenge himself on Gerrard, a man he believes to be of a lower station, he ironically ends up revealing his own nonaristocratic heritage. Given Paris's thorough knowledge of Don Diego's actual family history, it is not unlikely that Paris's father—a member of the landed aristocracy, who left Hippolita a substantial heritage—mocked his brother-in-law's heritage and self-importance. Wycherley, then, shows the importance of the wine trade and its ability to create wealth, while also problematizing commerce's ability to raise people above their proper station.

If Don Diego's grandfather made wine barrels, his father sold the casks in a tavern, and Don Diego shipped and sold wine, Wycherley figures Hippolita as the wine itself, illustrating her ability to be at once the product as well as the person successfully selling it to the aristocratic libertine wine lover. She recognizes her position as an unmarried woman and pursues a man that will love her, even if she is not of a member of the upper class or an heiress of 1,200 pounds a year. By equating Hippolita to wine, by connecting aristocratic, libertine masculinity to wine drinking, and by revealing the middle-class Formal family's mercantile history, Wycherley exposes the importance of wine to interclass relations. For the gentleman libertine, wine consumption and romantic pursuit are one and the same, meaning a healthy appetite for one is necessarily related to the success of the other. For members of the rising middle class, those gaining their position through commerce and trade, it is pivotal to recognize the role that wealth plays in their advancing social position, without losing track of how they attained those positions. As discussed above, the lucrative customs duties that merchants like Don Diego paid were absolutely crucial to the financial stability of England; however, as a middle-class merchant who gained power through wealth rather than nobility, Don Diego has forgotten it is aristocratic taste that has granted him wealth. Due to her effectiveness, it is perhaps unsurprising that Hippolita, a young heiress who chose to lie about her inheritance to ensure that her future husband was interested in her for love rather than money, ends the play having gained the husband and the freedoms she desired. Unlike her father, who sought the privilege of nobility through financial power, she seeks to harness aristocratic tastes to achieve her ends. As a character associated with the Spanish canary wine by which her father accrued his wealth, she seems to have exceeded her father in mercantile skill when seeking a marriage to Gerrard instead of her Francophile cousin; she, at least, recognizes that you do not sell a Spanish wine to a man with a taste for French claret.

INTERCLASS INTERACTION AND THE TAVERN IN RAVENSCROFT'S *THE CARELESS LOVERS*

In his 1673 play, *The Careless Lovers*, Edward Ravenscroft examines the expensive nature of wine and explores the relationship between daily commerce and alcohol.[27] As with the poem by Rochester discussed above, Ravenscroft investigates the libertine lifestyle, considering the ways in which alcohol fills a central role in the daily revelry of the rake. As a playwright, Ravenscroft problematizes alcohol (and, in particular, the middle-class environment in which it is served) as a substance that can potentially blur social class lines, even as it can, inversely, reinforce class hierarchies. The play features two romantic plots. The main plot focuses on Jack Lovell, who is deeply in love with Jacinta, the beautiful daughter of a wealthy alderman. Despite a prior understanding between Lovell and Mr. Muchworth, Jacinta's father, Muchworth has decided that he would prefer to marry his daughter to the foolish, conceited De Boastado, a man of the upper class. Thus, the play offers an intricate discussion of the balance between the desire for wealth—De Boastado must marry Jacinta to repair his fortune, which he seems to have squandered on fancy clothes, carriages, and extensive travel—and the desire for a higher-class position, Muchworth's primary motivation. The other plot features Mr. Careless, Jack's rakish friend, and his pursuit of revelry and of the female libertine, Hillaria, Muchworth's witty, rebellious niece.

Ravenscroft's play, which focuses extensively on this desire for wealth and aristocratic notoriety, uses a more middle-class setting than those found in many Restoration comedies to evaluate wine's connection to money and daily commerce. Because of the presence of the lower and middle classes in drinking establishments, Restoration libertine comedies tend to feature characters drinking in private homes (the drinking scenes in *The Country Wife*, for instance) or open public environs (such as the carnival setting of Naples in *The Rover*); writers focusing on libertinism use taverns and alehouse environments far less.[28] *The Careless Lovers*, however, sets a major scene, act 4, scene 3, in a Covent Garden tavern. After convincing his friend Lovell to enter the tavern, Careless and Lovell flirt with Careless's two constantly competing prostitutes, Clappam—mocked for her venereal diseases—and Breedwell—mocked for her many children. As the two women seek to undermine each other, Careless, Lovell, and the cross-dressing Hillaria drink claret and sack, two expensive beverages associated with the upper class. While prices from the period are by no means "easy to ascertain," Judith Hunter notes that in 1709, a pint of cheaper beer cost between one pence and one and a half ducats, whereas a pot of a nice, thicker ale or porter would cost about three pence (254). The price for wines, however, was much higher. Discussing the writing of the French visitor to London, Cesar de Saussure, Hunter writes, "the cheapest wine, Portuguese, cost about 2 [shillings] a bottle, and fine red claret as much as 5 [shillings]. This 'exorbitant' price he blamed on the great weight of the casks and the heavy duties on French goods" (254). According to this number, an entire bottle of claret—presumably purchased outright, rather than at a tavern—would cost about twenty times more than a single pot of beer.

When considering these differences in price in the context of the scene, Ravenscroft highlights the tavern in which social lines seem to blur. The two prostitutes, themselves lower class, aggressively seize the chance to portray themselves as rich, ordering upper-class drinks and treating the drawer, the waiter fetching the beverages, rudely. When asked if the tavern has good claret and sack, the drawer responds, "We have as good as any is in England" (l. 3). By pointing out the tavern's expensive foreign wines, the drawer both exposes the wine's imported nature and shows that these middle-class establishments have access to upper-class beverages, implying that the tavern is a place in which one can momentarily transcend class divisions. Furthermore, given that taverns in seventeenth-century British culture almost exclusively served types of wine (rather than ale, beer, and other liquors), the fact that Breedwell asked if they have these wines would most likely strike the drawer (and the play's audience) as odd, alluding to the fact that she is used to the more lower-class environment of the alehouse ("Legislation, Royal Proclamations, and Other National Directives," 18).

Believing the drawer is not fetching the wine quickly enough, Clappam continues to reveal her lower-class breeding by calling him a "son of a whore" and rudely asks him if they shall ever "have any of it?" (l. 4). By juxtaposing the polite manner of the drawer—"What wine do you please to drink, ladies?" and "I'll bring you that [wine that] shall please you" (ll. 1–5)—with the coarse behavior of the two prostitutes, Ravenscroft reveals the inability of the two women to assume the class roles they masquerade as when ordering the wine.

Clappam and Breedwell prove their inability to fulfill elite roles through their rough manner when speaking to Careless and Lovell. When drinking Careless's health, Breedwell says, "Here, Careless, you son of a whore, here's to you," to which he responds, "I thank you Mrs. Breedwell" (ll. 14–15). Likewise, Lovell politely offers "his service" to Clappam, only to have her retort: "Damn your compliment. 'My service to you'—you'd have said as much as that to an honest woman" (ll. 16–18). Here, Clappam rejects the role of "honest woman" into which Lovell attempts to place her, ultimately choosing to enjoy an aristocratic beverage without restraining herself to supposedly upper-class behavior. Clappam, perhaps realizing that she cannot properly maintain the illusion of class elevation, drunkenly decides to accept her lower-class standing.

This coarseness continues as Hillaria enters the scene, dressed in drag. As Hillaria joins the group, Lovell begins to make his exit. At this point, the company has been drinking one another's health repeatedly, and as Clappam and Breedwell start to drink to Lovell, he places "*four or five guineas in the glass*" in front of them (ll. 56–57). As he drops the money into the glass of wine, he states, "And to make it go down the pleasanter, there's that [the money] to sweeten your wine" (ll. 55–56). Perhaps fearing that he will become too drunk and be unfaithful to Jacinta, Lovell tips the women for showing him a good time, thanking them for "the good service you have done for me" (ll. 61–62). Clappam responds, "Were we but sure such sand lay at the bottom of the sea, we'd drink the ocean off" (ll. 58–59). Despite the physical dirtiness of the money (particularly to the mind of a modern reader), Clappam and Breedwell presumably drink the wine and view it as more enriching owing to its association (now made even more literal) with upper-class wealth. While Lovell uses his money to distance himself from the women that have provided a service for him, Clappam and Breedwell readily take the money, stating that they will do almost anything for Lovell's wealth. For Lovell, this assertion of his wealthy status is most likely a very welcome compliment, given that his potential loss of Jacinta stems from De Boastado's more aristocratic heritage. However, this image of the guineas dropping into the wine connects alcohol even more closely with daily commercial interaction, and more specifically with the lower-class desire to taste the wealth of the upper classes.

As Careless and Hillaria flirt with Clappam and Breedwell, one of the drawers announces that there are some sailors in an adjoining room of the tavern who wish to "entertain [the company] with a dance" (l. 156). Although this scene was most likely included in the play as another form of entertainment for the audience—the characters never verbally interact—Ravenscroft is clearly exposing the mixing of all social strata within the tavern, especially as Careless pays the sailors for their kindness, stating, "Give 'em what wine they'll drink, and clap't to our reckoning" (ll. 158–159). By covering the sailors' drinking expenses, Careless displays his wealth and class status, no doubt desiring to show off in front of the women while competing with the cross-dressed Hillaria for their attention. As with his and Lovell's interactions with the prostitutes, Careless rewards the lower-class figures with upper-class wine bought with upper-class money. The tavern, often suspect owing to the breaking down of class barriers, here appears instead as a place in which those of the elite can distinguish themselves from those below through monetary displays. Although Ravenscroft's tavern scene maintains class hierarchies, however, it staunchly rejects traditional gender dynamics in the main plot of the play, as the proto-feminist Hillaria successfully navigates the environ of the tavern to her advantage. In his play, Ravenscroft treats alcohol, and the monetary exchange that influences it, as important social markers for the aristocracy and for libertine behavior, regardless of gender.

ELIDING THE TRADE ROOTS OF WINE: ETHEREGE'S *THE MAN OF MODE*

Like Rochester's poem and the plays of Wycherley and Ravenscroft, Etherege's *The Man of Mode; or, Sir Fopling Flutter* (1676), treats alcohol as a necessity of the libertine lifestyle. While criticizing alcohol's ruining of aristocratic finances, Etherege, unlike Wycherley and Ravenscroft, intentionally avoids the connection between foreign commerce and wine to preserve English libertine masculinity, refusing to acknowledge the importation of wine when mocking foreign products and those who purchase them.[29] However, despite Etherege's clever elision, his interest in global commerce is more marked than Ravenscroft's and exposes an interest in current politics and cultural anxiety regarding France. Charles Ludington notes that during this period there was a "rising tide of Francophobia" that was no doubt related to economics, as "a Parliamentary report in 1675 painted a bleak picture regarding England's trade deficit with France" (26).

Compared to many Restoration sex comedies, alcohol is more seldom discussed explicitly in Etherege's play. Glasses and wine bottles would no doubt have been consistent props, but the stage directions and settings themselves do not refer directly to alcohol. The play instead emphasizes Dorimant's sexual intrigues rather than his alcohol abuse. When Dorimant does discuss alcohol, it is most often directed at the destructive drinking habits of the lower classes, for example the shoemaker in act 1, scene 1. By the end of the play, however, Dorimant, now engaged to the beautiful heiress, Harriet, sees wine as a disruptor of upper-class wealth, saying, "I will renounce all the joys I have in friendship and in wine, sacrifice to you all the interest I have in other women" (5.3.152–54). Dorimant decides to repair his fortune through marriage by avoiding the type of dissolute behavior that ultimately caused his financial problems.

The most significant discussion of alcohol as a commercial substance comes within the first scene of the play and is directed at lower-class characters, whose drinking Dorimant explicitly condemns. In the first scene of the play, Etherege examines domestic commercial activity as Dorimant meets with both an orange-woman and a shoemaker. During the interaction with the shoemaker, Dorimant and his friend Medley ridicule the lower-class worker for his drunkenness in a manner reminiscent of Charles II's proclamation against the drunken debauchery of inns and alehouses. In particular, the two libertines mock the shoemaker's frequent drunken fights with his wife. Dorimant also commands the shoemaker not to "debauch [his] servants" when the shoemaker alludes to drinking while in front of Dorimant's page, Handy (l. 322). Despite being famous for his own drinking, Dorimant ridicules members of the lower classes who cannot maintain proper control while inebriated. He also wants to ensure that his own servants do not become drunkards, a problem constantly discussed in early modern society and alluded to in Restoration drama.[30] It is therefore fitting that Dorimant see his own drunkenness as a privilege of his status, and the shoemaker's drunkenness as a problem; it not only disrupts the shoemaker's work, but it potentially jeopardizes the work of Dorimant's other servants. Furthermore, given the mockery directed at the shoemaker's drunken behavior and the fact that he plans to spend his entire half crown at the alehouse, Etherege suggests that the commercial aspects of ale and beer damage lower-class workers' ability to support themselves.

Despite this evaluation of lower-class drinking and the negative effect that libertine wine drinking has had on Dorimant's wealth, Etherege elides the discussion of the importation of wine throughout the play, a notable choice given the play's constant critiques of foreign finery. Charles H. Hinnant, for instance, notes that while Sir Fopling represents "the contemporary controversy over French imports," Dorimant consumes English products, "highlight[ing] a preference for domestic manufactures."[31] However, this discussion of foreign commodities does not extend to libertine drinking. Strangely for a play concerned with libertinism, the upper-class character most closely associated with wine is Old Bellair, an older gentleman. In act 4, scene 1, it is Old Bellair, rather than the libertines, Dorimant and Medley, who openly calls for the first bottle: "Stay, Mr. Medley; let the young fellows do that duty. We will drink a glass of wine together. 'Tis good after dancing" (ll. 392–393). The bottle that Old Bellair calls for is not named, meaning there is no way of knowing if it is French claret, Spanish canary, German Rhenish, or some other type of wine, thus drawing focus away from the wine's foreign nature. By refusing to name the type of wine drunk in the scene, Etherege purposely elides its role as an import, stressing instead its important role in the homosocial bonding of upper-class men. The proper English gentleman must engage in excessive drinking to celebrate his position in society.

Throughout the play, Etherege mocks the practice of purchasing foreign, specifically French, products over domestic ones, while intentionally ignoring the commercial roots of wine, one of England's most important and expensive imports. Sir Car Scroope, author of the play's prologue, initiates this discussion of the foreign versus the domestic:

> But I'm afraid that, while to France we go
> To bring you home fine dresses, dance, and show,
> The stage, like you, will but more foppish grow.
> Of foreign wares why should we fetch the scum,
> When we can be so richly served at home? (ll. 19–23)

Here, Scroope plays on the idea that Thomas Betterton, the actor who played Dorimant, had been sent to France to study their fashions for the improvement of the English stage.[32] As Scroope notes, however, foreign wares—even aristocratic consumer products such as clothing or plays—have the potential to corrupt British masculinity, making the audience more "foppish" by the minute.

As Hinnant points out, this preference for foreign commodities is investigated most strongly through the character of Sir Fopling, who brags about his French dress, his French caper, his French shoes, his French carriage, and his French customs, and who annoys almost every character in the play with his constant use of French words. Sir Fopling functions as the embodiment of an increasingly "Franco-fied" English citizenry, and his obsession is problematic for the British domestic market. Susan Staves notes, "Satire on fops during the Restoration and eighteenth century was prompted by a wide variety of motives ranging from concern over the moral evils of vanity through nationalistic worry over being inundated by foreign ideals and foreign goods to specific class tensions particular to the period" (428). By constantly purchasing French products, the English put money into the hands of a foreign power with whom diplomacy was always shaky at best.

It is all the more significant, then, that Etherege makes no reference to wine's foreign origins. Perhaps the most significant example of Etherege's avoidance of wine's commercial roots comes in act 4, scene 1, when Sir Fopling bewails his hangover from the previous evening: "I have sat up so damned late and drunk so cursed hard since I came to this lewd Town that I am fit for nothing but low dancing. . . . Pox on this debauchery" (ll. 319–325). Sir Fopling does not discuss the origin of the wine he drank the previous night with Old Bellair, Young Bellair, and Medley. He does not praise the wine for being a fine French claret, nor does he damn the wine for being Spanish or German; instead, he is merely irritated by his hangover while the playwright indirectly mocks him for not being manly (and English) enough to pursue heavy drinking. Sir Fopling's inability to drink heavily exposes one of the many ways in which fops fail to meet the Restoration standards of ideal masculinity. Furthermore, that Sir Fopling does not mention the type of wine is telling, because he has complained about every non-French product and custom with which he has come in contact. Sir Fopling's silence regarding the drink of the upper class suggests this import should not be noticed or criticized. Alcohol consumption is a necessity for upper-class masculine identity, and thus wine is not treated as a foreign product but merely as a substance brought up from a gentleman's cellar. Given the importance of the customs duties on wine to Charles's government, it makes sense that Etherege would avoid criticizing a substance that was central to both aristocratic male identity and the financial structure of the government.

ROYALIST MARKER OR CATALYST OF SEXUAL VIOLENCE? TRADE AND WINE IN BEHN'S *THE ROVER*

Like the poem and plays discussed above, Behn's *The Rover, Part I*, first performed in 1677, is intensely interested in the topic of money and commerce and its connection to wine.[33] Given the author's position outside the privileged elite, being a middle-class woman, Behn critiques alcohol and its effects on upper-class male privilege to a much higher degree than her male counterparts. While she celebrates the wit and revelry of her banished Cavaliers, Behn also exposes the damage that overindulgence in wine can cause, especially to the women who interact with these privileged men. Invoking the Royalist tradition of wine consumption as a way to honor the monarchy, Behn aligns the revelry of the Cavaliers with their support for their exiled prince. At the same time, as a female libertine, Behn investigates the effects of alcohol abuse on male libertines, specifically on their views of women and their own class privilege. By 1677, Behn had likely already befriended

Rochester, and thus her play was reacting to and investigating the types of destructive male behaviors for which he and his libertine circle were famous. Through the figure of Willmore, Behn shows that overindulgence in alcohol—a consumable product that costs money—leads libertines to equate women with wine, to misrepresent women as consumable products that are a mere "purchase" away, and ultimately to see themselves as entitled to women's bodies.

The Rover is set during the chaotic carnival of Naples, where the Cavaliers take a well-deserved break from their voyages to indulge themselves, and throughout their revelry, Behn connects libertine desire for flesh with the consumption of wine. While Willmore will eventually build these comparisons very directly in the second half of the play, his first sexual tryst with Angellica, the most expensive courtesan in Naples, features the poor Royalist rover clearly rejecting the monetization of the earthly pleasures of sex; especially since his lack of funds seems to restrict any such sexual romp between the two of them. Insulting her over her picture and her advertised price, he first asks what sexual favors he can get for a single gold coin: "I grant you 'tis here set down a thousand crowns a month—pray how much may come to my share for a pistole?" (185). After gaining her attention he offers her the single pistole in a more seductive fashion:

> —And yet I would at any rate enjoy you,
> At your own rate—but cannot—see here
> The only sum I can command on earth;
> I know not where to eat when this is gone.
> Yet such a slave I am to love and beauty
> This last reserve I'll sacrifice to enjoy you. (185)

Rather than the 1,000 pistoles she is usually offered, Willmore offers her the single pistole again, claiming that since it is the entirety of his wealth, he has paid more than any of her lovers before. Angellica having a fixed price for her favor does not gel with Willmore's view of sexuality; rather than a fixed price for each customer, Willmore believes his ability to gain her favor through seduction should constitute a type of bartering. Discussing commerce in the play, Richard Kroll writes that while "some transaction is undoubtedly involved, this is closer to barter than to trade, since Angellica can only think in terms of some absolute exchange: her full favors for a thousand crowns, nothing more or less on either side. Willmore cannot afford this sum, nor does the absoluteness of the proposition strike him as a proper form of commerce."[34] Unlike wine, which would have a set price, Willmore believes that any price set should be dictated by their mutual attraction.

Ultimately, Willmore's witty transformation of the single pistole as a sign of his absolute devotion works, and he successfully seduces Angellica, outflanking her business-savvy bawd, Moretta. While the two women may recognize the value of her "goods" in the sexual market of Naples, they do poorly when dealing with his arguments that sexuality should be divorced from commerce. We soon learn, however, that despite his persuasive speech, Willmore is extremely commercially minded. Kroll represents Willmore as a smart man of business, who is the character that "is most attuned to carnivalesque atmosphere" and whose "arrival in particular is cast in the general language of 'business' [. . . and] animates the very specifically the language of merchandizing, linking the Englishmen to the fluid environment of Neapolitan masquerade" (248–249). After having sex with Angellica, Willmore, the poor Royalist rover who has lost all his lands in England due to his loyalty to Charles I, quickly recoups some of his losses by asserting himself as the wealthy woman's lover, receiving new clothes and enough money to enjoy the carnival properly from the view of a court libertine.

At this point in the play, Behn connects her discussion of alcohol directly to global commerce. After his seduction of Angellica, Willmore fully equates the pleasures of women with those of wine. In the third act, Willmore conflates the two in conversation with his friends directly after his successful coupling. Responding to Willmore's desire for wine, Frederick suggests that perhaps a French wine would "do better" for their stated purpose of hearing the "story of [Willmore's] success" (191). Willmore, however, calls French wine "hungry balderdash," referring to it as an unadulterated wine that will not get them drunk (191). Willmore's disgust with French wine can be read in multiple ways. It could be that Willmore, a political exile from his own country, wishes to identify more closely with the Spanish, who at this point ruled Naples, wanting to drink the wine of the ruling class after being forced to leave his own homeland; this choice would still render the wine an import, technically, albeit from Spanish islands to a Spanish-ruled city. For the commercially-minded Willmore, the Spanish wine would likely also be cheaper due to its abundance and thus more desirable. It may also be that Willmore, a representative of the contemporary economic and political situation of 1670s England, does not want a wine imported from France. Ludington points out that although England had sided with the French in the third Anglo-Dutch war (1672–1674), the war had "actually led to a shift in public opinion against France, on the grounds that France posed a greater military and ideological threat than did the Netherlands," which led to further distrust of the French as a military power (25–26). Willmore's decision to drink Spanish canary, then, can be read as both a pining for a national beverage and Behn's comment on contemporary politics.

After Willmore declares his disgust with French wine, he expounds on the great qualities of "cheerful sack" or canary wine:

> [Canary] has a generous virtue in't inspiring a successful
> confidence, gives eloquence to the tongue, and
> vigour to the soul, and has in a few hours completed

all my hopes and wishes! There's nothing left to
raise a new desire in me. Come, let's be gay and
wanton—and gentlemen study, study what you want. (191)

Willmore's call to his comrades to "study, study" what they desire underscores his wish to drink and revive himself, and the stage directions state that he "*Jingles his purse*," implying that all the pleasures of Naples are to be bought and paid for. However, Willmore also implies that purchasing alcohol, rather than purchasing women, will lead to his sexual fulfillment. Canary accentuates his triumph with Angellica—a sexual liaison for which he did not pay—and it rejuvenates his eloquence and libido. The carnival of Naples that the Cavaliers have been enjoying abounds with "friends" that "beget new pleasures every moment" (191). Wine grants wit, and therefore is a necessity for Willmore's pursuit of female bodies.

By layering the imagery of the canary wine onto his sexual conquest of Angellica, Behn links indulgence in alcohol with the pleasures of the flesh. Behn strengthens this connection further by having Belville point out that Angellica seems to have driven the "little gipsy" (Hellena) from Willmore's mind. Willmore rebukes him for the comment: "A mischief on thee for putting her into my thoughts. I had quite forgot her else, and this night's debauch had drunk her quite down" (191). As with Angellica, Willmore configures Hellena as a bottle of wine to be either enjoyed or "drunk . . . down" and forgotten; alcohol serves as a tool to forget female bodies that are more difficult to procure. Willmore treats Hellena and their flirty repartee as a bottle of wine that needs to be pushed out of his system with more indulgence, thus configuring Hellena as another item to be consumed.

In comparison with Etherege's Dorimant, Behn presents her hero in a far more negative light, especially when he is in a drunken stupor. Whereas Etherege only alludes to Dorimant's heavy drinking, Behn portrays Willmore negatively whenever he has had too much to drink. During a drunken attempt to seduce Florinda, Willmore is unable to perform with the same verbal prowess he employed earlier in the play when flirting with Hellena and seducing Angellica. When speaking to Florinda, Willmore drunkenly tries to replicate his success with Angellica; however, his clever use of the single pistole—he verbally reconfigures his lack of wealth to his advantage—now becomes an attempted rape. Struggling with her, he insists, "That you would do't for nothing—oh, oh, I find what you would be at—look, here's a pistole for you—here's work indeed—here—take it I say" (202). In a bumbling, haphazard attempt to replicate his seduction of Angellica, Willmore seeks to force the coin into her hands, which to his mind renders her a prostitute ready to conduct business. Whereas the (somewhat) sober Willmore from the first two acts configured alcohol as something to be purchased and sex as something to be given freely after a clever seduction, the drunken Willmore sees sex as something that can be bought, no matter how unwilling the woman is to agree to the exchange.

Behn juxtaposes the witty cleverness of the earlier, less intoxicated Willmore with his disturbing behavior while drunk. Discussing the use of sexual violence, alcohol, and Cavalier imagery in the play, Susan J. Owen notes that—while "Drink is also a marker of Royalism" and a "marker of Cavalier sexiness and playfulness, as well as upper-class values"—it is also highly destructive.[35] She states: "Male sexuality in the play is presented as dangerous, desirable and ridiculous all at the same time. Through her treatment of drink, Behn brings out the ambivalence of libertinism for women. In particular, she shows how drink brings out the dark side of male sexuality. Drunk, the rake becomes predator" ("Drink, Sex and Power," 130).

The charming, irresistible libertine is transformed into the drunken rake who ignores resistance. When Willmore can no longer use his wit to charm women, he treats Florinda like a bottle of wine to be bought and consumed, sexually assaulting her and exposing the fine line between debauched court wit and drunken rapist. This moment, as well as the near gang rape of Florinda that occurs in act 5, exposes the violent behavior that was possible for the Royalist libertine fueled by alcohol, replicating the trope of the debauched Cavalier described by Airey. In Airey's words, Behn "offers her audiences a modified form of the debauched libertine; even as she romanticizes Cavalier behavior, she exposes the dark and frightening underside of the libertine ethos," ultimately depicting both the "comfortable," pleasure-seeking Cavalier and his potential for violence and destruction (102). Despite Behn's Royalist views, she critiques libertine abuse of alcohol and the exchange of money that accompanies that abuse, which often led to men feeling entitled to women's bodies and, ultimately, to acts of sexual violence.

Examining the libertine ethos closely, Behn questions the effects of the privileged male mindset, especially when under the influence of alcohol. Male aristocrats, overindulging in wine and taught by Rochester to see alcohol and heterosexual pleasure as synonymous, would therefore presumably take what they would when it suited them. In the case of Florinda, Behn shows that it is not just lower-class women who are vulnerable but upper-class women too are in danger, should they find themselves in the path of drunken, confused libertines. However, beyond questioning the conflation of heavy drinking with male sexual gratification, Behn also extends her view to Charles's court more broadly. The play itself, only alluding to the sovereign who has remained on the ship throughout the play, concerns itself with the "banished Cavaliers," those loyal subjects who are anxiously awaiting their return to England. Given the commercial aspects of the play and the role of wine as a staple import generating important revenue for the Crown, Behn shows that the revenue based on wine is inherently problematic; because of the Cavalier mindset that overindulgence in wine honors the Stuarts and the fact that consuming imported beverages supports him financially, those who view wine and women as essentially the same will likely treat them both in an equally indiscriminate manner.

CONCLUSION

Writers interested in the English court of the 1670s and the libertinism that permeated it used alcohol as a medium through which to celebrate, examine, and critique aspects of upper-class male privilege. Despite their collective interest in commerce, these writers all largely ignore the international trade that facilitated their characters' (and their own) consumption of wine, implying that wine was a necessity for the upper class—for the exercise of their privilege and to fit ideals of libertine masculinity—and for the financial good of the nation. To understand the contemporary cultural resonance of wine and its importance to Restoration drama is to develop a more holistic understanding of the ways in which British dramatists manipulated alcohol as a symbol. These cultural meanings expose the ways in which popular British writers responded to male libertinism, with all its attractive, dangerous, and destructive qualities, examining how it both existed within and helped construct class and gender dynamics during Charles's reign. In the coming decades, as discussed in the next chapter, the treatment of alcohol in satire would shift as more satirists, and especially those unaffiliated with and uninterested in the court, sought to discuss more middle-class environments, turning to inns, alehouses, and taverns for inspiration as well as the processes of trade and commerce that permeated them.

2

BOTTLING UP YOUR ANGER

Alehouse and Tavern Satire in Stuart England

> *Money, like wine, must always be scarce with those who have neither wherewithal to buy it, nor credit to borrow it. Those who have either, will seldom be in want either of the money, or of the wine which they have occasion for.*[1]

IN THIS PASSAGE FROM HIS seminal work, *An Inquiry into the Nature and Causes of the Wealth of Nations* (1776), commonly viewed as the founding text of free market capitalism and modern economics, Adam Smith compares money—here, referring specifically to gold and silver, the yardstick of early modern European economic development—to one of the most popular international trade items, wine. Indeed, Smith often uses wine to make points regarding his capitalist theories, indicating the heavy duties England placed on the trade item from the late seventeenth century and how these duties continued into eighteenth-century British policy (304). Using wine as an example, Smith looks back to the previous century, considering how the Stuarts had engaged in major trade wars, and ultimately, Smith, being one of the earliest proponents of free trade, saw these wars as extremely damaging to the quality of wine and alcohol, as well as the broader economic consequences of such a trade war. Elsewhere, Smith uses wine as an example of specialization. In "Book Four: Of Systems of Political Economy," he ruminates on Scotland and why his country does not grow grapes for fine wines. Clearly tongue in cheek, he posits that "very good wine" could be produced in his native country, but it would be "at about thirty times the expense for which at least equally good can be brought from foreign countries" due to all the expensive equipment and time it would take to produce it (294). Using this hypothetical, he showcases the importance of specialization, asserting that it would be more financially feasible to leave wine-making to countries such as France, to take advantage of mutually beneficial trade, and to expand Great Britain's own, more organically developed exports.

Smith, of course, fully realizes that his ideas regarding free trade were at odds with the mercantilist economic system that had begun to die out during the eighteenth century; Smith, himself, was in fact one of the main thinkers putting the very flawed theory of global economics to rest. According to the tenets of mercantilism, a system I discuss in more depth in chapter 5, a successful country should strive to limit imports of any kind, focusing on boosting domestic products and commerce while also building its reserves of gold and silver bullion. As an economic system, mercantilism stressed the importance of the financial strength of individual nation states, meaning that a sovereign country should seek to expand exports while limiting imports. Discussing the driving thoughts behind mercantilism, Thomas A. Horne writes, "The aim of mercantilism was national power and national self-sufficiency. It demanded that the state be preeminent in the internal economic affairs of the country and therefore sought to destroy internal barriers, municipal autonomy, and local standards of weights and measures. In foreign affairs mercantilism's demand for independence meant intense international rivalries with other sovereign states. International trade in this period was thought to be a contest where the gains of one state necessarily meant losses in another."[2] Because this system sought to limit imports, trade wars and the tariffs that drive them occurred intermittently throughout the last three decades of the seventeenth century as England placed embargoes on French goods, including wine and brandy.

Like Smith, the satirists I discuss in this chapter are deeply interested in wine and the ways in which it affects domestic and global commerce, but because their alcohol satires were penned during the very period Smith gestures to, most of these writers reveal their deeply embedded mercantilist thinking. Examining satires focusing on wine, ale, beer, and other liquors published from 1675 to 1714, this chapter focuses on seven understudied writers—John Earle, Charles Darby, Richard Ames, Ned Ward, and three anonymous authors—who address the role of alcohol in English commerce and trade and are particularly interested in wine, comparing it with other liquors, and especially the domestically produced and traditionally English beverages, beer and ale. Unlike the satirists of the previous chapter, who were greatly interested in libertinism and court intrigue, these writers focus more attention on middle-class drinking and the establishments in which it occurred. For several of these writers, taverns, oftentimes the sites of important business transactions, constituted a defining but problematic element of English culture. These satirists in particular tend to treat such drinking establishments as damaging to the financial security of the individual, creating a problem for the middle class that, they feared, would spiral out into the nation at large. However, this negative view of such spaces was not, of course, the only satirical view posited during this period. Several of these writers show a strong appreciation for the nuanced ways in which these establishments function as important sites of British culture and domestic commerce; indeed, Richard Ames and Ned Ward were themselves well-known not only for their overindulgence but also for composing their work in these very environments. Thus, in this chapter, I trace the myriad ways in which satirists examine such places and the beverages they serve, discussing one prose satire and several verse satires published during the last five years of Charles II's reign and through the end of Queen Anne's.

The first section examines three satirical pieces—John Earle's *The Character of a Tavern* (1675), Charles Darby's *Bacchanalia* (1680), and the anonymously published *The Paradice of Pleasure* (1700).[3] These satirists direct much of their criticism toward alcohol and its ill effects on trade and the monetary interests of the besotted tavern-goer. These writers focus a great deal of attention on foreign wine, critiquing its ability to intoxicate, to disrupt class dynamics and masculinity, and to ruin the drinker's life financially. Additionally, their satires tend to fit into mercantilist views of trade, examining how buying foreign (and especially French) wine puts money in the hands of England's competitors.

The second section focuses on tavern satirist Richard Ames's final poem, *The Bacchanalian Sessions* (1693); while focusing less on tavern environments in this specific poem than in his prior work, Ames examines alcoholic beverages and the people who drink them, but he also provides a much more nuanced view of the economic need for different types of alcohol than the satires that are directed mocking wine from a mercantilist standpoint. For Ames, alcohol is essential to global trade, and it plays an important role in class divisions.

Finally, I look at the anonymously written poem, *The Tavern Hunter* (1702), and Ned Ward's *The Hudibrastick Brewer* (1714). Here, the satirists provide a much different treatment of alcohol, largely presenting it as a consumable good and considering the acts of daily commerce that occur within the alehouse and tavern environment; while still critical of foreign wine, these texts also show its importance to English middle-class wealth and masculinity. The poetic works discussed in this chapter have seen little, if any, critical attention, and many of these works were likely produced quickly, meant to make the writers quick money and to supplement their income. Studying these texts provides a more holistic view of the ways in which alcohol, especially the luxury wine, was viewed within the early modern period. While still interested in ale, beer, wine, and other liquors, these satirists discuss alcohol as both a product of trade and driver of it, and although their respective views differ greatly, these writers all see alcohol as having a major impact on trade and the global connections that international commerce fosters.

TAVERN TIRADES: SATIRES OF COMMERCE, TRADE, AND WINE FROM 1680 TO 1700

In an age in which middle-class men increasingly gathered to discuss and debate current events and where social clubs were becoming ever more the norm, sites of drinking, such as alehouses and taverns, were important spaces of male homosocial interactions and were therefore the subject of mockery in the satires focusing on these gatherings. In the seventeenth and eighteenth centuries, alehouses tended to serve only ale and beer, whereas taverns sold wine; both types of establishments tended to serve food as well. The primary differences between the two were that alehouses oftentimes were viewed as being more aligned with the lower and middle classes, given the types of drinks they served, and taverns, because of the luxury status of foreign wine, were often portrayed as being more expensive, and thus connected to the middle and upper classes. The increase in middle-class consumerism that began during the late seventeenth century had aroused fears about the amount of money being wasted in drinking establishments. While prodigality and alcohol consumption were by no means new, the publication of satirical tracts discussing alcohol began to increase during this period with many minor satirists hoping to correct this problem of unfettered spending. For John Earle, Charles Darby, and the two anonymous satirists covered in this section, the tavern, and other such drinking establishments, were locations in which male bonds were reinforced and where domestic commerce and international trade were closely linked.[4] The middle-class merchant, who could very well have made his money through the wine trade, here ends up wasting that money on the very beverage meant to help him prosper financially. Further, such establishments sold foreign wine, an expensive import, ultimately contributing to problematic trade deficits, something to be discouraged according to mercantilist economics of the period. For these writers, the taverns offered the chance to examine the ways in which consumable items such as alcohol allowed for the crossing of class boundaries and the investigation of English masculinity and gender dynamics.

One such treatment can be found in Earle's pamphlet *The Character of a Tavern*, published in 1675 and about ten years after the author's death. After ridiculing taverns for five full pages, Earle summarizes for his audience what he has stressed throughout his sketch of the English tavern environment: "*In brief, A Tavern is a Scene of Confusion; a Gulf to Swallow up a Mans Money, and his time, which is yet more precious; a Nursery for Extravagancy, and a necessary place for Assignations between Cracks and their Cullies*" (6). To Earle, the tavern is a place of chaos and of extravagant spending and where men are taken advantage of by those who run the business itself. While he describes it early on as a "degree above an Ale-house" due to its being too expensive for members of the lower class, he implies that this more middle-class environment is still more dangerous due to the expense itself. Despite the lowest members of the working class being financially barred from the tavern space, there is still a confused jumbling of people of different classes as upper-class "Gallants" are mixing with what are clearly meant to be poorer members of the middle orders (1). In his discussion of Earle's piece, Adam Smyth states, "Careful hierarchies and distinctions are blown apart as previously separate worlds mix together and with hierarchies upset, authority is challenged."[5] While Smyth does not evaluate what these hierarchical elements have to say about commerce and trade, he correctly points out how chaotic the scene is meant to appear to the early modern reader.

The short prose satire provides a holistic view of the early modern drinking establishment, critiquing the sounds, music, and conversations, the debates and brawls, the lighting (or the lack thereof) and the sights, the food and drink, the patrons and servers. Earle's piece no doubt entertained his audience, offering a glimpse of a space with which most middle-class Londoners would have been familiar. While his piece satirizes the social environment of the late seventeenth-century drinking establishment and advises its audience to avoid such places, Earle himself seems to have spent enough time there to form the caricatures presented in the text, showing at once the moral superiority needed of a satirist and the observing, mimetic strength of one familiar with such places. In the course of his pamphlet, he mocks the drinkers, their conversations, and their frivolous wasting of money.

However, Earle saves his most damning criticism for the people operating the business, with each member of the staff employing their own techniques to cheat patrons out of their hard-earned money. The woman tracking the patrons' bills appears to write illegibly on the chalkboard. Earle writes, "under her all-commanding Canopy, *Casting the Nativityes* of your Estates in strange *Aegyptian Hieroglyphicks* and *Trithemian* Characters; And finds by the *Horoscope* of the *Board*, and frequent Ill *Directions* of *Score in the Half Moon*, that your Fortunes are *short-liv'd*, and your *Purses* declining into an *Irrevocable Consumption*" (3). Attempting to confuse the drunken onlooker about how expensive their bill has gotten, she writes in hieroglyphics, and unsurprisingly, when they have racked up many drinks, she is then refigured as a fortune teller, revealing that the customer's money is wasting away.

The drawers, those who draw the wine and wait on the customer directly, expect a bribe from those they serve, and if they are not satisfied, the drinker should expect to receive a less-than-savory pint of wine. The master of the house, the supplier of the wine, is only "esteemed" if he "is best at Brewing and Balderdashing Wines"; indeed, not only do they "cheat Mens palates," passing off cheap wine as Spanish canary, but they "destroy their Bodies" by adulterating their wine with dangerous chemicals (4). According to Earle, the tavern—commonly associated with hospitality, good cheer, and social gatherings—actually operates to separate men from their money and to poison and cheat them at every turn. Rather than a space of kindness and warmth, it is a place in which "'tis not you are welcome at all, but your Money" (5).

In addition to critiquing these elements of daily, domestic commerce, Earle highlights the ways in which taverns negatively affect England through global trade. The tavern's customers are styled not as Englishmen but as a "Hodge Podge of Nations," as their drunken conversation—a mixture of jests, play recitations, religious debate, ranting, and swearing—likens them to the biblical inhabitants of Babel. In the same sentence, Earle represents the men as distinctively non-English by parataxically linking them to the expensive, foreign wines stored in the cellar. He writes, "And below in the Cellar you shall see the *French*, the *Spaniard*, and the Natives of the *Rhine* [German wines] (notwithstanding the present Wars between them) lye quietly all together" (3). Rather than taking advantage of the military conflict between these nations, England is unintentionally providing them financial support through the wine trade. To the satirist, the difference between the expensive beverages and the people consuming them is negligible; both lack a sensible, English identity and both cede financial power to foreign nations. This view of wine, as disrupting the British mission for nation-state supremacy, underscores Earle's mercantilist understanding of trade.

While not focusing as fully on the owners of the tavern, Charles Darby's 1680 satirical poem, *Bacchanalia, or, a Description of a Drunken Club*, provides a lengthier, more grotesque, and more damning criticism of tavern patrons than Earle's treatment.[6] In this poem, the speaker, a spectator in a tavern, watches as a drunken club meets and quickly dissolves into chaos. Darby's poem, Juvenalian in its scurrilous, vehement (and extremely grotesque) treatment of drinking, examines a fear of male society spiraling into excessive spending and debauchery to the point that it endangers English masculinity. The poem opens with the speaker asking his audience not to accuse him of "Incivility" (1). He fears that the reader will judge him for revealing other men's private business. However, he notes that the loud group is doing nothing to hide its own activities, their voices only made louder by "transparent Wine" (1). From the outset, the speaker shows that the tavern is not truly a private space since its inhabitants (and their derelict activities) occur in full view of others. Adam Smyth notes the speaker's general desire for ironic distance: "The poem begins, paradoxically, with the narrator's attempt to distance himself from his subject. He artfully positions himself as an outsider, observing from afar—emphasising his chance happening upon the scene, rather than any planned encounter; his role as 'Spectator,' not participant; and his detached position . . . Indeed, not only does the narrator dissociate himself from the drinking group; he also shifts responsibility for this poetical vignette on to the drinkers themselves" (194).

Before discussing the idiosyncrasies of each member of the club, the speaker points to the mismatched nature of the men, explaining that none of the members fit into a single traditional group: "The Actors in this Scene were not of one / Age, Humour, Figure, or Condition" (1). The respective ages of the drinkers do not fit the proper mold for male companionship. One of the drinkers is "young as Hebe, [and] smooth as Ganimede," while the man next to him is so old that he is compared to "old Silenus" (2). Hebe and Ganimede were both divine cupbearers, while Silenus was the drinking chum and tutor of Dionysus; the young man being compared both to a female cupbearer and to the handsome male cupbearer (and homosexual lover) of Zeus, Ganimede, implies that this young, handsome man may be seated with an older man harboring lustful desires for him, suggesting that the homosocial space of the tavern may turn into a space of sexual deviancy.

Not only do these drinking circles challenge heteronormative masculinity, but they also constitute dangerous transgressions against the social order. The chaotic, thrown together nature of the group suggests a breakdown in class barriers, as none of the group is of the same "Condition" (1). In this context, condition would refer to "wealth, circumstances; hence, position with reference to the grades of society; social position, estate, rank."[7] Section III witnesses a nobleman, a man of a lower title, and a tinker all drinking together, despite the clear social and class divides between them. The poem's speaker sarcastically notes, "Cups reconcile Degrees, and Natures too; / He Noblest is, who can in Drink out-do" (2). For the speaker, the tavern and the drinking that happens within its walls create a breakdown in proper class boundaries; upper-class men are seemingly defiling their positions by associating with the working classes. As Michelle O'Callaghan points out, "Drinking rituals enabled the civil gentleman to forge alliances amongst his peers, amongst the nobility, . . . and even amongst merchants, who may be profitably admitted 'to their Brotherhood' for reasons of good finance" (63). Considering the important allusions to trade that I discuss below, this spectator—who may himself be of the upper class—no doubt worries that this overly fraternal behavior may spiral out of control, spilling out of the tavern and into polite society. What starts as connections between classes for the sake of business quickly leads to inappropriate fraternization between groups that ought to be separate.

When read in light of the Popish Plot and Exclusion Crisis, Darby's poem reflects societal fears about the uncertain succession, a common tension in satires of the 1670s and 1680s. Discussing these trends, Ashley Marshall notes, "With the Popish Plot and the Exclusion Crisis came much greater cause for alarm [than the events of the earlier years of Charles's reign], and unsurprisingly, satire of this period often reflects panic as much as indignation. To grumble about government ineptitude during the Third Dutch war is one thing; when Charles sprinkles bastards all over the land but cannot sire a legitimate Protestant heir, frustration gives way to sick anxiety."[8]

Given Darby's fears of social chaos, it is perhaps unsurprising that he would use one of the fictional wine drinkers in his group—who is described as overly obsessed with government policy and who drunkenly boasts that he understands all of England's statecraft, or "the Motions of the Powers above" (6)—to discuss this important political moment. In section XI, the speaker brings up Titus Oates and the Popish Plot, calling out the story's absurdity but also acknowledging the extreme social anxiety provoked by the unanswered question of succession.

Although Darby is satirizing the drunk who brags to his friends about his complete knowledge of politics, his mockery of the character allows Darby to join political discourse, quenching his audience's thirst for commentary. Darby's political drunkard also points out that a covert plot to assassinate Charles II would never have been entrusted to "blundering Fools," who leave important communications lying around for people to find (6). After ranting about the silliness of the plot, the speaker, agreeing with the sound reasoning of this drunk, notes, "Thus spake this Sage: whilst I, from thence, / Infer'd, amidst heaps of Intemperance, / Fools sometimes chop on Truth, and Drunkards stumble upon sense" (7). This scene is particularly interesting as it is one of the few times the speaker agrees with any of the members of the drunken club. Even as he mocks the type of drinker that rants about politics, he satirizes those that have failed to see through the falsity of the Popish Plot.

Additionally, the drunkard criticizes Jean-Baptiste Colbert—France's controller general of finance and one of the originators of the tariff—for his love of his own country's "French wine," boasting that he sees through Colbert's "French Design" or trade policies (6). The issues of religious fear and views of wine are, of course, deeply intertwined. James Nicholls highlights this anti-Catholic fervor embedded in the proto-Whiggish distaste for French wine: "France was seen as the major source of the Catholic threat, and French wines became targeted as both culturally popish (doubtless an idea bolstered by the role of wine in Catholic sacramental ritual) and as an economic drain which directed money straight to the coffers of the French treasury."[9]

Ironically from Darby's view, this same drunken speaker is giving money to the French through his love of alcohol, and while we are meant to read this member of the drunken club as a blowhard, Darby is also using his caricature to evaluate some of the most important mercantilist policies of Europe. Colbert's intermittent tariffs on English cloth (English's primary export) from 1654 to 1667 had started a major trade war between England and France. These tariffs were engineered to "protect and strengthen the French cloth manufacturing industry."[10] By 1678, Parliament had already instituted a trade embargo with France and taken steps to reconfigure French claret as a luxury item. Charles Ludington exposes these political aspects of wine, linking trade policies to the Exclusion Crisis and the rise of political parties, stating, "Given that wine was an outward symbol of the Court and Court interests, and that the soon-to-be Whigs had just imposed an embargo on French wines, it should come as no surprise that the politicization of drinks and drinking that occurred in the mid-seventeenth century returned with a vengeance" (27).

Tories, like the Cavaliers of the 1640s and 1650s, had begun to be associated more closely with wine, especially French claret, whereas the non-court-centered Whigs began to be more closely associated with domestic beverages of ale and beer, like the midcentury parliamentarians. Through the drunkard's offhand boast, then, Darby shows the importance of wine as an element of international trade and a significant feature in the contemporary political moment, placing it alongside his discussion of the Popish Plot.

In addition to these very direct discussions of English politics and economic policy, Darby also shows the very individual effects of French wine on the English citizen. On page 11, the satirical focus of the poem shifts to the repercussions of this self-destructive drinking bout, while highlighting the relation of these problematic behaviors to trade and commerce. In this section, the members of the club begin drunkenly passing out. While one man struggles to stay awake, most drift off almost naturally, and some blame their inability to drink more on alcohol itself:

> Though some [men] there are, that do affirm,
> 'Twas *Bacchus* did it; and that He
> Had Legal Right, to lock up each mans Brain;
> Since Every Room
> His own Goods did contain,
> And his proper Wine-Cellar become. (11)

Here, the men have become dehumanized, and in fact, they claim that "Every Room" has become Bacchus's wine cellar since the drinkers themselves have been transfigured to containers of wine, becoming the drunken god's personal "Goods." After a night filled with grotesque vomiting, the men awake, hungover, to find they must pay their bills. Although each feels he is being overcharged, none can debate the total, "Because 'twas all beyond Man's Memory" (13). As with the befuddled tavern customers of Earle's prose satire, these men have likely been swindled by those running the tavern but, regardless, the money must be paid.

After transforming the men from buyers of goods to goods themselves, and then emphasizing their loss of money, the satirist connects this loss of wealth to the international trade that produced that wealth, stating directly that this was the day that the "Poets Fiction" came true and that "*Bacchus* Conquered the golden *India's*" (13). Darby poetically states that the richness of India, a place with which trade was burgeoning during the second half of the seventeenth century, is lost to drinking, as the men—who have apparently made much of their money from this international trade—have spent all their money on wine.[11]

In the epilogue to the poem, the speaker reminds his audience of alcohol's ill effects on rational thought, bodily health, the proper management of time, the preservation of money and reputation, and the likelihood of eternity in heaven. He once again weaves together these points with references to trade, money, and commerce. Recalling the imagery of the storm, which is subtly linked to the hazards of international trade, he refers to the drinkers as "Hurricanes" that are seemingly ruining their commercial futures with foolish spending (14). Discussing their "abus'd Wealth," the speaker reminds male readers of their responsibilities, not just to family, but to people sustained by the parish, including widows and orphans (14). He states that the drinker's reputation is soon completely "Bankrupt," and he refers to the guilty soul's judgment in heaven as an "Audit" (14). Using the language of banking and money, Darby problematizes middle- and upper-class drinking, treating alcohol, like the Earl of Rochester, George Etherege, and Earle, as a major drain on one's personal finances; unlike the libertine authors of the previous chapter, however, Darby at no point treats drunkenness as a necessary privilege for the elite. Instead, he fears alcohol's damage to the middle class and stresses its effects on global trade.

Like Darby's poem, the anonymous writer of *The Paradice of Pleasure: Or, An Encomium upon Darby-Ale* (1700), using the pseudonym *Philo-Darby* (or "Darby Lover"), emphasizes the importance of international trade to England, while also stressing the devastating effects of wine on middle-class wealth.[12] The text itself is a response to a poem by Ned Ward, a lesser-known poet discussed more fully below. In 1698, Ward, a lover of French claret, had published *The Sot's Paradise*, along with the shorter poem, *A Satyr on Derby-Ale*, both of which mocked ale and the lower-class establishments in which it was drunk.[13] *The Paradice of Pleasure* not only seeks to defend Darby ale from its attacker, but it also considers to a greater extent than Ward's poems the role of alcohol in commerce and economics. Ward focuses mostly on ale's taste, its low alcohol content, its lower-class status as a beverage, and the consumer environment in which it is drunk; the writer of *Paradice of Pleasure* highlights the domestic nature of ale and the import status of wine, seeking to illustrate the ale's potential to enrich England and to mitigate wine's negative influence.

The writer first emphasizes Darby ale's ability to heal economic wounds. On page 3, he presents an image of a downtrodden English merchant. He writes,

> The Wealthy Merchant's Loss it does Restore,
> His Ills are lull'd, and he Repines no more:
> Wrecks nor Misfortunes can his Rest destroy,
> He drowns his Losses in a Flood of Joy.

While the speaker does not blame the merchant for seeking his fortune, he allows the unlucky merchant to "drown" his sorrows in a domestic product. The consumption of ale heals the wounds of international commerce for the English middle-class citizen.

Like Darby's *Bacchanalia*, the poem stresses the importance of international trade for England. The image of shipping returns in the next stanza when the writer wishes that he had the ability, like an alchemist or Midas, not to create solid gold, but instead "Liquid Gold" and "Metamorphize all to Darby-Ale" (2–4). In his vision, the Thames itself would change "its Christal hue, / And Ships shou'd in that noblest Liquor Plow" (4). Here, the Thames as a center for trade is imbued with the wealth that Darby ale would yield as a domestic product, presumably one that could be shipped to other countries. When read in light of the mercantilist ideologies underpinning the work, the imagery of the Thames becoming the hue of ale, described specifically as "Liquid Gold," implies that a successful export such as Darby ale would bring to England a vast wealth of gold bullion. Rather than causing further trade deficits with imports of foreign wine, the ships would instead return with money.

Extending his mercantilist view of alcohol further, the satirist also sees the importation of wine from foreign countries—especially French claret—as a major problem in England. The speaker notes that wine once held "sway" in England and was "the Nation's greatest curse"; only brewing "stem'd its Conquering Course" (4). While alluding to the fact that wine was not a major product for England due to its climate, the satirist imagines that it was the act of brewing ale that fended off the heavy importation that would have conquered England had it gone unchecked. He goes on to state that the Englishman that first brewed ale "taught at once, Frugality and Mirth" as "costly Wine . . . Had almost Bankrupt *Cornhill* and *Cheapside*" (5). The speaker is worried about the common man drinking the heavily taxed wine, which could lead all too easily to poverty.

A few stanzas later, the satirist imagines a scene in which Jove commissions Apollo and the other gods to discuss high mortality rates. Apollo, seeing the corruption that wine has produced in England, states,

> Wonder not, Ruler of the spangl'd Sky,
> That Souls throng *Styx*, and to *Olympus* Fly,
> When Wine, the *Brittish* Nation's chiefest good,
> Is turn'd distemper'd, and corrupts the Blood. (5)

Not only is the satirist pointing out the impact of wine on health and demeanor, but he rightly notes that it is the largest import ("chiefest good"). For the speaker, it is Darby ale that could fix this problem, as ale is presented as a healing "Cordial, to Revive Mankind" (6). If the speaker envisions wine as a problem, a beverage bankrupting English citizens, he implies that the cheaper, domestic ale will solve these monetary issues. Unlike Ames, who, as I discuss below, sees wine as playing a crucial role in England's financial status, this satirist sees ale as the fiscally responsible choice.

Just as wine is a corruptor of health *and* wealth, so is Darby ale a healer of both. The writer directly references several alehouses, providing a literal commercial endorsement of these establishments. But beyond this image of domestic commercial activity, the satirist also points out ale's potential as a major export.

Apostrophizing the Sun Alehouse of Golden Lane, a seller of Darby ale, the speaker tells the alehouse, "As far as *English* Banners are display'd, / Thy Name's Ador'd, and potent Ale convey'd" (7). Here, we have the reverse image of the Britain-conquering foreign wine: a world-conquering English ale. The only limits for ale are those of English ships, implying that ale itself acts as a colonizer. This idea is developed further in the next two couplets:

> Not to our Isle alone, thy Fame is known,
> But where the Winds do Course, or Ships are blown;
> The rough unpollish'd *Indian-Planters* own
> More Influence from *Thy Sun*, than from *their own*. (8)

While colonizing and trading in the West Indies, the ale of the Sun Alehouse creates "More Influence" than the very sun by which the foreigners grow their products, improving, in the eyes of the satirist and his English audience, the lives of the colonized. Furthermore, the "Liquid Cargo" is so loved by these natives that they are willing to "Barter costly Gems as Toys" for the easily produced English ale (8). Ale thus occupies a special place as a beverage that drives trade, a necessary export that increases Britain's ability to hold its important foreign colonies.

Not only does the writer demonize wine and praise Darby ale's restorative nature, he also shows how the environment of the Sun Alehouse has a positive influence on homosocial behavior and on English masculinity. Praising the alehouse-keeper Watt's establishment, the writer of *Paradice of Pleasure* provides a scene that contrasts greatly with the description of the drunken club in Darby's *Bacchanalia*. Whereas Darby's work mocks the chaos of interclass interaction, this satirist seems to praise it: "Each Rank, each Order, daily grace his House, / And at throng'd Tables roundly do Carouse" (8). While we see a mixture of different classes, it is not treated negatively but shows the positive aspect of so many different groups congregating. Darby ale unifies England. Further, it greatly improves masculine faculties:

> In chatting Clubs your Politicians sit,
> And as they Drink, they more refine their Wit:
> The Harrast Warriour there forgets his Toyls,
> In plund'ring Pints he finds more glorious Spoils. (8)

In this passage, Darby ale is presented as a masculinizing substance that crosses class divides; indeed, it has the ability to help the politician be more discerning when making state-level decisions, decisions that lead to the very wars in which the soldier of the second couplet fights. Interestingly, the soldier's "plund'ring Pints" provides two equally important readings: first, he finds another plunder of gold (i.e., the gold of the Darby ale itself), but he also relieves his mind of his past fights ("forgets his Toyls") and finds strength for *more* "glorious Spoils," or hard-won items captured for England. As opposed to Ward's treatment of ale as a lower-class beverage, this writer configures Darby ale as a key to national success. Without this beverage, he argues, England's trade prospects will be gloomy, its governmental policies will not be adequately debated and thought out, and its wars will be fought by men lacking any meaningful rest from toil. Further, England will not show a unified front, as they will not be able to gather around the domestic pint of Darby ale.

In these three tavern satires, the writers consider the roles that foreign wines play in English trade; for the most part, wine is shown to be highly damaging to English citizens at the individual level and more broadly to class dynamics, masculinity, and national commerce. Revealing their mercantilist views of the alcohol trade, these writers mock wine and its ability to put money into the hands of foreign powers. Additionally, while these writers differ on the ways in which they view interclass interactions, they ultimately see wine as disrupting English wealth in major ways, especially among the middle class.

THE QUARTS ARE NOW IN SESSION: ALCOHOL AND TRADE IN AMES'S *THE BACCHANALIAN SESSIONS*

In 1693, an anonymous friend of Richard Ames published a short pamphlet honoring the tavern satirist who had passed away the same year. In this text, the friend, who could very well have been Ned Ward or one of the other Grub Street writers who knew Ames well, provided not only a defense of the recently deceased, but also a fitting epitaph:

> Here lies one who liv'd free from ill Nature and Pride,
> He liv'd but too *fast*, and too *quickly* he dy'd.
> He lasht all the *Vintners* [Tavern keepers], whom he knew but too well,
> And the Ghost of *Tom Saffold* rejoyc'd when he fell.
> Light lie the soft dust, untrod let it be,
> As far from *constraint*, and as *easy* as he. (iii)

Ames, a heavy drinker, seems to have wasted away from a dissolute lifestyle that was not well suited to his career as an aspiring writer. In addition to this epitaph and the verse satire on Ames's enemies, the pamphlet contains a supplemental poem, *A Farewel to Wine*, that was written by Ames's friend and imitates Ames's most famous and popular poem, *A Search after Claret* (1691).[14] However, the central text in this pamphlet is Ames's *The Bacchanalian Sessions; or the Contention of Liquors* (1693), a verse satire that Ames had finished before his death but did not have the time or perhaps the money to get published.[15] As with his earlier work and like the tavern satires discussed above, Ames's final poem examines English consumption of alcohol, looking critically at wine and its role in English commerce and trade. However, unlike these other works, *The Bacchanalian Sessions* discusses more fully the impact of different alcohols on international and domestic trade. Within his poem, he mocks each type of alcohol and the kinds of people most associated with drinking them, and perhaps most importantly, the piece examines closely the negative impact these beverages have on English trade and commerce, on economic policies, and on class divisions; however, despite this largely negative portrayal of alcohol, the poem's anticlimactic ending subverts many of these criticisms, ultimately illustrating the importance of the variety of alcohols available to English society and exhibiting a proto-capitalistic sensibility.

Ames's poem, published after the Glorious Revolution that left James II exiled and William III and Queen Mary on the throne, represents an England that greatly needed funds for war. Discussing the major changes in economic conditions and policy under William III, M. J. Daunton notes, "William's need was above all for money to pursue his campaign against Louis XIV, and government expenditure tripled from less than £2 million a year before 1688 to £5–6 million between 1689 and 1702."[16] In his 1845 novel *Sybil: Or, The Two Nations*, Benjamin Disraeli stated that William "did not disguise his motives [for accepting the British crown]; he said, 'nothing but such a constitution as you have in England can have the credit that is necessary to raise such sums as a great war requires.' The prince came, and used our constitution for his purpose: he introduced into England the system of Dutch finance."[17] Here, Disraeli references the complexity and effectiveness of the "system of Dutch finance," which Jan de Vries and Ad van der Woude have argued was the first modern economy due to its advanced systems of finance, trade, and industrial techniques.[18]

However, despite William's desire for financial independence and his pursuit of military campaigns against France, a cautious Parliament chose to keep control over the moneys needed to wage war, lest the king gain too much power (*Progress and Poverty*, 508). Initially, it was through land taxes that parliament raised money for William's war; however, many "short-term expedients" such as "assessed taxes, stamp duties, customs, and excise" were used to supplement these funds (*Progress and Poverty*, 509). These excise taxes generated important revenue to fund England's involvement in the Nine Years' War against France: "The government's ambition of introducing a general excise in the 1690s was guaranteed to produce 'country' [non-metropolitan landowners] outrage against the threat of an over-mighty executive. The result was a succession of specific duties which were adjusted in a piecemeal fashion, such as doubling the excise on drink in 1691, and the introduction of new duties on malt and leather in 1697" (*Progress and Poverty*, 509–510). Furthermore, Judith Hunter notes that "a great part of the late seventeenth and early eighteenth centuries the country was at war . . . and much of the money raised by excise duties was used to pay for the army and navy."[19] Alcohol's importance to the British economy actually increased during the reign of William, as it helped fund his campaigns against France.

Ames's poem shows a strong awareness of this increasingly complex global activity and its effect on England and the country's tastes in liquor. *The Bacchanalian Sessions* discusses many different types of beverages, attempting (at least initially) to figure out which should serve as England's official drink. The god Bacchus calls all the (personified) liquors together on Mount Olympus, and he and a few other gods allow the alcohols to state their case for being considered the nation's official beverage and crowned with the laurel "Bays." The satirical target of this piece is much more wide-ranging than that of the tavern satires discussed above, which clearly criticized overindulgent customers and the tavern keepers plying them with wine. Ames's poem, which is less harsh and more urbane than the oftentimes Juvenalian grotesquery we see aimed at the tavern environments, instead mocks the effects that specific alcohols have on people, as well as the types of arguments that proponents of each liquor make on behalf of their favorite drinks.

Throughout the poem, Ames places discussion of international and domestic trade into the mouths of his personified liquors. He first sets up this dynamic on the second page of the poem, requiring that "each and every *Liquor*" leave behind its respective storage place to attend the meeting (2). Parading the containers of alcohol before the reader in a list, Ames implicitly alludes to international trade:

> In overgrown *Tuns, Pipes, Fats, Hogsheads* and *Barrels,*
> *Puncheons, Kilderkins, Firkins, Gallons, Quarts,* or what e're else
> Does good moisture contain, rolling through Streets and Allies
> With a motion like Ships between *Dover* and *Calais*. (2)

Ames begins with a reference to the ships in "motion" between England and France, "rolling" back and forth to export and import goods. Also, the very containers housing the liquors—"*Tuns, Pipes, Fats, Hogsheads* and *Barrels,* / *Puncheons, Kilderkins, Firkins, Gallons, Quarts*"—are specific to shipping, rather than the mugs, beer pots, bumpers, glasses, pints, and so on, that would house the liquors as they were drunk in public spaces.

While Bacchus allows (most of) the liquors a chance to plead their case during his court session, he refutes each liquor's claim to be the official English drink, despite many of them providing rhetorically sound proof of their popularity and worthiness for the bays. When the red wines step forward to present their argument, Ames employs military imagery to allude to the effects of war on pricing:

> The *Red Wines* together march decently all,
> Like a Call of New *Serjeants* which go by *Whitehall*
> In Coats party-colour'd, so these by Extraction,
> Were half of them *Spanish,* and half the *French* faction. (7)

Ames loops together these red wines, highlighting their foreign nature. When asked where they come from, the red wines respond, "*Down* the Gulph, *cross* the Alps, or the *Mediterranean*" (8). By referring to themselves collectively as red port rather than as claret, these wines attempt to rebrand themselves. Bacchus concludes that despite their former popularity, the name of claret is sullied in England due to the amount of "counterfeit, poor, pall'd, dull, flat, and insipid" wines that are passed off as such (9). Because of claret's bad reputation, Bacchus even claims that English wine drinkers have started favoring English-made wine over the famous import: "They [the tavern patrons] would drink a damn'd Wine of the Vintner's own making" (9). Unlike the other satirists discussed in this chapter, Ames actually mocks the idea of a domestic product outselling the French import, rather than patriotically championing that product. Thus, Ames alludes to the outbreak of war in Europe and the embargoes placed on French products, the fragile nature of large-scale trading, and the sheer popularity of French claret and other red wines that have caused an influx in counterfeit English-made clarets, something that has diluted this wine's popularity.

Ames employs a similar treatment of Nants, or Brandy. Brandy points to its extreme popularity in the past—especially when drunk in the form of spiced punch—as sufficient evidence of its merits; however, Bacchus rejects this position as well, stating that until "Brandy is cheaper" and the "Wars [in Europe] ended," people who enjoy brandy will have to wait to drink it, since it is too expensive at "twelve shillings the Gallon" (9). Here, Bacchus signifies the effect of international conflict on pricing, which in turn affects the popularity of certain products. In this instance, Ames exhibits proto-capitalistic ideas: that which is readily supplied, of the highest quality, and cheapest for the consumer will dictate popularity in the market.

However, somewhat surprisingly, Bacchus does not endorse beer or ale, despite their domestic status. When Beer and Ale plead their case, they stress that they are a domestic product, brewed all over England. Beer claims that he and Ale are the "best Liquors t' th' English Nation," due to their general popularity and their role as a shippable product (12). Invoking their status as a marketable trade good, Beer states that he and Ale are:

> A Drink much applauded, and thought very good,
> Not by English alone, but by Nations abroad;
> For 'tis plain that the French and Dutch do prefer
> Before their Rich Wines, the Bon Beer d' Angleterre. (12)

Beer portrays himself as being more popular among the French and the Dutch than their own wines. While the comment is clearly an exaggeration, Ames indicates the possibility of domestically brewed beer as an export. Ale further stresses that he and his brother are a boon to the English government; indeed, as noted by Hunter, "ninety per cent of the excise revenue came from the duties on ale and beer" (187).

Further, Ames subtly connects Bacchus's awarding of the laurel crown to the licensing of breweries in England, an additional source of government revenue throughout the seventeenth century. Using trade lingo, Ale declares,

> . . . we as a body call'd corp'rate may stand,
> And a Patent procure from your Seal and your Hand,
> That none without Licence, call'd *Special*, shall fail,
> To drink any thing else, but *Strong Nappy Brown Ale*. (13)

Ames's use of trade and fiscal terminology—"corp'rate," "Patent," "Seal," and "Licence"—shows a strong understanding of ale and beer's importance as a domestic product, as well as the history of brewing as a business. However, Ames also pairs these economic buzzwords with Ale's desire to control English tastes; by forming a "corporate" body, enforced by Bacchus's special license, Ale supposedly can ensure that no other types of liquors are drunk in England. As John O'Brien notes, the concept of a unified body of investors and works making up a corporate entity, a legal fiction, was a relatively new phenomena, beginning to develop in the early seventeenth century, and these corporate entities, capable of accruing a lot of capital for the nation in which they were "born," had a significant impact on the literary world.[20] Here, Ames is most likely alluding to the oftentimes questionable practice of brewery licensing that had been seen in England since James I's reign, which harmed small, family-owned breweries and allowed large-scale operations clear monopolies on the brewing trade.[21]

Further, Ames is likely alluding to the more recent activity of large-scale brewers who were invested in many different businesses and who made sure they received the most lucrative contracts through their royal connections. The large wealth gap this created, and the privileged positions that large-scale breweries enjoyed, would continue to develop throughout the eighteenth century ("Change is Brewing," 180–188). By revealing Ale's desire that everyone *only* drink ale and by having him use the language of trade, Ames gestures toward the increasingly industrial nature of brewing and the corrupt business practices being used by large-scale operations. Because the corporatized brewing that produced such alcohols often tried to monopolize the trade through favorable contracts and licenses, it makes sense, satirically, for Ale to seek to "monopolize" English taste buds.

Presumably, however, Ale's desire for monopoly would hurt not only the consumer but also the government through the loss of tax revenue. Peter Clark points out that by the 1690s, "The Crown's main concern with the drink trade . . . was confined to the excise, more and more the golden goose of government revenue," rather than on the licensing of breweries.[22] Under Cromwell's regime, increasingly complex and expensive duties had been placed on beer, necessitating the use of excise officers to track ale and beer production for taxation purposes;[23] perhaps unsurprisingly, these expensive duties had helped usher in more large-scale breweries throughout the seventeenth century, given that they could more easily handle the weight of such expenses.

Increases in domestic shipping also helped popularize beer, a beverage that was more easily transported in comparison to ale. As Peter Parolin notes, "The advent of beer profoundly changed the economy of drink in England."[24] Ale had been the English beverage for centuries, and up until the sixteenth century, the brewing of ale had been a domestic practice, mostly done by women for the private consumption of the family, but with the development of large-scale breweries, as Parolin notes, the practice was masculinized (28–29). As opposed to beer, English ale used spices rather than hops for flavoring. Hops, however, had the added benefits of allowing beer to last longer than ale without spoiling during the arduous shipping process, and John R. Krenzke points out many seventeenth-century brewers made the switched from ale to beer, writing, "Profit margins on beer were higher because more beer could be brewed with less malt and could be stored for longer periods" (117). Notably, Ale seeks to cut his brother, Beer, out of this monopoly as drinkers should only enjoy *"Nappy Brown Ale."*

Despite the fact that beer and ale generated internal revenue and that, as Ale demonstrates, these drinks are brewed all over England, Bacchus quickly refutes Ale's claim primarily on the basis of the class distinctions inherent to ale and beer (13). Bacchus mocks Beer and Ale, which continued to be associated with the lower classes throughout William and Mary's reign. Only "Ploughmen," "dull Country Vicars," "Carmen," and "Porters," he argues, enjoy drinking these liquors (13). To Bacchus, the prestigious title of England's chief alcohol must go to a worthy liquor that is not just widely consumed but also has cultural prestige. For Bacchus (and for Ames himself, considering his reputation as a claret drinker), England's national beverage needed to be a muse to poets, which the god notes is not the case with ale and beer. Like the more aristocratic and privileged Rochester and Etherege, Ames praises the ability of wine to facilitate artistic expression and wit; as a nonaristocratic writer, however, Ames demonstrates that different alcohols have different social functions and economic roles.

The poem ends somewhat anticlimactically with Bacchus declaring that every Englishman should choose the drink that best suits him. The god does not choose to crown any one liquor the winner, instead telling his fellow judges and deities, "Let each Mortal his skinful most soberly drink / Of the Liquor he likes, or what best he does think" (17). However, if we are to read Bacchus as representing the claret-loving author's views, wine, and especially French claret, seems to be the most favored liquor of the poem, given Bacchus's declaration that they nearly

[53]

won the prize, and Ames implies in the poem that it is one of the most crucial drinks to England's position in the global marketplace. Indeed, as mentioned above, claret would have been awarded the coveted title had it not, unwisely, attempted to enter the competition under the name of red port (8).

The fact that the poem ends without a crowning of the bays reflects the importance of having a number of drinks to choose from, allowing the market to satisfy not only the needs of individual citizens, but the financial needs of the kingdom with England (and other European countries) as consumers. Almost implying proto-Smithian ideas of free market, Ames argues that the different tastes of English citizens impact international trade, domestic commerce, and economic policy in profound ways the individual cannot easily track; indeed, he attempts to provide a literal god's-eye view of how alcohols fit into these major trade dynamics. By leaving his poem open-ended, he asks his audience not to side with their drink of choice, nor only to consider the choices of others within their own country, but also to see the vast web of tastes that make up a burgeoning, global consumer culture.

HUNTING AND BREWING: ALCOHOL AS THE POET'S ALLY IN *THE TAVERN HUNTER* AND *THE HUDIBRASTICK BREWER*

Despite the diligent work of many satirists, alehouses and taverns unsurprisingly remained popular at the start of the eighteenth century; in fact, this century would see the development of two new drinking locales: the public house, which served wine, beer, ale, and other spirituous liquors, and, as discussed in chapter 5, the highly vilified gin shop that almost exclusively slung cheap shots of gin. The continued growth in the popularity of taverns as places of homosocial male bonding would reinforce the commercial desire for poetry focusing on such locales, especially poetry of a satirical bent that presented the archetypical figures to be seen there. However, unlike the satires of the previous decades, the two satirical pieces discussed in this section do not as ardently condemn wine drinking, drunkenness, and the foolishness of tavern behavior; while they critique such places, they consider more fully taverns and alehouses as businesses and as important sites of domestic commerce. As we shall see, these satires consider how such spaces offer financial security not only to those working at them but also to the satirical writers reflecting on such locales. In the anonymously published poem, *The Tavern Hunter*, the satirical poet critiques wine in a similar fashion to the tavern satires discussed above, pointing to claret's high alcohol content, its effect on the middle classes, and the ways in which it undermines English masculinity. However, this writer also forms, within the majority of the poem, an interesting, underlying conceit: the poet and tavern keeper can form a mutually beneficial relationship. The anonymous poet seeks to prove himself both an ally to any business-savvy tavern keeper, and a wealth of knowledge to the reader thirsty for good wine. In a similar way, Ward argues in his apologetic poem *The Hudibrastick Brewer* that his own decision to run an alehouse and to brew beer is not at odds with his role as a poet. Providing both poetic and pragmatic examples of the ways in which his new vocation fits succinctly with his satire and versification, Ward demonstrates alcohol's deep connection to writing, and he argues that being a businessman and being a poet are not mutually exclusive. In this section, I argue that both these satires—while at certain points mocking alcohol in more traditional ways—seek to expose the ways that wine, beer, and ale can serve to bolster middle-class businesses and writers.

Like the other satirists of the alehouses and taverns discussed above, the anonymous writer of the 1702 poem *The Tavern Hunter; Or, a Drunken Ramble from the Crown to the Devil* examines commerce and alcohol from several angles.[25] Like the satires of Earle, Darby, and the anonymously penned *Paradice of Pleasure*, the poem satirizes prodigal spending and the ways in which wine puts money in foreign pockets. However, the poem also examines closely acts of daily commerce in ways that differ greatly from the satires previously discussed. The poem focuses on two men's proto-pub crawl as they visit eleven different taverns, traveling to one after the other and describing the types of people they meet at each place. The anonymous poem has been attributed to Ned Ward, which is very probable given its subject, style, and execution. As a satire, *Tavern-Hunter* offers a perplexing mixture of positions and genres as a majority of the poem (over 400 lines) seems to praise and celebrate the homosocial activities of wine drinking, carousing, and general debauchery. Within the main narrative portion of the poem, the speaker and his friend travel from tavern to tavern, providing descriptions of early eighteenth-century drinking environments: the patrons buying the alcohol, the vintners running the establishments, the behaviors of the staff waiting on customers, the decor of each locale, and the humorous actions of the two main characters. Akin to our contemporary online reviews, the poem in a sense offers a "rating" for each establishment.

While the bulk of the poem (and the humor of the poem itself) focuses on these general commercial aspects, the first fifty-six lines ridicule the "drowthy degenerate Nation" of England for its prodigal pursuit of wine (3). The speaker complains of wine drinking and tavern hunting, activities he and his companion pursue throughout the poem, which, he argues, have caused England to forget its traditional beverage of small beer, the beer of low alcohol content that was a staple of the lower- and middle-class diet. This sudden pursuit of wine is especially problematic for the rising middle class. The speaker notes,

> Nay, those who had liv'd and were Rich by the Sale
> Of *Belch*, as some call it, but I say *Good Ale*,

> Were prodigal grown, and to saucy to Quench
> Their drowthy Salivals without *Flask of French*,
> Contemning at Home their own wholsom and Nappy
> Malt Liquors, that made them so rich and so happy. (3)

The speaker points out that many people who once made a great profit by selling malt liquors, ales, and beers (domestic products) have started drinking French and Spanish wines, imports that strengthen other countries' economies. Echoing Rochester's "Regime de Vivre," he goes on to compare these types of drinkers to a "Young Libertine" who spends all his money on "some soothing Jilt," money that he made by marrying a rich "loving Old Wife" (3). In noting that these new wine drinkers initially made their money by selling traditional, domestically brewed alcohols, the satirist indicates a broader problem: the middle classes are now drinking alcohols more traditionally aligned with the upper class. In the second stanza, he states,

> Each city *Mechanic* too proud is to Dine,
> Sup, talk or make Bargains, but over his Wine.
> The Flask of *French Claret*, Monteth, and *Flint Glasses*,
> Are Tavern delights only worth his Embraces. (4)

The "city *Mechanic*," a member of the lower or middle class, conducts trade and parts of his business within a tavern. For the satirist, the mechanic's lavish taste in wines shows a desire not only to drink in a tavern for the convenience of conducting day-to-day business, but also to enjoy a French import. Additionally, due to the embargo on French claret, which was only dropped in 1697 with the end of the Nine Years' War, claret would have still been difficult to find and would most likely have been more expensive than its Portuguese, Spanish, and German counterparts (*The Politics of Wine*, 42). A luxury item, claret represents a fiscally irresponsible decision that will no doubt have problematic effects on middle-class financial prosperity.

When the poem shifts toward its primary purpose, to "taste [and discuss] the delights of the Bottle," it begins with the speaker and his friend entering the Crown Tavern in Ludgate, one of eleven establishments they will visit throughout their trip (5). This tavern, we are told, is nice enough for a king, and the building's rent is so high "That few *German* Princes are able to pay-it" (5). Immediately, the middle-class speaker evaluates the tavern based on its location. The environment of "this glorious Mansion" itself seems problematic to the speaker because it is overly "lofty" (5). Rather than choosing a more modestly sized building for their tavern, the owners have chosen a very large place that costs much more than they should be spending. While the speaker praises the speedy way in which the owner's wife conducts business ("So brisk in her Bar, and her Business we found-her," 5), he also takes note of her extremely ornate earrings and necklace, perhaps wondering if these consumer products are a sign of extravagance. Afterward, he describes the vintner, her husband, as an extremely thin man whose kind welcome is "Express[ed] in Gesture as much Complesance, / As any new Beau just came over from France" (6). While the speaker's companion ends up mocking the physical differences between the wife and husband, the speaker is more critical of their desire for fine clothing and pomp, hyperbolically stating that not even Queen Elizabeth herself, "Tho' mounted on Throne could more graceful appear" than the owner's wife (5). The satirist uses the figures to consider and to question the vast success that the alcohol business can impart. As is the case in the beginning section of the poem, the satirist shows how wine often drives people to live above their class status; however, in this case, the owners of the tavern are able to do so successfully, at least for the moment.

By the time the speaker and his drinking companion arrive at the Devil, the last tavern on their quest, they are (understandably) very drunk, having had *at least* a pint of claret at all but one of the other taverns. Still, the speaker offers a very detailed judgment of the establishment, supplying only minor criticisms and many accolades. He notes the comfortable size of the private room into which they are led and the general cleanliness of the place: "a little snug Room very neat, / No Cob-webs o'er-head, neither Spawl under-feet" (15). He also praises the orderliness with which the place is run. Despite the tavern being busy, the speaker states,

> Our Wine was brought in without Ringing and Bawling,
> Two Candles, a handful of Pipes without Calling,
> A Chamber-pot too they were careful to bring-in,
> Which few Drawers use under seven times Ringing. (15)

Despite its foreboding name, the Devil is a tavern in which things run smoothly, and the necessary requirements for the customer's comfort—candles, tobacco pipes, a chamber pot—are brought in ahead of time. The speaker points out that although the place "seem'd fond to be busy," every aspect of its operation seemed to have been premeditated or "study'd to make ev'ry Company easy" (15).

The only criticism the speaker offers for the Devil Tavern mirrors his criticism of the Crown Tavern at the beginning: the tavern's size is too large for financial stability. He notes that the owner's "mansion is large, and his Charges are great, / His Trade much too little to gain an Estate," pointing out that the careful selection of the location is paramount for commercial success (15). He goes on to jest about the size of the Apollo Room, the largest room of the tavern. This room, which was famously frequented by Ben Jonson and his friends in the late sixteenth and early seventeenth centuries, is so large that, according to the speaker, it would not only hold all nine Muses, but all of Mount Parnassus. While the speaker alludes to the ability of the location to provide poetic inspiration, he also criticizes it, seeing the excessive space as a potential obstacle to the owner's success. As with his earlier criticisms of the extravagancy of wine, he sees these same deficiencies in the fiscal choices of the tavern keepers.

By beginning his poem with a diatribe against wine drinking and then systematically—and somewhat conversely—discussing the specific environments of each of the taverns in turn, the satirist achieves three main commercial purposes. First, as discussed above, the poem critiques the drinking of imported wine, questioning the purchasing of expensive French claret. The poet also satirizes English drunkenness due to the rise in wine's popularity, and he nostalgically praises the days when middle-class men drank small beer. At the end of the poem, the satirist returns to his original critiques of wine, as the speaker and his friend get so drunk they can no longer function, once again evaluating wine for its damaging effects on English masculinity. Discussing the pair's decision to finish "their Drunken Design" in their cozy, private room at the Devil Tavern, the speaker notes,

> And each time we piss'd we had hold of a thing,
> Which both of us took for the Pack-thread, or String;
> But finding our Lines were abundance too short,
> It hindred our flights, and prevented our sport. (16)

Fittingly, it is in the *Devil* Tavern, the last stop of the evening, that things take a grotesque turn. The speaker and his friend become so drunk that they are no longer able to sustain erections or pursue their sexual interests. Like the vomiting, hungover men in Darby's *Bacchanalia*, the two men are ridiculed in a grotesque, Juvenalian fashion. Mocking their emasculated state, the satirist criticizes wine's ability to prevent sexual coupling. The anonymous satirist fears a loss of English masculinity, arguing that wine imported from France decreases British male sexual potency. It comes as no surprise, then, that the last image of the poem is that of the speaker and his friend returning to their respective homes and having beautiful, tantalizing "Dreams of Small Beer," which would not have created this effect (16). The speaker ends his poem by reminding his audience of the less intoxicating domestic beverage, which does not endanger one's personal wealth or virility.

The second commercial purpose of the poem is located in the speaker's desire to critique the consumer environment of drinking establishments. Throughout the poem, the speaker chronicles specific, interesting interactions in these public spaces. While some taverns only receive cursory treatment, the satirist provides unique details about each place, and these details give the reader clear insights into each location's positive and (more often) negative aspects. Whether it is overpriced shellfish, the off-putting, bickering spouses that run the bar, the owners attempting to charge outrageous prices, or even the overly religious atmosphere, the taverns the satirist mocks are discussed thoroughly, providing the contemporary reader with information on what places to avoid. The satirist supplies those that have the consumer impulse with the direction they need to make educated choices within the market. He also provides feedback to the vintners who own and run these establishments, documenting what is expected of them as business owners. Should the tavern keepers read his poem and realize the faults at work in their businesses, they can change the environment to please the customers and to increase their profits; furthermore, in addition to indicating aspects of businesses that could be improved, the writer presumably sees his poem as a kind of advertisement for the establishments he deems worthy.

Finally, the satirist's "reviews" are surrounded by many funny scenes as the speaker and his friends go from tavern to tavern, interacting with the strange figures with whom the eighteenth-century reader would have been familiar, such as the former apothecary who runs the Younger Devil Tavern and scares away his clientele or the solemn Quaker who operates the Fountain Tavern and makes one feel awkward due to his pious demeanor. By reading these entertaining scenes drawn from some of the very taverns the readers themselves would have visited, the satirist emphasizes that his poetry is made specifically for those of the city. He, like his readers, frequents the same establishments, and he deals with the same problems. By showing off his own interpersonal skills and his savvy, businesslike manner, he presents himself as a member of the group he hopes will read (and purchase) his poetry. He positions himself as a knowledgeable source with a shrewd talent for evaluating businesses, and as a purveyor of entertaining and accurate poetry. He also insists that his writing may have a pragmatic purpose for existing. The writer is thus developing a popular form for the newly emerging and highly competitive literary marketplace.

Like Earle and Darby, the poet and pamphleteer Ned Ward (1667–1731) clearly connects alcohol, trade, and commerce in his poetic satires. Ward, the leading publisher of satirical discussions of alcohol during the reigns of William and Mary and Anne, is perhaps most famous as fodder for Alexander Pope's 1728 publication of *The Dunciad*.[26] While Ward's writing may lack some technical skill, his detailed observations display a unique intimacy with everyday city life in London.

As a poet, Ward demonstrates a clear understanding of the commercial rewards of selling poetry to middle-class Londoners. Focusing on familiar locales, Ward provides a plethora of details about the kinds of daily occurrences that one could see in the city, especially in its most public spaces. His best-known work, the periodical *The London-Spy*, was a monthly publication that lasted from November 1698 to May 1700, and its popularity led to six editions. Throughout his work,

Ward treats alehouses and taverns as important spaces of human interaction, regarding them as a hub for the discussion of news, politics, and business; as we shall see, he also sees these public environments as spaces of poetic inspiration—often composing his work in taverns—and for lucrative employment; he worked as a tavern keeper from 1710 until the end of his life.

Ward targets different forms of alcohol—and the people that imbibe them—for satirical lashing throughout his works, but he fluctuates between the alcohols he chooses to mock in his poetry. Most of the time, Ward, like his friend Ames discussed above, praises French claret, which often functions as an anti-Whig beverage, since it was one of the main products affected by the embargoes against France, embargoes defended by the Whigs. Fitz-Wilhelm Neumann notes, "The French Wars [the Nine Years' War] eventually led to the distinction between 'claret' and 'port,' in the same way that they led to a polarization between Whigs and Tories. When Bordeaux wines [clarets] became less available due to the embargo policy against France, claret rose to a commodity of even higher distinction."[27] Broadly speaking, Tories tended to prefer claret over the Portuguese equivalent, port, for this reason; although, as Ludington argues in his book, these divides—Tories drinking claret, Whigs drinking port—were by no means consistent or absolute.

Still, Ward, as a defender of Toryism, tended to praise claret. Satirical poets focusing on everyday London saw that partisan politics provided both easy targets and a hungry audience, and Ward, one of the major producers of tavern poetry in the previous decade, transitioned more and more to political writing, discussing the victories of the Tories and damning the Whigs. However, Ward's 1714 poem, *The Hudibrastick Brewer; Or, a Prosperous Union between Malt and Meter*, shows a melding of his two styles: the poetry of alcohol and drinking establishments and a not-so-subtle discourse on contemporary politics.[28] Like the satirist in *The Tavern Hunter*, Ward discusses the role of the drinking establishment in daily consumer society. In his poem, Ward defends his decision to work in alehouses and taverns and to brew while continuing to write verse in his spare time. In his biography of Ward, Howard William Troyer explains this dramatic shift in occupation:

> What moved Ward at the very height of his success as a writer to turn tradesman, it is not too difficult to conjecture. The career of a pamphleteer and journalist was frequently a precarious one . . . Of Ward's more widely known colleagues and rivals [John Dunton, Tom Brown, John Tutchin, William Pittis, William King, and Daniel Defoe] engaged in the profession in 1700 only Defoe remained active as a journalist, and his subsistence was fortified both by political patronage and trade. Ward himself in his early years had been sharply aware of the proximity of Grubstreet to a debtor's prison.[29]

Through his endeavors as a brewer and proprietor, Ward was able to have a consistent income and fuel for his poetry, having long recognized that the alehouse provided a wealth of material for his verse. As a writer, Ward knew very well that his best writing was observant of the middle-class environments his readers saw every day. Troyer points out, "For over a decade his success had been directly dependent upon popular taste and appetite, an appetite easily satiated" (170). Neumann argues that Ward was a chief figure of middle-class Tory writing, stating that "the Wardian reporters [of his periodicals and poems] focus on the middle class, depict their habits of conspicuous consumption and self-fashioning as well as the presentation of new commodities—food and drink included—on the metropolitan stage" (47). *The Hudibrastick Brewer*, then, functions as a defense of Ward's choice to take on a secondary career as a brewer and manager of a brew house, and he does so from a middle-class perspective, arguing that he is being pragmatic about his income.

While Ward mostly focuses on his reasons for brewing and alehouse keeping, he also refers to contemporary politics, digressing from the central point of his poem while defending his decision to run a business. One of his major points is that being a brewer and vintner does not interfere with his objectives as a poet. On page 6, he specifically addresses the Whig members of his audience:

> Pray, therefore, let no *Whig* pick Quarrels
> With *Ned*, about his *Tubs* and *Barrels*,
> Or think his *Pegasus* [his poetic endeavors] must halt,
> Because so grosly fed with *Malt*,
> Like *Brewer's* Horse that drags a Score
> Of Beer from *Ale-house* Door to Door.

Ward, a High Churchman and a Tory, preemptively strikes out at Whig critics who would mock him, achieving two purposes. First, he implies to his audience that people who criticize his move to brewing are most likely doing so because of political bias; he refers to Oliver Cromwell a few lines later as a point of reference to defend himself. He points out that Cromwell, the man who defeated and deposed a British king, had himself been a brewer, and that therefore the brewing of ale and beer should not be stigmatized. At the surface level, Ward uses the comparison to Cromwell to provide a very specific example of a successful person who practiced brewing, but politically, he preemptively strikes his Whig critics, portraying them as covert anti-royalists who treat Cromwell as an idol.

Using Cromwell as an example, Ward argues that, rather than being mutually exclusive professions, brewing and poetry are in fact symbiotic. He likens the writing of satire to the process of brewing:

> Besides, the *Bard* that will be nibbling,
> At th' Art of *Brewing* well as *Scribbling*,

> May from the wicked Weed call'd *Hops*
> Draw bitter *Satyrs* for the Shops
> Of Pampleteers . . . (5).

In these lines, the brewing of beer provides a unique perspective on the world, giving the satirist the chance to "Draw bitter *Satyrs*" while also providing him with a steadier source of income. Although he notes that wine has traditionally been associated with poetic insight, Ward treats ale and beer as a muse to poetry, a stark difference from his earlier work in which he praised wine. He posits that "*Good Ale* turns all to poetry, / When drank by *lovers* of the Muses," and provides specific examples of how alcohol assists a writer in composing:

> I've often by Experience found,
> When jaded Muse has been a-ground
> For want of some damn'd crooked Word,
> To make two *Ultimates* accord,
> That then one *nappy Dose* inspires,
> My *Brains* with what my *Verse* requires. (22)

In three couplets, Ward shows how alcohol plays a vital role in his process. When trying to find the perfect word to make two seemingly dissimilar ideas fit ("make two *Ultimates* accord"), a quick drink of ale or beer relieves his stress and inspires him. As in the writing of the court-focused satirists of chapter 1, alcohol is portrayed as a substance necessary to the production of poetry. However, for Ward, the use of alcohol is not directly tied to the elite's ability and privilege to write. He stresses that alcohol and poetry (*Malt* and *Meter*) are meant to provide the author with an income; both are consumer goods that provide money to the writer/brewer.

Ward likewise argues that one must drink the right types of alcohol to reach the proper level of inebriation and to harness the type of bitterness needed for satirical thought. He argues that cheap brown beer only produces burping, flatulence, and poor puns when drunk by poets. Rather, the very ale sold by Ward's alehouse provides the poetic inspiration for satire:

> Therefore the *Bard* that would *inspire*
> His Muse with *Hudibrastick Fire*;
> Must lay aside *Brown Drink* for *Pale*,
> And tipple [Ward's] *salubrious Ale*. (26)

Ward states that he brews his beer himself while invoking the Muses. A somewhat shameless advertisement for his own alehouse, Ward implies that his establishment will likely be the gathering place of other aspiring poets, enticing the average drinker to come to the alehouse to see famous authors. Indeed, when he later moved to the more socially respected Bacchus Tavern in Moorfield, Ward was known for displaying his own volumes, which seems to have benefited his business, and while Pope would ridicule Ward somewhat mercilessly later in his writing, he appears to have visited Ward's tavern in 1717 (*Ned Ward of Grub Street*, 175).

Like Darby and Earle, Ward recognizes the ill effects that alcohol, and especially highly potent wine, can have on people who overindulge. Despite his consistent praise for claret throughout his poetry, Ward points out that too much wine inhibits the creative process. He writes,

> Nor does the *home-spun Juice of Malt*,
> Like *foreign Wine*, alone exalt
> The *Fancy*, but if drank in Season,
> Strengthens and modulates our *Reason*. (22–23)

Placing emphasis on the domestic nature of beer and the foreign nature of wine, Ward gestures toward the international trade required for wine that sends money elsewhere; however, he also shows that wine has a way of robbing British poets of their nationality, causing them to not only discard the traditionally English beverage but also their very ability to reason and develop thoughtful writing. Furthermore, like the anti-wine satirists discussed above, he also recognizes that in addition to having a lower alcohol content, at the most practical level, beer is cheaper. The struggling writer can raise his creative facilities through "*small Expenses*" rather than by being "*lavish*," meaning his alehouse can maintain the poet when they are having trouble selling their work, which he terms "the *starving Times*" (23–24). Thus, for Ward, drinking ale and beer, running a tavern, and writing poetry all fit together. He recognizes the English alehouse for its ability to provide a stable source of income, its contribution to domestic commerce, its ability to inspire the satirical writer, and its role in English culture more broadly.

Both the anonymous writer of *The Tavern Hunter* and Ward recognize the daily acts of commerce at work in the tavern and alehouse. Not only do they see poetry as a way of engaging creatively with these sites of commerce, but they also see such spaces and the alcohol consumed there as providing unique opportunities to supplement the poet's income. By embracing a semi-entrepreneurial spirit, both writers set up their poems to facilitate greater success for the person running those respective establishments (in the case of Ward, this person is himself), while also using pragmatic approaches to sell their own work more efficiently.

CONCLUSION

In this chapter, each satirist shows an interest in examining and critiquing trade and middle-class wealth through the medium of wine and other alcohols; additionally, each of the satirists displays an intimate understanding of the alehouse and tavern environment, showcasing the types of commerce and behaviors that occur in such sites of homosocial bonding. For these writers, alcohol plays a key role, for good or bad, in the life of the middle-class citizen. In a world that was increasingly driven by money and trade, the ability of the middle class to grow would, understandably, be a source of anxiety for writers focusing on the middle class. Further, because of mercantilist views of trade, foreign wine represented a major form of contention among writers who feared the ability of foreign nations to siphon off middle-class money. By looking at the extravagancy of middle-class tastes and by considering the role international trade plays in alcohol consumption, these writers highlight the tensions of class and masculinity that would necessarily play a role in the discussion of sites of drinking.

3

SOT-WEED OR INDIAN WEED?

Pipe Tobacco and Satire, 1689–1709

Pipe tobacco, like alcohol, pervaded English society during the late seventeenth and early eighteenth centuries. Although it was a relatively new product, having been introduced to England in the early 1580s, it had already become a staple item by Queen Anne's reign with enough imported to allow each British citizen to smoke two pounds annually.[1] For many drinkers heading to the alehouse, coffeehouse, or tavern, the plumes and smell of tobacco smoke were expected; indeed, most establishments provided tobacco to those who wished to smoke free of charge.

While Sir Walter Raleigh had popularized tobacco in the English court in 1586, it did not become more widely smoked until three decades later. Under John Rolfe's direction, planters for the Virginia Company of London, desperate to find a lucrative cash crop, began growing broadleaf tobacco in 1612, with the first tobacco crop arriving in England in 1613.[2] By the late 1610s, tobacco had become an important commodity for the English, with colonial tobacco production booming throughout much of the seventeenth century. As was the case with alcohol, the duties placed on English colonial tobacco provided important monies to the English government throughout the seventeenth and eighteenth centuries.

The fact that tobacco enjoyed such popularity was due in part to its ability to transcend both class and gender lines. In her article on the English consumption of goods, Carole Shammas proves conclusively that early modern tobacco meets the criteria to be considered a mass-consumed commodity.[3] She writes, "For a good to be considered a mass-consumed commodity in any given place, two things must happen. It must be bought by people of varied income levels and they must be buying it on a more or less regular basis" (179). As a commodity, tobacco was relatively cheap, which meant the working classes had access to it. Furthermore, the availability of tobacco in lower-class alehouses, along with the replaceable nature of the clay pipes used in Britain during this period, meant that smoking was a habit particularly suited to the non-elite. Sara Pennell notes, "the tobacco-pipe was amongst the first 'essentially disposable' commodities outside of printed ephemera, 'its life in use . . . normally measured in hours or days.' The pipe could be, and was, as ephemera as the tobacco smoked within it; if it was dropped, cracked, broken by being tucked into one's belt (a common way of carrying), or left behind on a tavern table, its inherent cheapness did not impede farther consumption."[4] Not only was the tobacco readily available, but the apparatus by which it was smoked was easily replaced when damaged. As with tobacco itself, many alehouses provided these clay pipes to their patrons.

Given this wide availability, it makes sense that women, too, would have enjoyed smoking during this period. However, while it is clear that snuff—tobacco ground down to a powder, soaked in perfumed chemicals, and inhaled through the nose, which is the focus of the next chapter—was particularly popular with women during the eighteenth century, pipe tobacco's popularity is much more difficult to ascertain. There is evidence to suggest that women did consume tobacco in this way. The chronicler Edmund Howe wrote in 1631 that tobacco was "commonly used by most men and many women," and according to Angela McShane, throughout the seventeenth century "Court records and other anecdotal sources tell us that many women used tobacco" at a time when snuff taking was not widely popular in England.[5] Furthermore, Jordan Goodman notes that

> it is doubtful whether we will ever know if there was any gender or age prohibition about smoking before the nineteenth century. . . . Until other evidence is forthcoming it is best to leave the issue as it stands, by stating that no conclusive proof exists that points to any proscription against anyone of whatever age, gender or social class consuming tobacco. . . . Though we may find the image of a pipe-smoking woman uncomfortable because of our own gender assumptions and constructions, there is little evidence of this in the seventeenth century.[6]

In fact, many seventeenth- and eighteenth-century physicians thought that women should use tobacco based on contemporary Galenic views of the body. According to humoral theories of medicine, male and female bodies were structured differently. Men were primarily associated with hotness and dryness, women with coolness and wetness; based on this misogynistic system, female composition was seen as "unnatural," and thus to take something that made one hotter and dryer, such as tobacco, made a woman's composition more like a man's, and therefore less chaotic.[7] Undoubtedly, men would have been the primary users of pipe tobacco. However, while there is no doubt that some men thought women should refrain from tobacco use and while they were likely forced to restrain their tobacco use more than men, it does not seem to have been culturally stigmatized during this period.

Because of tobacco's huge economic influence during this period, its role as a colonial cash crop, and its ability to cross class and gender lines, British satirical writers grew concerned with its power to affect British identity, particularly due to its Native American origins. Because of the association of tobacco with Indigenous religious rites, ceremonies that British writers often rendered as devil worship through their Eurocentric lens, satirists feared the adoption of "savageness" into English culture.

This chapter considers four satirists who deal with tobacco and the tobacco trade within their work, wrestling with its positive influence on their country's financial stability and with the possible effects it could have on British identity. I begin by looking at the history of tobacco from English explorers' first contact with Native people through the first decade of the eighteenth century. While King James I's financial policies would shape tobacco consumption throughout the seventeenth and early eighteenth centuries, his polemical writing on the product would also set up many of the racialized portrayals of tobacco we see in the satires that come later. In the chapter, I tend to discuss bigoted treatments of Native Americans—and of the African enslaved peoples who picked tobacco—using the term "racialized prejudice," rather than "racist," because ideas of skin color difference between Europeans and these ethnicities were seen as mutable, rather than stable; accordingly, the idea that races had different inherent traits was not a widely established viewpoint in the early modern era. After considering these cultural elements, I then examine Aphra Behn's final play, *The Widow Ranter* (1689), in which the playwright uses tobacco to serve two key functions: to define tobacco as a specifically English trade item, intentionally omitting its Native American origins, and to examine English aristocratic identity and its ability to work within a system based more specifically on financial success. I then consider the works of Ned Ward and Lawrence Spooner. Using xenophobic arguments initially popularized by James I and other early seventeenth-century anti-tobacconists, Ward and Spooner both seek to curb the popularity of pipe tobacco in their satirical works, connecting lust, gluttony, and Native American savagery to excessive use of the product. While Ward and Spooner mocked smokers by suggesting that the Native American tobacco habit was "savagizing" Britons, Ebenezer Cooke, who like Behn had personally experienced colonial life in the Americas, considers tobacco and the colonial space in which it is grown in more nuanced ways.[8] In his most well-known text, the verse satire, *The Sot-Weed Factor* (1708), Cooke's speaker—the eponymous "factor" (or midlevel trader) who has lived in England his entire life—seeks to metonymize the lower-class common planters of the Maryland colonists with the very tobacco plants they grow. Presenting the plant of tobacco as synonymous with the person cultivating it, Cooke's persona generally treats the raw, uncultivated material of tobacco as engendering laziness and American savagery; the factor, then, intentionally separates this uncultivated material from the "product" of tobacco, which he seeks to present as a cultured English trade item.

Taken together, the satirists discussed in this chapter consider tobacco's role as a central consumable trade item that had exerted a major influence on British culture since Elizabethan times. Given pipe tobacco's transcendence of class and gender lines, these writers investigate its ability to change British identity through importation from the colonies; further, they investigate (and in Behn's case, purposely omit) its Native origins, presenting and oftentimes promoting the racialized views produced by these origins. While all four satirists mock colonial life and especially the lower-class behaviors found there, it is Behn and Cooke who move beyond James I's xenophobic critiques of product, exposing more fully the nuanced ways it helped develop the British economy.

THE ROOTS OF COMMODITY: TOBACCO FROM ELIZABETH TO ANNE

Among the many people that accompanied Sir Walter Raleigh on his 1585 trip to the New World was the astronomer and mathematician, Thomas Harriot, whom Raleigh hired soon after his graduation from Oxford in 1580. At the age of twenty-five, Harriot accompanied the group sent by Raleigh to start a colony on Roanoke Island, off the coast of what is now North Carolina. While this colony failed spectacularly, Harriot would write about the findings of the expedition in his 1588 tract, *A Briefe and True Report of the New Found Land of Virginia*.[9] Among the many important findings of this trip, including maize and potatoes, was what he refers to first as uppówoc, or tobacco. He writes, "There is an herbe which is sowed a part by it selfe and is called by the inhabitants *uppówoc*: In the West Indies it hath divers names, according to the severall places and countries where it groweth and is used: The Spaniardes generally call it Tobacco" (16). Notably, Harriot uses primarily the plant's Algonquian name, while merely listing the one commonly used by the Spanish as a secondary descriptor.

In addition to describing the process by which the Natives smoke tobacco, Harriot also provides a detailed list of the pharmaceutical applications of the plant. He notes tobacco's ability to purge excess phlegm and other humoral chemicals and to "openeth all the pores and passages of the body," stating that it is because of the Natives' use of tobacco that they "know not many greevous diseases wherewithall wee in England are oftentimes afflicted." (16). Just as he chooses to label tobacco under its Algonquian name, Harriot points out that these medicinal properties are proof that the Indigenous peoples may know elements of medicine the English do not, and when describing tobacco's role in Algonquian ceremonial practices, he does not completely reject it (and its supposedly medically beneficial qualities) based on a perceived connection to witchcraft; in fact, Harriot engages in tobacco smoking with the Algonquians in a way that many of his contemporary audience would likely have viewed as spiritually problematic or even blasphemous. Harriot writes, "We ourselves during the time we were there used to suck it after their maner" (16). Discussing *A Briefe and True Report*, Kelly Wisecup argues that Harriot's labeling of tobacco in his writing was meant to combat these anti-tobacco views, refocusing the reader's attention on its medical and commercial potential rather than on its ceremonial usage: "[Harriot's] catalog highlighted tobacco's uses as a medicinal herb and a commodity rather than its status as a vehicle with which to access metaphysical powers."[10] Further, Wisecup writes, "While Harriot smoked the same herb and employed the same 'manner' the Algonquians did, the catalog form allowed him to emphasize tobacco's appearance and utilitarian features and in this way to separate English use of tobacco from practices of witchcraft" (63). Thus, employing categorization and proto-scientific cataloging, Harriot emphasizes tobacco's ability to promote health, while also implying its possible (and eventual) commodification for English markets.

Harriot's treatment of tobacco—with its medical applications and its potential as a cash crop—would be a defining element of the English tobacco debate; however, another powerful voice in this debate would be King James I, who shortly after ascending the English throne would publish a scathing condemnation of the plant in his 1604 pamphlet *Counterblaste to Tobacco*.[11] This piece and other anti-tobacco pamphlets of the Jacobean era, such as Philaretes's *Work for Chimny-sweepers: Or a Warning for Tabacconists* (1602) and John Deacon's *Tobacco Tortured, or, the Filthie Fume of Tobacco Refined* (1616), are among the earliest examples of nationalized stances against tobacco and consumer items more broadly.[12] In his condemnation of the product, James attacks tobacco's supposed medical benefits, positing that its effects disrupted the humoral balances in the body, and as David Harley notes, James's views and arguments were not entirely consistent with the contemporary Galenic theories of the day.[13]

However, James directs his main attack at tobacco's Indigenous origins. Whereas Harriot catalogs the plant as a potential remedy for ailment and as a novel commodity, James's text, published eighteen years since the introduction of tobacco to England, stresses its Native origins, its perceived connection to witchcraft, and its negative effect on Christian morality. James proffers many xenophobic views of Native Americans, condemning their role in introducing colonizers to tobacco and continually stressing that tobacco endangers Christendom. Sabine Schülting notes that "Tobacco, as the 'Indian weed,' was associated with all the vices which were ascribed to Native American societies in European colonial discourse: devil worship, unbridled sexuality, a lack of culture, and foolish ideas of economic value."[14] While Harriot may present Algonquian ceremony with some racial condescension, James—a king famous for his obsession with witchcraft—projects more fully Judeo-Christian religious doctrine onto Native culture.

Further, James connects the "sins of lust and drunkenness" of the body to what we would now term the addictive qualities of tobacco ("The Beginnings of the Tobacco Controversy," 45). As James writes, just as "no man likes strong heady drink the first day," so "great takers of Tobacco" are "by custom . . . allured" to the plant. However, when this moral strategy did not work, he turned to money. In his analysis of the pamphlet, Iain Gately states that realizing that his "rhetoric had failed James resorted to the only other weapon against tobacco at his disposal—taxation."[15] It may be that James hoped to make tobacco prohibitively expensive, as we shall see in chapter 5 with the numerous Gin Acts, which sought to combat gin consumption in a similar way. Or, it may be as Susan Campbell Anderson has argued, and James was not as morally opposed to tobacco as his famous pamphlet makes him out to be.[16] He may have seen, like Rolfe, the ability of tobacco to be a financial powerhouse. Regardless, James ended up raising taxes on tobacco 4,000 percent from what they had been under Queen Elizabeth.

Although their relationship sprung first from rocky soil, the Stuarts would go on to cultivate a great deal of revenue from tobacco. While he may have differed with Harriot's view of Native American ceremonial uses of tobacco, he recognized, like Harriot, its potential as a commodity for England. By 1613, England received its first official tobacco shipment, which kicked off an extremely lucrative enterprise for the English government, and by 1621, James and his ministers had created laws that "required all tobacco grown in Virginia and Bermuda first to be shipped to England, landed, and have duties be paid before being transshipped for sale elsewhere in Europe (*Tobacco*, 72). To increase the yield from imported tobacco, planting in England was prohibited."[17]

In a similar manner to Parliament's 1651 Acts of Navigation discussed in chapter 1, this law ensured that government duties were paid by requiring merchant ships, in this case those specifically carrying tobacco, to dock and be inspected in London. Alan Taylor comments, "Eventually [James] learned to love the large revenues that the crown derived from taxing tobacco imports."[18] Despite his antipathy to tobacco, James provided the Virginian colonies, at their request, important tax breaks to facilitate colonial trade and to counter Spanish trade; furthermore, as Woodruff Smith makes clear, this economic development "gave the Virginia variety [of tobacco] substantial access to the English market and allowed it to be sold for a price that attracted customers of middling income," despite "Serious smokers continu[ing] to prefer Spanish-American tobacco."[19]

Like his father, Charles I expressed a public hatred of tobacco but clearly recognized its financial significance. Charles inherited from his father trade laws that facilitated governmental wealth from tobacco taxation. Todd Butler notes that despite the "obvious vehemence with which James attacks tobacco . . . the official policy regarding tobacco that he bequeathed to his son Charles was more nuanced and practical."[20] Charles would continue his father's trade policies, ensuring that the American colonies grew all the tobacco for English consumption and trade, and that England's tobacco would continue to generate lucrative customs duties while attempting to keep out Dutch traders.

However, in his trademark approach to policy (asserting royal prerogative and indiscriminately ruffling the feathers of a Parliament that would ultimately defeat his armies, and capture and execute him), Charles angered those around him with his treatment of the tobacco trade. Indeed, as McShane points out, "the taxing of tobacco without parliamentary approval was one of the many crimes visited on Charles I's unfortunate head" (41). Along with angering Parliament, Charles also enforced the deeply unpopular law that prohibited large-scale tobacco growth in England, ordering his soldiers on at least one occasion to cut down tobacco crops and trample the plants with their horses. These types of policies even led to riots ("The New World of Tobacco," 41). However, the most dramatic association between Charles I and tobacco comes during his captivity. After the Rump Parliament handed down Charles's capital sentence, his royal physician, George Bate, claimed that parliamentary soldiers "blew the smoak of Tobacco, a thing which they knew his Majesty hated, in his sacred mouth, throwing their broken Pipes in his way as he passed along."[21] As Stephen Coleman notes, smoking tobacco in a public space, apart from an alehouse, was already considered disrespectful (427); to blow smoke in the face of the monarch was almost unthinkable.

During the English Civil Wars, trade routes between England and the American colonies unsurprisingly eroded, and many specific laws dictating trade were left unenforced. This lack of control led to a spike in tobacco smuggling during the period, as well as increased reliance on Dutch merchants for shipping (*Tobacco*, 98). Gately writes, "Some Englishmen had enjoyed the taste of anarchy the civil war had offered and continued to cultivate and smuggle tobacco during Oliver Cromwell's protectorate, and after the restoration of the monarchy" (98). However, with the establishment of the Commonwealth and its devolution into the Protectorate, the English government sought once again to establish trade rules concerning tobacco. With the Navigation Acts of 1651, Cromwell attempted to rein in smuggling; indeed, Gately argues, "Tobacco was . . . a problem for the English government, which it turned to its advantage by using [it] as a justification for renewing its grip on colonial trade" (99). In addition to requiring English trade ships to land first in London docks, the acts also banned shipping that involved "intermediary nations" (99). Ultimately, these restrictions increased hostilities with the Dutch (which was part of the laws' intent) and decreased the autonomy and trading power of the English colonies.

During Charles II's rule, as well as his brother's short, unsuccessful reign, tobacco laws remained very similar to those enacted by their grandfather, their father, and during the Protectorate. J. M. Sosin points out that the Restoration of Charles itself had major effects on trade, especially in the months following his ascendancy. He writes, "In the newer, expanding trades, competition was intense, as the number of men engaged in commerce increased. With the boom in tobacco imports the number of London traders dealing in tobacco tripled" (50). Due to the increase in the number of people dealing in tobacco, the market became flooded, resulting in "collapse in the price of the weed in the 1680s and the threat of economic ruin" in the colonies (*Tobacco*, 106). Such problems would persist even as tobacco's popularity grew, and shipping problems in particular would occur during the reigns of William and Anne due to trade line issues resulting from the Nine Years' War with France (1688–1697) and Queen Anne's War (1702–1713). However, the issue that would most greatly shape the tobacco trade during the period would be the shrinking of the traditional labor pool, indentured servants, meaning that tobacco would be increasingly picked by enslaved Africans.[22] This change would help set the stage for the type of chattel slavery that would develop with the racist ideologies beginning to form in America.

Throughout the seventeenth and early eighteenth centuries, the tobacco trade played a key role in British economics. As we shall see, Behn, and later in the eighteenth century, Cooke, consider the economic and cultural importance of tobacco within the colonial space, presenting the incapacity of the English trader to understand fully the cultural significance of the plant. For Ward and Spooner, however, the physical and moral repercussions of pipe smoking outweighed the revenue brought to England, and ultimately they see the desire for tobacco—gluttony according to Ward, lust to Spooner—as beyond the control of the average, sinful person; the people capable of fixing this problem, according to these writers, are those who have significant interests in maintaining tobacco's profitability and who are, notably, people living in the British Isles.

HAZARDING ONE'S PROSPECTS: TOBACCO AND TRADE IN BEHN'S *THE WIDOW RANTER*

"He had learned to take tobacco," Behn's narrator tells us in the last pages of *Oroonoko*, shifting momentarily away from description of Oroonoko's grisly torture and execution, "and when he was assured he should die, he desired they would give him a pipe in his mouth, ready lighted, which they did."[23] Oroonoko's request for tobacco may come across as odd to a modern audience, especially given his general antipathy to the customs of his European enslavers, but as Susan B. Iwanisziw clarifies, Oroonoko's tobacco smoking indicates his symbolic denigration to the status of colonial commodity through slavery.[24] In her essay on *Oroonoko* and tobacco, Iwanisziw argues that Oroonoko's use of tobacco while being burned alive symbolizes his commodification as he figuratively undergoes the same processes used for curing tobacco, emphasizing the Crown's colonial desires for enslaved people and tobacco during James II's reign. Indeed, as Iwanisziw points out, Oroonoko's name is from the Spanish strain of tobacco common to Virginia (77). At the same time, Behn also speaks to the pervasiveness of tobacco usage in colonial settings. Despite being an enslaved person, Oroonoko has clearly grown accustomed to smoking, alluding to both the economic importance of tobacco (it is an abundant crop) and its ability to cross class and racial lines.

Representing the commodification of enslaved people, Behn satirizes the insidious nature of the slavery project, as Iwanisziw indicates, by mimicking tobacco curation when Oroonoko is put to death. However, Behn's choice to present Oroonoko as tobacco at the moment of his death should give the reader pause for a secondary reason: despite Behn's desire to illustrate the brutality and pain caused by slavery, she chooses to connect Oroonoko to tobacco curation, rather than the processing of sugar cane that actually occurred in the English colonies of Surinam. While Behn does point to sugar as the root of the South American plantation system early in the text—writing "Those then whom we make use of to work in our plantations of sugar are negroes, black slaves altogether, who are transported thither in this manner" (78)—the process of refining sugar is notably absent in the text, partially due to the narrator's insistence that Oroonoko, because of his innate nobility, is exempted from the difficult labors that are beneath his elevated class status as a prince. While tobacco only appears once in *Oroonoko*— albeit at a crucial moment in the text—this commodity permeates the plot of Behn's less famous tragicomedy, *The Widow Ranter; Or, the History of Bacon in Virginia, A Tragicomedy*, which was written in the same year as *Oroonoko* and was performed and published posthumously. As with her more famous prose work, Behn uses tobacco for satirical purposes, and like Oroonoko's death scene, she also seeks to omit the role of the Other in cultivating the colonial commodity. Like *Oroonoko*, Behn's play omits tobacco's Native American roots and does not discuss the use of tobacco in American Indigenous religious ceremonies and beliefs; however, in her final play, it seems more an intentional choice than an authorial oversight, given her insistence to exoticize the Native peoples of her play. Behn seeks then to define tobacco as a uniquely English good, perhaps hoping to highlight her support for Stuart taxation of the plant.

The Widow Ranter presents a highly romanticized version of Bacon's Rebellion of 1676, in which Nathaniel Bacon revolted against colonial leadership and fought an unsanctioned war against Native American tribes. The historical Bacon arrived in Virginia in 1674, entering the colony at an important turning point. Virginia's colonial governor, Sir William Berkeley, had presided over two largely successful stints in office, having begun his second tenure at the start of the Restoration in 1660; however, the overproduction of tobacco and a resulting drop in prices, along with increased taxes, had created widespread economic hardship. It was around the time of Bacon's arrival that, as James D. Rice notes, "A growing chorus of complaints blamed the commissioners of Virginia's county governments for levying such heavy taxes, which unfairly burdened small planters who grew little tobacco or had little to spare."[25] In addition to being understandably concerned with these economic issues, Bacon was also particularly angered by Berkeley and the colonial council's alliance with specific Native tribes—despite the long-standing nature of these alliances. To gain support from the common planters, he spread conspiratorial claims that Berkeley had monopolized the fur and tobacco trade for personal gain, providing dangerous Native tribes with colonial guns (*Tales from a Revolution*, 40). Using his (apparent) charisma, leveraging his elite status, and weaponizing anti-Indigenous fervor, Bacon began fighting against Native tribes in open defiance of the governor's council in the spring of 1676. By the end of the rebellion, Bacon managed to push the colonial government out of Jamestown and to set fire to the village; Bacon's aspirations were short lived, however, as he contracted typhus later in the year and died in October 1676, bringing an end to the conflict.

While Behn's play highlights the importance of tobacco in colonial life, it does not do so via the fictious rendering of the political events of Bacon's Rebellion, instead investigating tobacco through comedy. Tobacco plays little to no role in the tragic plot, which concerns the fictionalized Bacon's deteriorating negotiations with the Indian king, Cavarnio, the resulting battles, and a love triangle between the Indian queen, Semernia, and the two rival warriors. Rather than emphasizing tobacco's role in the political crisis, Behn investigates tobacco's role in British colonial society within the comedic storylines. The play consists of three intertwined plots: the tragic one concerning Bacon; the lower comedic plot concerning the uncouth, inept members of the Privy Council of Virginia, and the English trader, Hazard; and the comedic plot centering on the Widow Ranter and her pursuit of General Bacon's second in command, Captain Daring. These two comedic plotlines depict the centrality of tobacco—both as a consumable material and as a product of trade—to the English colonies, examining the ways in which long-term colonists, both male and female, realize (and attempt to demonstrate) its communal importance.

Through the character of Hazard, an Englishman just arriving in the colonies, Behn examines the effects of the colony's tobacco-based economic system on traditional English class dynamics. Entering a society in which tobacco plays a key role in business and communal interactions, the Englishman unfamiliar with the tobacco trade quickly reveals his seeming incompatibility with the social environment. Through conversations surrounding tobacco, Hazard is introduced to the ways in which the tobacco-based economy has destabilized class divisions in the colonies. He learns that tobacco-infused wealth provides a nontraditional (and thus problematic) path to public office, and that it has reshaped the marriage market. While traditional English dynamics win out in the end, Behn plays with the foreign, colonial environment, subtly criticizing English upper-class identity within these systems. While primarily satirizing the ways in which English systems have been inverted in the colonies with disastrous results, Behn also uses tobacco to mock members of the aristocracy who are unable to adapt to new cultural environs. As with her use of wine in *The Rover, Part I*, discussed in chapter 1, Behn uses an important, consumable good—with all its economic and commercial implications—to critique aspects of English aristocratic identity.

Before examining the use of tobacco in the play and the way it illustrates the trade-based, communal characteristics of colonial smoking, it is important to recognize the ways in which Behn removes the Native American origins of tobacco throughout the text, as well as her possible reasons for doing so. Discussing John Dryden's *The Indian Queen* (1664) and its sequel, *The Indian Emperor, or the Conquest of Mexico by the Spaniards* (1665),[26] Robbie Richardson notes that, while "Exotic settings were a common feature of Restoration drama," Dryden's New World settings are "evoked both implicitly and explicitly as a means of imagining Britain's own fantasies of global conquest."[27] Dryden's use of the Native American is very rudimentary, functioning more as a type of "generalized exoticism" (*The Savage and Modern Self*, 17). Behn likewise treats Indigenous people as an exotic spectacle in *The Widow Ranter*, a text to which Dryden penned the prologue. In act 2, scene 1, a scene set in an Indian pavilion, Behn introduces Carvarnio, the Indian king, and his queen, Semernia, "sitting in state" and attended by a great many of their tribe.[28] Despite the traditional connections of tobacco to Native Americans seen in James I's *Counterblaste* and other anti-tobacco pamphlets, something that a royalist like Behn would likely have been aware of, tobacco is not mentioned at all in this scene. As we shall see, tobacco is a consistent element in the play but is absent here.

This lack of tobacco in act 2, scene 1 is rendered more noticeable due to its juxtaposition with the following scene. In act 2, scene 2, the Widow Ranter holds a small party at her hall. As with the previous scene, Behn uses the body of the Other to render her settings exotic but chooses here to incorporate Black bodies, rather than Indigenous ones. The stage directions read: "Enter the Bagpiper, playing before a great bowl of punch, carried between two Negroes, a Highlander dancing after it" (275). Given that Surelove starts the scene off by noting the smell of a "dessert of punch and tobacco," most likely many of the people would be smoking in the scene (274). Rather than connecting the exoticism of the Native Americans with tobacco, Behn instead presents enslaved Africans carrying punch and preparing for the Widow Ranter's gathering. It may be, as indicated by Iwanisziw (90), that Behn is alluding to the increased use of chattel slavery during a period that saw both a higher demand for tobacco and a smaller pool of indentured servants to harvest it. Behn's use of rum—a drink derived from sugar, which was almost exclusively produced by enslaved peoples due to the extreme toil and danger necessitated by the rendering process—highlights these connections. However, given that tobacco does not appear in the first scene with Carvarnio and Sermernia, we are clearly meant to associate tobacco more closely with Scots and enslaved peoples than we are with Native Americans.

In act 4, scene 1, Behn once again neglects tobacco's Native roots, making no mention of tobacco during her representation of a Native American religious ceremony. Within the play's stage directions, Behn details a Eurocentric vision of Native American religion; she describes a scene at a temple complete with "an Indian god placed upon it, Priests and Priestesses attending," who "dance about the idol, with ridiculous postures and crying (as for incantations)" (299). Although she provides several fake Indigenous words and alludes to an Indian god, Behn does not reference tobacco in the scene, despite the fact that it would likely have made the play's Indigenous religious rituals more authentic.[29]

It may be, as Daniel Yu has recently demonstrated, that the representation of tobacco in religious rites were seen as dangerous due to their "homologies with communion" which "threatened the sanctity of the [Protestant] rite."[30] Discussing Daniel Defoe's *Robinson Crusoe*, Yu argues that Crusoe's material use of tobacco, equated with Christian rites of communion, connects in part to the novel's "transgressive religiosity" rather than its secularism: "Tobacco, the sacred substance that catalyzes Crusoe's conversion, persistently reappears in the narrative as a reminder of the material basis of his religion and its dangerous proximity to heathenism" (104). Although Behn is far from the most religiously focused writer of the period, she may have wanted to avoid reminding her audience of tobacco's association with Native idolatry, instead seeking to emphasize the Englishness of the trade good. By redefining tobacco as an English good, rather than one adopted from Native Americans, Behn more closely aligns tobacco with the English colonial community she presents in her play, avoiding the type of criticism of tobacco that, as discussed above, had long been associated with the Stuarts. Thus, through her work, she seeks to bolster tobacco as a uniquely English product, seeking to defend it as a material that can continue to generate wealth for the Crown.

Her treatment of tobacco as a distinctive product and cultural material of the Virginia colony allows her to imagine a world in which trade and commerce yield greater power than traditional class and gender dynamics. Using the character of Hazard, an upper-class man new to the Virginia colonies, Behn presents tobacco as a product that the newly arrived Englishman should absolutely understand for economic purposes and for social cohesion, but he fails to do so. By omitting the Native American origins of the trade good, she pushes her audience to think of tobacco as an English product that will greatly impact England's financial and cultural future.

From the first scene of the play, Hazard functions as a metaphorical stand-in for the audience, allowing Behn to introduce the multiple-plot structure of the play and the alien environment of the colony. At the start of the play, Hazard arrives in Jamestown and finds his way to an ordinary, or inn, where he runs into his old acquaintance, Friendly. During their conversation, Friendly presents Hazard and the audience with an overview of the differences in colonial life. After Friendly mentions that he has inherited a large tobacco plantation from a wealthy uncle, Hazard describes his own financial position: In England, he almost ruined himself with drinking and gambling, but his brother gave him a small cargo and free passage to Jamestown to seek his fortune.

Friendly then pushes Hazard to woo the soon-to-be-widowed (and wealthy) Mrs. Surelove. Ever fiscally minded, Friendly suggests that Hazard also pursue the eponymous Widow Ranter, a woman worth over £50,000, advising Hazard, as it were, to diversify his investments in the marriage market, rather than focus solely on Mrs. Surelove. According to Friendly, the widow, who was Colonel Ranter's indentured servant until she married him shortly before his death, offers a unique opportunity to an eligible bachelor just setting up in Virginia. Friendly then describes the Widow Ranter's strange, somewhat outrageous behavior, especially her lack of gentility and traditional femininity.

Friendly presents the widow's "pleasant" and "primitive quality" of low birth as unproblematic, alluding to the relaxed, more colonial approach to class (255). Mrs. Surelove, meanwhile, is a "young gentlewoman" of good parentage and whose "breeding's the best this world affords" (255). This short description of the up-jumped Widow Ranter and her comparison to the upper-class Mrs. Surelove provide an important insight into Hazard's character. While both women are wealthy, Hazard is only interested in someone from his own station. While she has taken on the "humour of the country gentry," Widow Ranter still exhibits her low birth in the eyes of the English, class-conscious Hazard, which clearly factors into his dismissive treatment of her in the play.

The other comedic plot, which begins after Friendly leaves the inn and as the various council members file in, ridicules from its very first scene the upstart group of lower-class figures who, we learn later, have gained significant power in Jamestown and whose ineptitude has led to the current political crisis with Bacon and the Natives. Behn is careful to tie tobacco and rum punch to the communal rituals of the council. Upon sitting down in the ordinary, the men call for pipes and tobacco, and discuss the types of alcohol they plan to drink; while their tobacco smoking does not tie them to any particular class, Behn uses the liquors they discuss to betray their non-elite background. One of their first comments of concern is the nature of Timorous's hangover, which he blames on drinking Colonel Downright's "high burgundy claret" (258). As discussed in chapter 1, French claret and other such wines would have been the fashionable drink of the middle and upper classes, causing contemporary audiences to see the stark class difference between Colonel Downright and Timorous. This reference to claret, to which Dullman pejoratively refers as "your English French wine," shows the popularity of spirituous liquors like brandy and rum punch in the colonies, and presumably Restoration audiences would have been surprised to hear wine spoken of in this way. Further, the fact that a claret originates in Bordeaux, not Burgundy, underscores Timorous's ignorance of wine. As the men continue their conversation, Timorous argues that punch and brandy will eventually become more popular than "the lousy juice of the grape," and he states that upper-class men just need "a little Virginia breeding" to correct their taste in alcohol (258). Timorous, a nonaristocratic member of the council, is unused to wine and mocks it, while Colonel Downright is a member of the upper class. Behn, then, uses alcohol to satirize the improper subversion of power and order that has happened in the colony, as these extremely dishonorable men have gained seats on the council.

After discussing alcohol and beginning to smoke, the men mock the innkeeper, Mrs. Flirt's lover, Parson Dunce. Mrs. Flirt, giving as good as she gets, points out that more than a few of these men have less-than-reputable backgrounds. She states that prior to Jamestown, Timorous was "but a broken excise-man, who spent the king's money to buy your wife fine petticoats, and at last not worth a groat, you came over a poor servant" (259). Like most of the other councilmen, Timorous seems to have been transported as a criminal to the colonies, condemned to indentured servitude until his sentence was served. The practice of transporting, shown famously in Defoe's *Moll Flanders* (1722), was a cheap source of labor and much appreciated by the colonial leaders.[31] The practice began in the early seventeenth century, and James Davie Butler notes that in 1619 as many as fifty convicts were sent to the Virginia colonies in one trip.[32] While being an excise officer means that Timorous was likely middle class, other councillors present, including Dullman and Boozer, prove that the Privy Council is made up of many former members of the lower orders. Dullman criticizes the "scoundrels" who "live upon scandal" and claim that he "was a tinker and running the country, robbed a gentleman's house there, was put into Newgate, got a reprieve after condemnation, and was transported" to the colony (259). Dullman also alludes to Boozer's time as a "common pickpocket, and being often flogged at the cart's-tale" before he became an informer and then came to Virginia.

It is not without a bit of irony that twenty lines later, Flirt insists that Hazard join the council, which is made up of "very honourable persons, I assure you" (259). However, Hazard, who has observed this entire conversation, clearly recognizes the foolishness and low birth of the councilmen, noting in an aside that he would have "sooner take[n] them for hogherds" than for council members (258). Despite their lower stations, Behn also shows that her dissolute aristocratic hero, who is meant to be seeking his fortune in the New World, is clearly incapable of taking the steps to do so. As the scene continues, Hazard shows his inability to engage in tobacco-focused conversation. Hazard shows no ability or inclination to prevail in the tobacco trade, the most customary method of economic growth in the colonies. Timorous asks Hazard if he has any cargo with which to trade, and if Hazard truly sought success in this commerce-based environment, he would most likely begin hashing out a deal with the councilman, trading his cargo for tobacco that he could send or accompany to England for sale. However, Hazard, who does not quite understand the centrality of tobacco to Virginian life, responds, "I was not bred to merchandizing, sir, nor do intend to follow the drudgery of trading" (260). Dullman, perhaps responding to the newcomer's haughty tone, points out that "Men of fortune seldom travel hither, sir, to see fashions." Here, Dullman seems to be mocking the fact that upper-class people rarely come to the colonies except out of desperation, correctly guessing Hazard's financial ruin and lack of drive.

Intrigued at Hazard's lack of enthusiasm, Timorous asks if Hazard will "hire [himself] to make a crop of tobacco this year?" (260). Hazard responds that he "was not born to work, sir," prompting Timorous to also mock Hazard, insinuating that the clothes on his back are his only possessions. Although a contemporary audience probably would not be inclined to side with Timorous, it is perhaps unsurprising to the modern reader that he would take offense at Hazard's proud demeanor: "Not work, sir, 'zoors your betters have worked, sir; I have worked myself sir, both set and stripped tobacco, for all I am of the Honourable Council." Discussing the position of the characters at the end of the play, Iwanisziw writes, "the immigrant Englishman Hazard, despite his lack of fortune adamantly refused to dirty his hands with tobacco cultivation. His upper-class identity would militate against manual labor in any case, but Hazard's unwillingness to apply himself to agriculture only emphasizes the distinction between the gentleman/aristocrat and the vulgar planter" (91). While perhaps not apparent at first, the row that occurs between Hazard and the three council members is primarily rooted in economic and class dimensions. If Timorous, Dullman, and Boozer are meant to be mocked, Behn implies that the unsuccessful, dissolute lifestyle of the aristocrat does not quite fit within a colonial community built on the tobacco trade. Just as he refuses to engage with the product itself, he is ill suited to discuss any aspect of the tobacco trade in conversation, a major necessity for life in colonial Virginia.

For Hazard, honor is connected directly to being "nobly born" (256), whereas for Timorous, Dullman, and Boozer, council members who were born lower or middle class, honor is linked with physical labor and the success in trade that raised them from their former statuses. Their back-and-forth should therefore be read with class distinctions in mind:

> HAZARD: Is it your custom here, sir, to affront strangers? I shall expect satisfaction.
> TIMOROUS: Why, does anybody here owe you anything?
> . . .

> TIMOROUS: Let him alone, let him alone [Boozer], how should he learn manners, he never was in Virginia before. (260)

Timorous clearly does not understand the upper-class reference to dueling that Hazard makes. If Timorous is a fool unworthy of the Privy Council, he also reveals the extent to which Hazard is unaware that Virginia's atmosphere and society are starkly different from England's. While Behn clearly develops this scene to expose the council members' inept, cowardly, and rude behavior, she also makes clear that Hazard is not meant to be taken as a businessman, and in a place like this English colony, noble birth, divorced from any knowledge of trade and tobacco, is of little worth. While the drunken, tobacco-smoking councilmen are Behn's primary satirical targets, Hazard's inability to contribute economically also serves as a butt of her humor. As with *The Rover*'s Willmore, Behn shows the problematic nature of a dissolute aristocracy divorced from honorable purpose.

While inept, corrupt, and undeniable lushes, Timorous and the other councilmen are clearly interested in discussing financial matters, since business has allowed them to ascend to their affluent positions in the colony. Through this discussion, Behn draws attention to the differences between the aristocratic Hazard and the low-born councilmen. At the Widow Ranter's feast mentioned above, Timorous, Dullman, and Friendly discuss the way business is conducted in London, and Timorous and Dullman are critical of the direction in which English trade is headed. Timorous believes that once the problems with Bacon have ended, Virginia will be "one of the happiest parts of the world," clearly alluding to the restoration of trade that may have been suspended by the wars (276). One of these supposed issues may be that Timorous and others like him were behind the trading of British firearms to the Indians. Thus, Timorous would see this trade as a lucrative enterprise, despite the dubious treatment of these trades in Behn's play. He notes, however, that affluent members of the London Court of Aldermen showed little enthusiasm when he visited them: "Some were nodding, some saying nothing, and others very little to purpose, but how could it be otherwise, for they had neither bowl of punch, bottles of wine or tobacco before 'em to put life and soul into 'em as we have here" (276). Here, Timorous stresses the importance of intoxicating liquors and smoke to business dealings. Given the nature of the character espousing this opinion, audiences are meant to see the humor in this statement; Timorous believes that all business dealings should involve two substances, alcohol and tobacco, in which he is constantly overindulging.

However, less than fifteen lines later, Timorous also mocks the "young merchants" of England whose "Exchange is the tavern, their warehouse the playhouse, and their bills of exchange *billet-doux*, where to sup with their wenches at the other end of town" (277). This line is less hypocritical than it first appears. While Timorous believes that alcohol and tobacco, two central trade items to

England and its colonies, are important for fueling business discourse, he also marks out elements—the taverns, the playhouses, and mistresses—that may lead to distractions from financial pursuits. Furthermore, as a businessman, Timorous places a lot of emphasis on his holistic knowledge of trade ("I myself have stripped tobacco," 260), on knowing one's product. By this line of reasoning, the disconnectedness of English businessmen from the items in which they trade constitutes a problem, one that would presumably be solved if those same men used alcohol and tobacco themselves and visited the Virginia colony, ideas that Timorous suggests are crucial. Whereas the young businessmen of England model their behavior off the licentious actions of elite (and financially ruined) men like Hazard, Behn shows that Timorous and the other councilmen engage with their product and recognize its importance within colonial systems of trade, something that Hazard consistently refuses to do.

At the end of the play, Timorous and the other drunken councilmen are removed from their offices. Timorous, for one, does not seem bothered by this change, and it comes as no surprise that Timorous—a man who promotes engagement with the commodity that fuels his success as a businessman but has not exhibited any specific skill in statecraft—comes to the conclusion that he "has never thrived since I was a statesman, left planting, and fell to promising and lying; I'll to my old trade again, bask under the shade of my own tobacco, and drink my punch in peace" (324). Anita Pacheo connects this "expulsion from the council" to "the class politics of Tory comedy," arguing that

> it would be imprudent to claim that Behn's last play advocates the admission of the humble into the sphere of public life. But the clowns' fate is also consistent with the links Behn has drawn between them and Falstaff, who is similarly ejected from public life at the end of *Henry IV, Part Two*. Their manifest unfitness for government may not therefore be solely a class judgment but equally a recognition that festive disorder has no place in public office.[33]

For Pacheo, their riotous lifestyle and behavior, not their low-born status, has led to this expulsion. I would point out, however, that this ending acknowledges Timorous's unfitness for council affairs while also stressing his past commercial success.

Thus, Behn uses Timorous and his companions to represent a mad world in which commerce and trade allow one to rise quickly and undeservedly to positions of power. Yet by contrasting Hazard with these men, Behn also subtly satirizes English aristocracy, exposing the extent to which upper-class men cannot fully engage in a society that is built chiefly on exports such as tobacco, a model to which England was striving. The licentious and lazy libertine figure is not prepared—both because of his lack of experience in trade and his lack of drive—to engage in this type of system successfully. Considering the financial revolutions that would occur over the next half-century, during which the landed gentry would cede affluence to the power of new financial institutions, Behn gestures toward an anxiety at the loss of aristocratic power.

Hazard's rejection of tobacco and the financial power of trade is also reflected in his interactions with Widow Ranter. Like Timorous and his compatriots, Widow Ranter views the consumption of tobacco and knowledge of the tobacco trade as essential components to being a colonist; however, whereas her male counterparts are most interested in discussing trade as it relates to class, the widow instead connects these commercial ideas to gender. During her interactions with Hazard and her primary romantic interest, Captain Daring, she reveals her sexually enterprising nature, her view of her body as merchandise, and her wealth as a financial incentive to potential husbands, showcasing her deft navigation of the marriage market. In her interactions with Hazard especially, Widow Ranter demonstrates a similar mindset to Timorous, arguing that an intimate knowledge of tobacco is essential for Virginians; however, while Timorous's views focus almost solely on business dealings, the widow shows that knowledge of tobacco is crucial to the colonial marriage market. Through her sexual interest in Hazard, Widow Ranter reveals not only the ways in which tobacco is a lubricant in business transactions but also that it underpins important cultural institutions like marriage.

Widow Ranter first appears in the play in act 1, scene 3, attending a morning gathering at Mrs. Surelove's house. After exchanging a few pleasantries with Mrs. Surelove and Friendly's lover, Chrisante, the widow calls for rum punch and tobacco, providing the audience with a glimpse of the "extravagancy," or outrageous behavior that Friendly mentions to Hazard in the first scene. If Mrs. Surelove is shocked by the widow's desire for alcoholic punch in the morning, she shows little surprise at Widow Ranter's desire to smoke, and almost immediately after, the stage directions say that the widow "falls to smoking" (265). The women's conversation quickly turns to marriage, and Widow Ranter reacts enthusiastically to the news of the downturn of Mr. Surelove's health. For Widow Ranter, who was raised from an indentured servant to affluence through her marriage to an elderly husband, the news is excellent, as it will allow Mrs. Surelove to remarry and have her pick of younger men. Like Chaucer's Wife of Bath, Widow Ranter celebrates the widowhood that allows her to pursue men in whom she has an actual sexual interest. She praises her deceased husband, calling him a "sweet-heart" for dying early enough for her to reenter the marriage market a wealthy woman and still young and sexually desirable (266). Discussing the play's treatment of female characters and class, Heidi Hutner notes, "In an odd twist for the class-conscious Behn, however, Ranter is a positively portrayed lower-born woman, a former servant who moved up the social scale by marrying her now-deceased former master. Her behavior reveals her social background—she drinks, swears, and smokes a pipe, but she also negotiates her desires effectively and remains, in contrast to all of the other female characters in the play, uncontrolled and unvictimized by men."[34]

Part of this refusal to be victimized rests in her unique position as a widow. Like many widows in early modern literature, Widow Ranter realizes after her husband's death that she is in complete control of her sexual interests, as well as the money and property left to her, allowing her to decide whether or not to yield these freedoms to the control of a new husband. Responding to Chrisante's query whether she worries about being "bound body for body" in marriage, the widow states, "Rather that [Daring] should love no body's body besides my own, but my fortune is too good to trust the rogue, my money makes me infidel" (266). Because she is so wealthy, the widow cannot trust Daring, who may throw aside her sexual needs after gaining control of her wealth. It is clear from this interaction that the widow desires another marriage, provided the man be willing to fulfill her sexual and emotional needs and remain faithful. Like Timorous and the councilmen's business discussions, the widow's interest in marriage fits succinctly with the commercial aspects of Virginian culture, which are at odds with the mentality of the libertine Hazard.

Just as Widow Ranter shows interest in different business opportunities as a trader of cargo, she diversifies her sexual interests by pursuing more than one man. As implied by Friendly in the first scene, Hazard soon learns that he could easily gain the widow's affections (and wealth) for himself. Upon meeting Hazard, Widow Ranter instantly shows her interest in the young libertine, her commercial pragmatism in the tobacco trade mirroring her practical recognition of her own status as a commodity in the marriage market. When Hazard first arrives, she asks, "Come, sir, will you smoke a pipe?" (267). In addition to this being an offer to Hazard to engage in the communal ritual of pipe smoking, to be more connected to the colony, the widow also implies a sexual intimacy in the ritual via the phallic nature of the pipe. Hazard, perhaps conscious of the sexual underpinnings of the invitation, responds that he does not smoke. In a fashion similar to Timorous and the other drunken councilmen, the widow illustrates the importance of tobacco as a commodity in which a colonist should partake: "Oh fie upon it, you must learn then, we all smoke here, 'tis a part of good breeding—well, well, what cargo, what goods have ye?" Noticeably, the widow demonstrates the close connection between smoking tobacco and dealing in it. That it is "a part of good breeding" to take tobacco stresses the communal importance of smoking; to refuse to partake reflects one's outsider status, especially when one trades in the product itself. Thus, the widow shows that to be in the know in the colony, to establish good deals and to succeed, one should smoke.

A similar rule applies to the marriage market. Like Timorous, Widow Ranter correctly guesses that Hazard has cargo to trade, despite his lack of interest. The widow shows off her vast means by expressing a willingness to trade any amount of tobacco for his cargo, whether it is "lace, rich stuffs, [or] jewels" (267). In a clever bid to parlay a mutually beneficial business relationship into a potential sexual one, she tells him that she lives "hard by, anybody will direct you to the Widow Ranter's," providing her name and evidence that she is well known both for her plain dealing and for her wealth. Displaying her understanding of the marriage market, Widow Ranter also correctly guesses that Hazard aims to marry well to secure a fortune, noting that "the first thing [young men] do when they come to a strange place, is to enquire what fortunes there are" to be made via marriage. She goes on to advertise herself as an object to be purchased: "we rich widows are the best commodity this country affords, I'll tell you that." Widow Ranter connects business relationships and knowledge of trade with matrimony, illustrating the extent to which Virginia's marriage market is deeply connected to its primary cash crop. Ultimately, however, Hazard chooses the more passive, genteel widow Mrs. Surelove, as his future wife; just as Hazard rejects Timorous and the other councilmen's interest in business and their accompanying desire for communal tobacco smoking, he dismisses the business-minded Widow Ranter as a potential spouse. Behn, then, plays with the idea that the dissolute (and lazy) aristocrat would reject newer forms of wealth, such as those that are much more trade based and that change the conduct of the marriage market.

For an English audience, witnessing a culture built on the trade of this major cash crop would have been a novelty. Rather than take on the traditional, Stuart anti-tobacconist stance, largely based on xenophobic views of the Indigenous peoples, Behn seeks to distance its connection to the Native people of her play and embraces tobacco; indeed, Behn stresses tobacco's role as an important trade product. While pushing her audience to ignore tobacco's Native American roots and think of it as a traditionally English product, she provides, through the character of Hazard, an Englishman's view of the colonies, and she underscores the importance of tobacco as a product to be both consumed by colonists and traded for English goods. Despite mocking the lower-class characters extensively, Behn shows the development of a culture that is distinct from England's, founded more on economic principles than on birth. Although Hazard and the aristocratic principles he represents win out in the end, the playwright asks her audience to consider the ways in which an increasingly trade-based country such as England could come to mirror aspects of this foreign space. Behn satirizes aristocratic power through tobacco, illustrating potential economic changes on England's horizon, suggesting that new wealth could one day displace aristocratic power.

SOT-WEEDED AND SAVAGIZED: TOBACCO IN WARD'S WRITING

As with the alehouse and tavern poets of chapter 2, many English writers understood tobacco's importance to the English economy and also reveled in their usage of the product.³⁵ Surprisingly, Ned Ward's treatment of tobacco fluctuates between mild enjoyment and skepticism. Despite his heavy consumption of wine (especially claret) and beer and his clear belief in these alcohols' essentialness to English culture, he was much more critical of tobacco and its role. There are points, specifically in his famous eighteen-month periodical *The London-Spy* (1698–1700), where he discusses smoking tobacco and treats it favorably; indeed, he enjoys it.³⁶ In the first installment, published in November 1698, Ward's journalistic speaker meets his London acquaintance, and his recording of the sights of the city is initiated with a visit to a coffeehouse, where he and his friend immediately begin smoking. Tobacco's role is key in blending into the environment and for studying humankind: "When we had each of us stuck in our mouths a Lighted pipe of Sot-weed, we began to look about us" (1:9). Despite making fun of the pungent smell of tobacco in the coffeehouse, he seems to enjoy his tobacco. Later, in May 1699's installment of the periodical, Ward's persona in *The London-Spy* goes to buy tobacco at a shop and makes fun of several of the store's patrons who clearly do nothing else but smoke; however, in the same passage, it is also clear that he plans to enjoy tobacco himself and praises the enthusiastic demeanor of the vendor where he purchases the tobacco (7:6–7). Despite often complaining of the stench of tobacco in his writing, he also mocks foppish men who are overly sensitive to the smell of tobacco (9:5).

However, his views of tobacco's ability to harm the individual and society greatly outweigh the moments in which he is more relaxed toward the product. Discussing the anti-tobacconist writers of the Jacobean era, Sandra Bell notes,

> At a time when expansion into the Americas promised to carry English customs and values to the New World, the new import appeared to be undermining that very Englishness within England itself. The custom of taking tobacco was changing the nature of the English body, and for many this extended into a potentially destructive change in the body politic. England's imperialist drive into the Americas, which was motivated at least partially by tobacco, was threatening to undermine rather than expand England's power.³⁷

Like these writers of the early seventeenth century, Ward often represents tobacco as a savagizing substance, an idle and gluttonous indulgence that leads one to become less English and more Native American. Indeed, the *Oxford English Dictionary* cites Ward as being the coiner of the term "sot-weed," which analogizes the overuse of tobacco to becoming stupid with drink.³⁸ In his writing, Ward presents these behaviors as problematic for English identity as they are easily transmittable to his country through the material of the tobacco itself; his discussions of tobacco within his works, such as *A Trip to New-England* (1699) and *The Secret History of Clubs* (1709), thus reveal a satirist seeking to curb British tobacco consumption by reminding readers of its Native origins.³⁹

In 1698, Ward published *A Trip to Jamaica*, first employing his travel writing style, which he later applies to London itself in his *London-Spy*.[40] *A Trip to Jamaica*, a mixture of prose and poetry, provides a detailed account of Ward's time at sea on the way to the island. Building off this modest commercial success, Ward published *A Trip to New-England* a year later, using many of the same literary techniques: descriptions of strange sights, the mockery of archetypes, interspersed poetry as further commentary, and evaluations of the commerce that facilitates travel. In comparison to *A Trip to Jamaica*, Ward provides a deeper discussion of the culture of New England. In his biography of Ward, Howard William Troyer gives the writer the benefit of the doubt regarding his supposed trip to Jamaica due to the specificity, the accuracy of his description, and his mentioning the trip elsewhere. With his account of *A Trip to New-England*, however, Troyer establishes that it is highly unlikely that Ward ever traveled to the American colonies, and could have gleaned any of the details of the poem from "any tavern about London."[41] In *Jamaica*, Ward had focused more attention on the trip itself, whereas with his sequel, he provides a greater analysis of strange animals, the behavior of the New England colonists (to whom he refers as the "Native English" and the "American English") and the nature of the Indigenous peoples. Here, I refer to the New England colonists using the "American English" since Ward's use of the phrasing "Native English" is clearly meant to mock the effects of Native American culture on the colonists, implying that the colonists themselves—through cultural osmosis—have been savagized and made more like the Natives of the New World; further, it also insinuates that the colonial lands are now the Native home of the English, despite the settlements supposedly functioning as colonies.

Ward mocks both the American English and Native people primarily based on their idleness, a quality that he insinuates is a result of the American English becoming more like the Native Americans. Ward also connects the immoral behavior of the American English to the Indigenous peoples through his use of tobacco and alcohol. Unlike James I or, as we shall see, Spooner and Cooke, Ward depicts in this text a reciprocal corruption of both cultures, rather than solely a savagizing of English colonists. Ward shows a racialized, prejudicial treatment of Native Americans, presenting them as lazy and as dependent on alcohol; however, he highlights the British colonists' negative influence on the Natives, noting wryly that the vice of drinking is one that "(to the Reputation of Christianity) they learn'd of the *English*" (16). Ward aligns tobacco smoking with the idleness of inns and the laziness of the English planters. In his first descriptions "Of the Native English in General," he focuses on the colonists' extreme abuse of tobacco, writing, "The Women (like the Men) are excessive *Smokers*; and have contracted so many ill habits from the *Indians*, that 'tis difficult to find a Woman cleanly enough for a *Cook* to a *Squemish Lady*, or a Man neat enough for a *Vallet* to Sir *Courtly Nice*. I am sure a *Covent-Garden Beau*, or a *Bell-fa* would appear to them much stranger *Mon-*

sters, then ever yet were seen in *America*" (10). Here, Ward blames Native American "ill habits" for corrupting the American English. What is perhaps most problematic for Ward is that their excessive smoking has made these Anglo-American people incapable of living a traditional English life. These lower-class figures are no longer eligible to maintain honest livings in England, and in fact they would be perceived as "monsters" more frightening than the actual exotic animals he discusses.

However, Ward notably begins by pointing out the non-gendered aspect of the colonists' tobacco use; not only do the women smoke, but they smoke excessively, calling into question their proper English femininity. In his text, Ward mocks both men and women for their excessive smoking, but it is the women to whom he pays particular satirical attention. Ward goes on to argue that this rampant consumption of tobacco infiltrates every aspect of the female colonists' lives. The habit is observed not only during their rest times, but presumably in their sexual lives ("They *Smoke* in Bed"); in their daily act of preparing meals ("[They] *Smoke* as they *Nead* their *Bread,* [and] *Smoke* whilst they're *Cooking* their *Victuals*"); during their work; in their religious practices ("*Smoke* at *Prayers*"); and even during their daily bowel movements (10). Ward seeks to show how the obsession spreads to every facet of the female smokers' lives, pointing to the embedded nature of tobacco within their lives, and more broadly, the culture of the entire colony.

If his evaluation of English colonists and their love for smoke very directly blamed Native Americans, Ward's later satirical piece, *The Secret History of Clubs*, considers more specifically the role of trade in tobacco's prominence in Britain. *The Secret History* was, like much of Ward's work, refined from earlier ideas; it had first appeared as a short pamphlet, *The Secret History of the Calves-Head Clubb, or, the Republican Unmasqu'd* (1703), which discussed a secret club in which republican-minded men toasted the death of Charles I.[42] This satirical piece saw several editions over the next decade. By 1709, Ward used the same model to satirize other groups of people within society, such as thieves, syphilitic people, atheists, and, in the text I discuss here, smokers. The 1709 version of the text examines many interesting clubs, and Ward uses each group to scrutinize a specific phenomenon in society; perhaps the most important to history is his discussion of the molly clubs, secret gatherings of queer men.[43] As with many of the club descriptions that make up the prose satire, chapter 27, "Sam Scots Smoking Club," provides a fairly simple, humorous anecdote meant to mock a common aspect of London life. In the case of this chapter, Ward's targets are people who smoke excessively in London taverns and inns. In the opening anecdote, a male club, led by Sam Scots, intrudes on an inn near St. Clement Danes Church. Because the innkeeper is understandably annoyed at the group's excessive smoking, he convinces his other, non-smoking guests to play along with his scheme: to drive them from the premises by yelling out that there is a fire. Following this anecdote, Ward tells his reader that the smokers eventually lost all their health, their friends, and their sexual potency because of their obsession with tobacco. He then ends the chapter in his usual way, with a poem that satirizes other aspects of his subject he did not address in his anecdotal discussion of the respective club.

The poem itself is perhaps Ward's most direct attack on tobacco. In the first two stanzas, he mocks smokers—referring to them as "Sots" in line 1—for willingly "sacrific[ing] their Lives to such a Weed; / Whose only Virtues are to Smoak and Stink" (317). As in modern culture, the stench of tobacco smoke was a common target of complaint and mockery for both the product and the user in the eighteenth century. In the final pages of *Gulliver's Travels*, for instance, Jonathan Swift ridicules human stench by having the disillusioned, Houyhnhnm-obsessed Gulliver—upon returning to the human world—plug his nose with tobacco leaves to avoid the Yahooish smell of people.[44] While Ward notes that wine is helpful when it is not abused, he insists that tobacco provides no positive qualities for smokers themselves, arguing that it must have been some "Devils dream" that first convinced someone to smoke (317). Like James I, Ward conflates Native American deities with the figure of the Christian devil. In the fourth stanza, Ward points directly to James and his anti-tobacco views in *Counterblaste*. After imagining that the plant had never been imbibed, he writes,

> Well might the Royal *Scot* so much exclaim
> Against an Herb, that did such Mischief breed,
> Which in his happy Days had scarce a name
> Besides that odious Term of *Indian* Weed. (318)

In these lines, Ward begins a subtle critique of the "Royal *Scot*," reminding us of James's exclamation against tobacco while questioning his integrity. He states that James's *Counterblaste* would make sense had tobacco not flourished during his reign and garnered other names (or "Terms") as a product. The "odious Term of *Indian* Weed" includes the same racialized implications apparent in the "Devils dream" above, and Ward implies that the plant would have been relegated to a Native American habit only had it not been for James and his government.

In the stanzas that follow, Ward blames governmental greed for the spread of tobacco smoking. Expanding on his criticism of James's hypocritical stance on tobacco, Ward argues that this type of product would never have gotten popular if the government were not so interested in taxing it. He writes,

> Nor would the nauseous Product e'er have grown,
> Within these Realms, so popular a Vice,
> Had it not brought large Incomes to the Crown,
> And been a grand Promoter of Excise. (318)

In addition to exposing the strange positions of James I and Charles I regarding tobacco, these lines question the impact that government regulation and taxation have on the popularity and spread of consumable items. Using the synecdoche of "the Crown," Ward links the first English monarch to push for extreme tobacco taxation—James himself—to its spread.

By alluding to the Native American origins of tobacco while also mocking Stuart financial policies, Ward shows that the dangers of tobacco stem not only from its effects but also from its ability to generate wealth. Ward represents tobacco smoking as an enjoyable experience, when properly controlled; the problem lies in gluttonous overindulgence, which he argues engenders idleness and apathy in the working classes. According to Ward, this overindulgence will only increase when moral institutions—namely, the English government, which is expected to curtail such idleness and gluttony—choose to capitalize on the situation.

"THOU TAWNY MONSTER": TOBACCO, NATIVE AMERICANS, AND THE SATIRE OF LAWRENCE SPOONER

Between 1703 and 1705, Lawrence Spooner completed two verse satires against pipe tobacco. The first poem, *A Looking-Glass for Smoakers*, appeared in 1703, and focused primarily on the negative effects (medical, financial, and spiritual) of tobacco on the smoker and those closest to them.[45] Throughout the poem, the speaker, implied to be Spooner himself, claims that his choice to take up pipe tobacco was initially medicinal but soon became a debilitating habit. Throughout the seventeenth and eighteenth centuries, there would be many physicians arguing—according to Galenic views of the body—that smoking actually promoted good health due to its ability to "dry out" the subject, thus counteracting humoral imbalances in the body. No doubt the writing of Thomas Harriot had helped promote this view of tobacco. While many people recognized that smoking was not good for breathing, tobacco's benefits as a medicine persisted throughout the early modern period. Defoe, for instance, has Robinson Crusoe not only inhaling tobacco smoke, but also chewing a green tobacco leaf and steeping the rest of the leaf in rum, which he takes a "Dose of" after laying down.[46] As with Ward's work, Spooner's first poem references tobacco's Native American origins, referring to it as the "Indian Weed" (17) and the "Indian Herb" (21); however, unlike Ward, Spooner satirizes tobacco and the desire to smoke by sexualizing the act of smoking, infusing it with racialized prejudicial beliefs about rampant Native American sexuality. He posits that the impulse to smoke is nearer to lust than to gluttony and idleness, as seen in Ward's writing. This treatment, which appears marginally in *A Looking-Glass*, is developed more fully in his later work, *Poetical Recreations: Or Pleasant Remarks on the Various Rumours upon the Publication of My Poem, Call'd, A Looking-Glass for Smoakers*, published in 1705, which seeks to defend against a supposed popular backlash to his earlier poem.[47] As with James's pamphlet, these poems employ racialized, bigoted ideologies to link English tobacco consumption to Native American sexual licentiousness; by alluding to sexual diseases, the possibility of racial hybridity, and the threat of interracial sexual violence, Spooner seeks to combat tobacco's popularity in England by stoking fears of the loss of English identity.

In the earlier poem *A Looking-Glass*, Spooner conflates Native American sexuality with tobacco through the figurative use of venereal diseases. After a lengthy section discussing the inability of people to quit tobacco, Spooner argues that even if a man is able to smoke tobacco on occasion without forming a habit, his wife and children are likely to take up the habit as well. He writes,

> If therefore you have the *Indian* Itch,
> Tho but a little, lest your Offspring catch
> The Mischief from you, purge your self with haste,
> Lest it should prove a Leprosy at last. (39)

While not directly naming pox or syphilis in these lines, Spooner's use of contagion imagery brings to mind any itchy disease that a man might pass to his wife and then, in turn, to his children, alluding to tobacco's long association with Native American licentiousness and with venereal diseases. This subtle reference to syphilis is compounded when considering that it is more than likely that Spooner is connecting this "Indian itch" to James's and the other anti-tobacconist pamphleteers' critique of tobacco as originating as a remedy for sexually transmitted diseases.

Spooner layers deviant Indigenous sexuality onto tobacco more explicitly later in the poem, when he describes tobacco as an alluring foreign prostitute. On pages 87–88 of the pamphlet, Spooner notes the dangers of large gatherings such as "merry Meetings, Markets, and the Fair," at which people tend to follow the behaviors of the "jolly Crew [surrounding them], / Who to be temperate yet never knew." Combined with this imagery of presumably drunken frivolity is the image of a prostitute roaming the place for a client:

> I say be watchful; for this *Indian* Witch
> Is always present there, she'll strive to catch
> Away your heart, and there's enow,
> That for your Love unto her will you woo. (88)

In this passage, Spooner is likely playing off Philaretes's anti-tobacconist pamphlet, *Work for Chimny-sweepers*, which as Kristen G. Brookes points out, had "figure[d] tobacco as a 'swarthie Indian' who 'pla[ying] the painted English Curtesan,' and been corrupting 'fair Albion from within.'"[48] Spooner, like Philaretes, uses sexuality to show the corrupting nature of tobacco's influence. By connecting tobacco specifically to lust, Spooner stresses the influence that male groups have on individual male behavior; places of merrymaking with high concentrations of frivolous men will attract the enterprising prostitute, and the group of men themselves will reinforce lustful behavior. Furthermore, using the phrase "*Indian* Witch," Spooner mixes the Christian rendering of Native American religious beliefs—that Indians, like witches, are serving the devil—with the image of the man-baiting sex worker, while also reminding the reader of the Native rituals with which tobacco is often associated. According to Spooner, tobacco constitutes a grave, almost sexual sin that the proper, Christian Englishman must avoid at all costs.

While modern readers may find these racialized and sexualized representations of tobacco disturbing, Spooner's personification of tobacco in *Poetical Recreations* offers a far more startling and racialized treatment of the product and its threat to England, connecting importation to invasion, mocking skin color difference, and projecting fears of Native American sexual abuse of English women. As mentioned above, the poem seems to have been written as a defense of his earlier piece; it is, however, hard to tell if this is mere posturing on the part of Spooner, as there seems to be no evidence of pamphlets responding to Spooner's writing or position. Elaborating on his intended audience for the second poem, Spooner notes that when thinking about tobacco, he "fell unexpectedly into a second Chain of Thought, respecting a Dialogue, for the gratification of Young People" (4). This sequel is thus much different from the previous poem, with much of the writing criticizing the commerce-based thinking that allows tobacco to infiltrate English culture and with a greater use of fear tactics meant to restrain young would-be smokers.

The last twenty-four pages of Spooner's sixty-three-page poem are devoted to the dialogue mentioned above. This portion of the poem, entitled "Poetical Recreations: A Dialogue Betwixt *Tobacco* and a *Fair Virgin* about a Match," describes the personification of Tobacco, disguised with a mask, and his unsuccessful marriage proposal to a young, eligible Englishwoman. Despite his masquerading, the speaker informs the reader very clearly that the man, Don Tobacco, is "Outlandish"—most likely meaning "Of or belonging to a foreign country; foreign, alien; not native or indigenous" with a second (and more modern) meaning of "unfamiliar, strange."[49] We are informed that his "Fortunes were too low" to be an appropriate match to the young woman, given his foreign status (40). Most disturbing, however, is when the speaker of the poem—an English gentleman who chooses to keep an eye on the couple for the woman's safety—alludes directly to the potential for sexual violence. Before the virgin sees the young man, the speaker tells the reader:

> As for the Spark, I knew him, and his Name,
> I knew his Mother, and from whence he came:

> I also knew what Pranks he us'd to play,
> By staining Virgins Honour every day.
> And 'cause I had a fear, lest he might try
> To offer to her some Incivility,
> I did resolve to stay to rescue her,
> If I should see a real Cause there were. (40–41)

In this passage, Spooner's speaker reveals an intimate knowledge of the character of Don Tobacco. He begins by highlighting the figure's non-English identity; although the speaker "knew his Mother," implying that she was English, it is clear that he does not know Don Tobacco's father, who it is later revealed to be Native American. Don Tobacco's racial hybridity is a taboo which Spooner demonizes throughout the poem, implying that the divide between English identity and Native savagery is tenuous at best.

Because of the speaker's intimate knowledge of Don Tobacco and his past deeds, Spooner affirms that the speaker's voyeurism is warranted, that his spying on the young man and woman protects her from a likely sexual assault. Even before the actual dialogue begins, Spooner stresses the absolute foreignness of the man, as well as his potential for violence. Projecting fears of racial hybridity, Spooner uses shifting pronouns in reference to Don Tobacco and mocks tobacco's connection to Native American religious rituals, once again molding Native religious beliefs to fit his own Christian narrative. On page 45 of the pamphlet, Don Tobacco discusses the healing powers of tobacco with his prospective marriage partner and he brags that his product can be used to concoct a healing oil of which "there's scarcely found / The like, they say, upon our *English* ground." Here, Don Tobacco identifies himself clearly with his English heritage, showing that his tobacco and his medical expertise are important to England as a whole. As with *A Looking-Glass*, Spooner mocks the healing powers of tobacco through its connection with venereal diseases, having Don Tobacco point out that it is helpful with "Scabs also, and famous for the Itch / In high or low, in poor Men or the rich" (45).

However, Spooner does not allow Don Tobacco's racial hybridity to remain hidden long, as the character soon suffers a verbal slip. When asked by the young woman if there are other medical applications for his product, he responds,

> Yes I can make a Smoke that, Authors say,
> Was useful for to drive the Fiends away:
> And our Forefathers that were grave and wise,
> Unto their *Indian* Gods did sacrifice:
> Or plainly (to prevent their after Evil)
> They offer'd up this Smoke unto the Devil. (45–46)

Directly after stressing his own Englishness, Don Tobacco, no doubt unintentionally, announces that his own ancestors were, in fact, Native Americans who sacrificed tobacco smoke to their own gods and to the Christian devil. While the young woman does not immediately notice these comments, Spooner uses the moment to establish his view of what a hybrid English/Native culture would look like, combining a Native pantheon with a type of sacrifice to the Christian devil.

However, Spooner's main satirical treatment of tobacco comes in connecting Native American skin color to the product of smokable tobacco. This racialized approach begins on page 48 when Don Tobacco's mask falls from his face, revealing his Native American identity. The moment is clearly based on the Philaretes's Jacobean era anti-tobacconist pamphlet, *Work for Chimny-sweeper*, in which the masked tobacco figure is revealed for his duplicity. Discussing Philaretes's pamphlet, Schülting writes, "Tobacco's pernicious character is inseparable from its geographic and cultural origin, which, however, is hidden and has to be 'unmasked' by the writer" (107). Schülting also notes that for writers like Philaretes, "the effect of tobacco consumption in England . . . consists in a dissolution of identities" (107). For Philarates's pamphlet and others based on it, Schülting notes that "This paradox also structures early modern representations of tobacco—as a European commodity of mass consumption on the one hand and an 'Indian weed' on the other" (107); in these types of pamphlets, she notes that "the imminent danger tobacco (purportedly) presents to European culture, it is identified as a kind of 'illegal alien' and—discursively—sent back to America" (107). Like Philarates, Spooner presents Don Tobacco as a dangerous alien who snuck his way onto English soil, mimicking the citizens to corrupt from within.

When Don Tobacco's mask slips, his difference in skin color is instantly recognizable to the young maiden. Spooner then plays on English fears of the intermixing with Natives, invoking a racialized, sexualized image of white women inappropriately attracted to men of color reminiscent of Iago's black ram comment in *Othello*:

> Madam [spoke Don Tobacco] what makes you look in Scorn
> Upon me thus, because an *Indian* born?
> 'Tis said you *English* Women sometimes chuse
> A Black to lie with, and the White refuse. (48)

This reference to Blackness exposes the ways in which African and Native American ethnicities were essentially interchangeable to English eyes. Connecting the sexual connotations of tobacco to early modern views of racial difference, Anderson writes, "Whether American or African—the two apparently indistinguishable in a contemporary English mind—the representation of non-Europeans carried similar connotations; both evoked images of transgression, savagery, and sexual liberty" (144). Further, this equating of African with Native American was shown substantially in advertisements for tobacco. As noted by Catherine Molineux, eighteenth-century tobacconists of London represented the Native American and the African as one and the same within advertisements for their products, an approach that had a long tradition in British culture.[50]

Unsurprisingly, these references to skin color are not accompanied with the denunciation of slavery or the fact that chattel slavery produced the very tobacco itself. Because of his bigoted views and the fact that he is inciting the racialized fears of other Englishmen, Spooner does not address the destructive colonial practices that produced the cash crop, nor the colonial systems that profit off such atrocities. Rather, the smoking of tobacco, instead, is a treated as a type of pollutant not just to physical health but also to English whiteness. Playing on these racialized, misogynistic fears for his satirical purposes, Spooner aligns English tobacco consumption (a habit that was enjoyed by men and women) with the English feminine desire for non-white men, implicitly arguing that the lustful enjoyment of the former will necessarily generate the latter. Given Don Tobacco's mixed heritage and the threats of sexual violence that begin the poem, Spooner imagines in tobacco the invasion of savagery and the Other into England through intermarriage.

Spooner represents his young woman in what would have been deemed a positive light for his contemporary audience with her full-throated rejection of her potential lover, who, before the loss of his mask, seemed to have made some positive impressions on her. After realizing his Native heritage, the young woman verbally accosts him, pointing out many negative traits of tobacco and smoking, such as the habit's expensiveness and its negative impact on one's health; however, she also mocks Don Tobacco, calling him "Thou Tawny Monster" and "Thou Sooty Idol" (49). Here, she connects the color of tobacco with Native American skin color difference, presenting him as both monstrous and pagan.

At the beginning of the poem, Spooner's speaker alludes on page 41 to Don Tobacco's infamous treatment of women, mentioning his many "Pranks" involving women and using the word's early modern connotation of "wicked deeds."[51] In that case, as opposed to the one quoted here, Don Tobacco's "staining" of Englishwomen is implied as rape rather than promiscuity on the part of the woman. Presumably, the earlier usage is supposed to instill a fear of violence; whereas, here, Spooner seeks to shame women into giving up pipe smoking. Despite the speaker's exposition on Don Tobacco at the beginning of the poem, Don Tobacco claims in these lines that he has never stained the honor of a woman, a statement the young woman utterly rejects. She goes on to argue that Don Tobacco has ruined many betrothals and marriages, once again conflating tobacco with unbridled sexuality:

> Ne'er got a Stain! An healthful Woman never
> Got Credit by thee, no nor shall they ever;

>   . . .
>   How many Virgins had gain'd bravest Matches,
>   But that the Suitor these brave Lasses catches
>   Kissing with thee, and they never care
>   For smelling of their pleasant Breathings more. (55–56)

In this passage, the young maiden alludes to other women's failures on the marriage market when men have witnessed them "kissing" Tobacco, connecting the unhygienic aspects of pipe smoking with the loss of chastity and even of Englishness itself.

As Brookes notes, as far back as the early seventeenth century, antitobacconists insinuated that turning the inside of the body black with pipe smoke could make an Englishman become African (160–161). Craig Rustici also points out that geohumoralists—those who connected humoral theories to specific elements of geography—asserted that tobacco could make Englishmen "less phlegmatic and more like the idealized state attributed to inhabitants of the temperate, middle zones" of Virginia.[52] However, he questions how these same geohumoralists, would view an overuse of tobacco, asking, "could the 'excessive,' 'great and immoderate,' even hourly taking of tobacco that James deplores in the *Counterblaste* and his 1604 'Commisso pro Tabacco' seem to dry the body so thoroughly that English smokers would become like Native Americans?" (124). Schülting also notes that in the minds of early modern Europeans, the "embracing of 'savage rites' [such as smoking tobacco] inevitably left a mark on the (white) bodies of European smokers. Skin colour was not (yet) unchangeable 'racial characteristic,' but was read instead as a signifier of the spiritual state of the people" (100). To some early modern readers, tobacco could be seen as negatively transforming, in a very literal sense one into a different race, something Spooner uses metaphorically in his text. Thus, the young maiden not only presents tobacco smoking as a disgusting habit that can turn away men for reasons of hygiene, but also insinuates that it can cause eligible women to appear less Christian and less white.

Near the end of the poem, Spooner has his young maiden provide a broader view on how England would be improved if tobacco smoking were completely stamped out. She notes, for instance, that people of the lower classes would have more money to feed their starving families, using a similar argument, as we shall see in chapter 5, to one that would be repeatedly used against gin during the Gin Craze. For the young woman (and, by extension, Spooner), tobacco consumption directly correlates to sources of wealth. To fix a problem that greatly affects the laboring class, the young woman argues that it will take the moral fortitude of the men rich from the tobacco trade to limit British consumption:

>   I also long to see our richer Men
>   Value their Vertue, and their Health, and then

> Thy trade will soon be fall'n, and we shall
> Our Don Tobacco, *poor* Tobacco call. (58–59)

Here, Spooner equates moral and financial health between classes. The poor family's health is based on the father's thriftiness and avoidance of tobacco. The moral health of the rich English trader, however, is contingent on his decision to quit trading in tobacco, for the sake of his country's health. Notably, this moral fortitude will not greatly diminish the English trader's wealth but will only affect the standing of Don Tobacco ("*Thy* trade will soon be fall'n," my emphasis). Thus, Spooner's personification of Tobacco, standing in for American tobacco plantations and planters, necessarily implies that American savagery itself will only continue to gain power in England if wealthy English traders do not put morality before income.

This argument near the end of Spooner's poem, like the poem that concludes Ward's *The Secret History of Clubs*, calls out the type of large-scale tobacco trading that resulted in the ubiquity of English pipe smoking. For Ward, tobacco constitutes a type of gluttonous and idle enjoyment produced by governmental greed on the part of Stuart leadership; the American colonies, as flawed as they are, only provide the good, not the heavy traffic itself. Spooner, however, attributes the problem of excessive tobacco consumption more fully to America itself, a land where, he implies, Englishwomen are vulnerable to interracial sex and rape, where the mixing of English and Native American blood easily occurs, and where rich, savage tobacco planters are first taught how to infiltrate English society. Like James, the other Jacobean anti-tobacconists, and Ward, Spooner denounces the effects of Americanization on English identity; however, as we shall see with Cooke, the English satirist, by largely ignoring the Native American origins of tobacco, can embrace the commercial importance of tobacco to the colonial world while also highlighting the need for traditional English social hierarchies.

PLANT OR PLANTERS? METONYMY AND CLASS IN *THE SOT-WEED FACTOR*

Like Behn, Ebenezer Cooke considers the English trader's ability to navigate a society that is structured much differently from Britain's. In his poem *The Sot-Weed Factor*, Cooke uses the trader figure to evaluate Maryland as a colony; like Behn, Cooke overtly satirizes the colonial environment—showing the ways in which these spaces are wild and strange—while also subtly satirizing the Englishman himself.[53] However, whereas Behn's play represented a period in which tobacco exportation from the colonies was much the same as it had been since James I's time, Cooke's poem was penned after William's reign, which saw the development of increasingly complex systems of trade, including the factor system alluded to in the poem. Given that an English factor would likely have been viewed as much more of a cultural outsider than Behn's Hazard, who becomes a resident of the Virginia colony by the end of the play, the social environment of Maryland is more difficult for the Englishman to navigate. While Behn's Hazard is ultimately successful, despite rejecting the newer, colonial systems of wealth, Cooke's tobacco factor fails to adjust to his surroundings, and he incorrectly metonymizes the lower-class planters he meets with the plant itself, leading to his financial ruin at the end of the poem. Although Cooke constantly mocks the wild atmosphere of the British colony and its inhabitants, he also develops a secondary satire of the factor himself, representing the ways in which Englishmen fail to understand the colonial environment.

Cooke's factor does not fully understand the foreign environment in which he finds himself nor the tobacco product itself, resulting in near-constant frustration throughout the poem. While Cooke would later "walk back" his satirical persona's hostile treatment of Maryland, the original 1708 version of the poem, as we shall see, features an Englishman financially and emotionally devastated by his experiences there, condemning the whole society in a Juvenalian rant in the final stanza. Somewhat strangely, the poem's narrative marginalizes tobacco smoking and only features one character—a poor common planter—that engages in the activity. However, the ways in which tobacco functions as a cash crop are a major part of the story. Because of Cooke's complex satirical persona, the limited descriptions of tobacco seem to be an intentional act of omission, misdirection, and subversion, not unlike George Etherege's avoidance of French wine in *The Man of Mode*. Many scholars, including Robert D. Arner, J. A. Leo Lemay, Edward H. Cohen, Gregory A. Carey, and Cy Charles League, have pointed out that Cooke's speaker is not just an Englishman mocking the wildness of the British colonies, but is in fact himself a main target of the satire.[54] However, because of this multifaceted satirical approach, the role of tobacco and the commercial aspects of the poem have gone largely unexplored by critics.

In his poem, Cooke uses his satirical persona to investigate tobacco's role in Anglo-American society. As a writer publishing his work in both Maryland (where he lived for the next several decades) and in London (where he often went on business), Cooke chooses to mock the savage, lower-class squalor of the Maryland planters while also satirizing the condescending English trader who is far less morally upright and shrewd in business than he believes. This twofold nature of his satire—the factor's mocking nature and the fact that he, too, is a target of the poem's irony—should also be applied to Cooke's treatment of tobacco. Despite the small portion of the poem devoted to tobacco smoking, the product is used subtly throughout the poem, contributing to the satirical treatment of the lower-class planters. By representing these planters as synonymous with the very plant they grow, Cooke, like Ward, represents tobacco as a "sot-weed," a plant that seems to instill laziness, using his satirical persona of the factor to expose its ability to alter Britishness. Like Spooner, Cooke's factor seems to imply that tobacco itself has the innate ability to alter and stain white skin; however, within Cooke's poem, it is the act of growing the plant that generates these changes, as Cooke consistently connects the lower-class planters to their unharvested crop, and the American soil where it is grown, rather than the final sellable product that the factor tries (unsuccessfully) to obtain and take back to England.

As a writer aware of the important economic contributions of tobacco to the colonies and to Britain, Cooke, unlike Behn, connects tobacco back to its Native American origins, albeit marginally; however, by concluding the poem with the factor's bumbling financial mistakes, Cooke implies that tobacco is indeed an important crop to Britain, despite its somewhat savage cultivation, and that ultimately his factor's anger may be distorting much of the treatment of the cash crop.

Cooke's satire, written in Hudibrastic verse, focuses on an English factor, a low- to midlevel businessman who trades merchandise from England for colonial tobacco. The sot-weed factor arrives in Maryland at the beginning of the poem and quickly (and quite unintentionally) shows himself to be foolish, proud, and completely unprepared for the new environment. Over the course of a few days, the factor interacts with several tobacco planters, an indentured servant, a Native American, card-playing women who may or may not be prostitutes, drunken townspeople, a swindling Quaker, and a corrupt (and inept) lawyer. The factor is consistently startled by this less-civilized world, mocking it, all the while exhibiting behaviors that undermine his condescending self-satisfaction. After being duped by both the Quaker and the lawyer and losing any chance at financial success, the factor ends the poem by calling down an indignant curse on Maryland itself.

In the first thirty lines of the poem, Cooke establishes the factor's proud, anti-colonial sentiments; by linking the "uncivilized" colonists with the tobacco plant they cultivate, the factor attempts to distinguish himself from the common planters whom he sees as being beneath him, and it may be that the factor sees himself as higher-level merchant than he actually is.[55] Discussing the trading system of the period, John F. Wing notes, "Smaller planters increasingly sold their crop to factors and large planters rather than deal with powerful London merchants. This in turn speeded the loading and dispatch of vessels for the return voyage by reducing the time spent searching for cargoes."[56]

In the first line, the speaker refers to "a way-ward Curse," that forced him to take his "leave of *Albion's* Rocks" (1014). This curse, his lack of a good support system ("Friends unkind") and of funds ("empty Purse"), has forced him to leave his native land, and is bookended by the speaker's Juvenalian curse on Maryland at the poem's conclusion. After unloading the goods he brought to exchange for tobacco, the factor looks up to see that a "numerous Crew" of planters have surrounded him (1015). A few lines later, the speaker provides his first sketch of the colonists, discussing their ragged dress and their lack of socks, shoes, and hats (something the factor ironically later finds himself without). After highlighting their lack of traditional English clothing, the speaker mocks their physical bodies and provides an alternative (and distinctly non-Anglican) version of how the people came to exist:

> These *Sot-weed* Planters Crowd the Shoar,
> In Hue as tawny as a Moor:
> Figures so strange, no God design'd,
> To be a part of Humane Kind:
> But wanton Nature, void of Rest,
> Moulded the brittle Clay in Jest.
> At last a Fancy very odd
> Took me, this was the Land of *Nod*;
> Planted at first, when Vagrant *Cain*,
> His Brother had unjustly slain. (1015)

The factor wants his audience to understand the alien nature of the planters, first mocking their dark skin tone, and then providing an alternate history for the group. Rather than admit that the planters are British colonists, he imagines them as descendants of Cain from the biblical story in Genesis.

By placing the planters in Cain's lineage, the speaker stresses their savage nature; that these colonists were "Planted" by Cain connects them to the dark-hued earth. Jim Egan notes that "The colonists are quite literally a people produced by the soil itself."[57] The fact that these colonists, viewed as mere "*Sot-weed* Planters" by the speaker at this point, are portrayed as springing out of the ground connects them to their crop. In his article on English identity in *The Sot-Weed Factor*, Egan argues that through his satire, Cooke hopes to show that nativization—the capability of British colonists to become more like their Native counterparts— would "replenish rather than diminish the quality of" Englishness (397).

One point that Egan does not address in his detailed evaluation of Englishness and nativization, however, is the possibility that through the factor's allusion to Cain, Cooke may also be referring to contemporary debates over the origins of Africans and Native Americans, such as the theory posited by William Whiston in his 1725 essay, *An Exposition of the Curse upon Cain and Lamech: Shewing that the Present Africans and Indians Are Their Posterity*. In Whiston's theory, and ones like it, Africans and Native Americans were argued to be the offspring of Cain, whom God cursed for Abel's murder with a specific mark—here, argued to be skin color difference—and was then expelled from East of Eden and into the Land of Nod;[58] and while Whiston's essay was published seventeen years after Cooke's text, the use of a specific mark, related to skin color, had been around since the seventeenth century when theorists likewise had opined that perhaps Africans were descendants of Ham, Noah's son, whose descendants were commonly viewed to have been marked as well due to Noah's curse on his son's line. The idea that Indigenous peoples, both Native Americans and Africans, were the offspring of Ham was popular throughout this period. With the start of the African slave trade, slaveholders would mix and match these types of theories to justify their actions (*The Forging of Races*, 39–41). In alluding to these origin theories, the speaker connects the planters racially with Africans and with Indigenous peoples.

However, in these early descriptions of the planters, Cooke demonstrates the many eighteenth-century theories on skin color difference that competed with the "descendants of Ham" model. One predominant view was the climate theory in which skin color was caused by factors such as soil color and the presence of an intense heat and sunlight. As Dror Wahrman notes, stories of Englishmen and women taken captive by Indians seemed to support this, since many claimed the captives were indistinguishable from the Natives after their return to English colonies;[59] the layer of Cooke's satire directed at the savage nature of the British colonists plays on this idea.

However, another theory that complemented this thinking, as well as competing with it, was the theory that Native Americans and Africans rubbed their bodies to create or enhance their darker color, thus "manufacturing their skin color" with various oils and soot (*The Making of the Modern Self*, 97–99). Cooke employs this theory as well, implying that the use and cultivation of tobacco renders the planters more like their Indigenous counterparts. Interestingly, in addition to each of these theories, Cooke's factor actually puts forth his own view of how the Native peoples came to be when speaking to his guide later in the poem. The factor posits that the Indigenous peoples were in fact ancient Phoenicians that were unintentionally left behind in America. Presenting these many competing theories allows Cooke to establish the uncertain effects of the Native land on colonizers.

However, there is also the problem of who is in fact picking and curing the tobacco, as we saw above in the writing of Behn and Spooner. Within the poem itself, it is low-level planters and not enslaved Africans who are performing the labor, despite the fact that, as noted, indentured servitude was no longer a steady source of workers for the colonies. While it may be that in the poor areas mentioned, one would not have ordinarily seen enslaved peoples, it could just as likely be that Cooke is actively avoiding the discussion of slavery, something about which his London audience may not have wished to read.

The speaker's habit of seeing the colonists as merely "planters," and as extensions of the product for which he has come to trade, is a consistent element in the poem. Throughout the text, he continually describes the vulgar, drunken behaviors of these lower-class members of Maryland culture, and tends to connect them specifically to the uncured, unrefined tobacco they cultivate for their livelihood. After staying a night at a planter's home, the sot-weed factor is offered both a horse and the planter's own son as a guide for his journey. During their trip to one of the towns, the two travelers come upon a scene of drunken revelry: "But I espy'd the Town before me, / And roaring Planters on the ground, / Drinking of Healths in circle round" (1023). Here, the drunken planters are pictured as rooted into the very ground. After the factor and his guide tie up their horses and fail to find proper lodgings, they end up joining the group and drinking rum punch with them. Once again, Cooke connects the colonists—who are waiting for the court of law to begin—to tobacco, the chief product of the colony:

> We sat like others on the ground
> Carousing Punch in open Aire
> Till Cryer did the Court declare;
> The planting Rabble being met
> Their Drunken Worships likewise set. (1024)

Cooke drives the point further by playing with a double meaning of the phrase "the planting Rabble," describing the group both as planted in their positions outside the court of law, unable to move from their drunken stupors, and as a "Rabble" that plants tobacco. Given the trade dynamics, by which a factor would more often work with larger-scale planters, the presumably middle-class factor projects his British class ideals onto this proto-American society. After satirizing the "court" proceedings, he repeats a similar image: "A Herd of Planters on the ground, / O'erwhelm'd with Punch, dead drunk we found" (1025). By repeatedly recycling this imagery of planters lying on the ground, Cooke, like Ward, presents British colonists as having become completely lazy, drunken fools when outside England; taking the connection between tobacco and American idleness a step further, Cooke causes the reader to associate the planters with the earth that provides their sustenance. However, throughout the descriptions of their drunken revelry, the imagery of tobacco smoking is noticeably absent, as though the factor wishes to keep the cured, smokable tobacco product, something he will "civilize" through his commercial pursuits back in Britain, separate from the colonists themselves.

This association between planters and soil hits its climax the following day when the speaker awakens at the inn where they spent the night. After a restful sleep, the factor looks around the inn for the planter's son, whom he left downstairs drinking with the local townspeople. The planter's son apparently continued to drink throughout the night and is in terrible shape from the resulting hangover. The speaker notes that the young man is lying naked on one of the inn's main tables, and states that "One wou'd have judg'd him dead and cold" because of his lack of movement (1025). After "wringing" the planter's son's nose, which is bloody from a drunken fight, the factor finds him "not so fast asleep" as he first thought (1026). At this point, trying to bring the young man to his senses, he offers a strange use of metonymy: "Rise *Oronooko*, rise, said I" (1026). Cooke, who supplies his own detailed footnotes that provide cultural context for his readers in London, explains in a footnote that "Planters are usually call'd by the Name of *Oronooko*, from their Planting *Oronooko-Tobacco*" (1026, n30). Given that Cooke wrote this poem for an Anglo-American audience as well as an English one, this odd tradition is most likely factual; however, by having his persona call the planter's son by the title of the very tobacco leaf he cultivates, Cooke once again analogizes the lower-class laborer with his daily work, rather than the act of smoking the tobacco itself.

While Cooke clearly limits the presence of tobacco smoking within the text, it does appear at one point, providing the poet with an opportunity to distinguish pipe smoking as a somewhat noble habit despite its non-European origins. The first planter the sot-weed factor visits, the father of the young man discussed above, is very hospitable to the businessman on his first night in the colony, offering him shelter, food, and alcohol. After the factor eats an unsatisfying meal in the planter's home, an environment that the factor describes as being rather filthy, the planter pulls out his tobacco pouch to smoke. The factor states,

> Then out our Landlord pulls a Pouch,
> As greasy as the Leather Couch
> On which he sat, and straight begun,
> To load with Weed his *Indian* Gun;
> In length, scarce longer than ones Finger,
> Or that for which the Ladies linger:
> His Pipe smoak'd out with aweful Grace,
> With aspect grave and solemn pace. (1017)

Prior to the act of smoking, the factor describes the squalid environment, using textile imagery to connect the "greasy" leather couch in which the planter sits and the tobacco pouch that contains the consumable material.

The factor then describes the planter "loading" his short pipe, which he refers to derogatorily as an "*Indian* gun." Here, the factor mocks the de-anglicized colonist in two separate ways: by alluding to the non-imported status of the pipe and by underscoring its Native influences. As an Englishman, the factor highlights the local, or colonially produced, nature of the pipe. While traditional English pipes were white clay and featured a longer stem and belly bowl design (see figure 3.1), the working-class planter's pipe is shaped in a fashion that brings to the factor's mind the Native American, ritualistic pipes that he likely heard of when in England. Rather than one of the mass-produced, imported English pipes, the planter smokes out of a pipe that conjures English fears of the Indigenous (and to the English,

Figure 3.1 A traditional English clay tobacco pipe, which features a thick stem, a large prominent flat circular heel, and a small bulbous barrel-shaped bowl. London, England, ca. 1640–1670. Courtesy of the Science Museum Group.

demonic) rituals described by James I. For the factor, the planter's decision to smoke out of one proves the influence of the land on Englishness.

Imported pipes, the kind the factor would wish the planter to smoke, were widely available. Anna S. Agbe-Davies notes that "Local and imported pipes are often found side-by-side on seventeenth-century sites in Virginia," attesting to the availability of such pieces in the colonies.[60]

Rather than an imported (and properly English) one, the planter smokes one that has a design greatly conflicting with the many pipes he would have seen in the alehouses, taverns, and coffeehouses of his homeland. The factor also highlights the hybrid nature of terracotta pipes popular in the Maryland region, many of which were "Native American-derived."[61] As Al Luckenbach and Taft Kiser note, colonists like Emanuel Drue of the Jamestown region were experimenting with Native-inspired designs. Looking closely at Drue's work, Luckenbach and Kiser note that these designs were intermixed with many more traditional English belly bowl–style pipes among Drue's work in the 1660s. However, many of these so-called Indian designs were greatly impacted, in addition to the Native influences surrounding them, by the expensive duties placed on the traditional, imported English pipes. Discussing the local clay pipes of seventeenth- and

Figure 3.2 A clay pipe of the late seventeenth century, recovered from a pond at the Rich Neck Plantation site of Jamestown. Courtesy of Archaeological Collections, the Colonial Williamsburg Foundation.

eighteenth-century Jamestown, John L. Cotter writes, "Anyone of modest means who worked with clay and wanted to smoke would have fashioned clay pipes by hand and devised a simple way of utilizing the heat of the kiln to fire them—anticipating the blossoming of American ingenuity. Doubtless such a workman would have few scruples about neglecting to contribute to the Crown the duty imposed on imported pipes—nor would his companions, to whom he may have sold pipes in excess of his own needs."[62] Figure 3.2, a local clay pipe from the Rich Neck Plantation site in Colonial Williamsburg likely made in the late seventeenth century, features a similar design to those described by Cotter in his work at the Jamestown archaeological site, structure 127.[63]

Like the one pictured in figure 3.2, the pipes Cotter examined from this particular site have "very characteristic construction details," including eight-sided bowls that he describes as "unique" among the hundreds of pipes in the Jamestown collection (145). Additionally, he writes that "The rounded bowls are subconical and of a shape often described as 'Indian,'" adding that "any white settler's handmade pipe would have come closer to the Indian prototype than would the delicately rounded bowl of the molded import types" of England (145). While Cooke, a man who lived much of his life in the Maryland colonies region, would presumably have recognized these types of pipes as common to the region, he presents the pipe itself in an alien light through his English-born factor.

However, the factor associates the savage, hybrid nature of the pipe, along with its sexualized description ("scarce longer than ones Finger, / Or that for which the Ladies linger"), from the commodity itself, a product on which the self-important factor is ultimately resting all his financial hopes; further, he does not treat the ritual of smoking as uncouth. Interestingly, when referring here to the tobacco product, Cooke uses the term "Weed" rather than his usual "sot-weed," initiating a kinder treatment of tobacco. Then, when describing the ritual itself, he no longer describes it in Native American terms, but instead as a "pipe," which when lit "smoak'd out with aweful grace" and "aspect grave and solemn pace." While he references the Native American influences on the planter's pipe, which is indirectly compared to the English pipes the factor is used to, Cooke treats the act of smoking itself respectfully, rendering it in an almost noble light.

While the factor may associate "sot-weed" with the laziness of the planters, alluding to the idleness often associated with tobacco, and while he treats pipe smoking positively, Cooke provides the kindest treatment of tobacco near the end of the poem when the speaker discusses the tobacco he purchases to take back to England. After mocking all the lower-class planters throughout the poem, the factor's treatment of the Quaker with whom he trades focuses on religious rather than class terms. It is in this conversation that the factor begins to speak like a tobacco trader, using shipping jargon that much of his English audience probably would not have understood, but that his Anglo-American audience likely would have. Discussing his business deal with the "sly Zealot," the Quaker, the factor describes their agreement, seeming momentarily proud of his own clever business acumen:

> A Bargain for my *English* Truck, [Commodities for barter][64]
> Agreeing for ten thousand weight,
> Of *Sot-weed* good and fit for freight,
> Broad *Oronooko* bright and sound,
> The growth and product of his ground;
> In Cask that should contain compleat
> Five hundred of Tobacco neat. (1029)

The repeated comma punctuation in the first five lines with a lack of a full stop propels the reader to keep reading onto the next line, replicating the speaker's excitement at how well his deal seems to be going. In these lines, the excited factor goes beyond calling his commodity "sot-weed." Not only does he point to the "sound" nature of the product, but he also presents it in a lighter hue, disconnecting it from the racial elements employed earlier in the poem. He presents the leaf as a "product" that is shippable ("Cask"), and then for the first time in the poem, he refers to the plant by its most popular name, tobacco. In these lines, the factor shifts away from describing the filthiness and savagery of British colonial society and adopts (temporarily) the excited nature of a businessman on the cusp of success.

However, as we have been abundantly warned, the Quaker is not to be trusted. Whereas the factor has shown a condescending attitude toward the poor common planters, he quickly strikes a deal with the Quaker businessman, perhaps projecting a middle-class status onto him. The next four lines come as the quick, inevitable punchline to the joke, facilitated by the short pauses via commas:

> The Contract thus betwixt us made,
> Not well acquainted with the Trade,
> My Goods I trusted to the Cheat,
> Whose crop was then aboard the Fleet.

The sot-weed factor admits that he was duped by the Quaker and realizes now that he was "Not well acquainted" with the way trade is conducted in America. Lemay notes that these types of stories—in which Americans took advantage of English traders—were commonplace before 1708 (90). Furthermore, League also argues that the anecdote of the Quaker, as well as the ability of the lawyer to swindle the sot-weed factor in court, betray the speaker's immaturity and naivete: "Here, more fully than almost anywhere else, Cooke signals the callowness of his narrator; no one would trade as foolishly as the factor, and the implications of his gullibility are obvious. Any observation or judgment he makes is compromised. . . . His incompetence renders his comments on the colony the petulant whine of a failed business man" (23). League's description is apt, especially given the speaker's near-constant condescension. Carrying a British understanding of class into this new world, the factor thought himself on equal footing with the Quaker, whom he sees as a trustworthy member of the middle class; rather than taking steps to protect himself during the transaction, he believes that his similar class status with the Quaker grants him a type of protection.

After the failures in his business dealing and in court, the speaker bitterly retreats back to the ship in which he will return to England, his paltry and near-worthless cargo in tow:

> Raging with Grief, full speed I ran,
> To joyn the Fleet at *Kicketan*;
> Embarqu'd and waiting for a Wind,
> I left this dreadful Curse behind. (1031)

Much of the factor's "dreadful Curse" on Maryland is specifically aimed at colonial trade. He wishes that the lowly "Slaves" of Maryland will be eaten by cannibals, preying on them the way the Quaker did the factor himself. While Cooke explains via footnote that he does not refer to any of the "*English* Gentlemen" living in Maryland, his factor hopes that "never Merchant's, trading Sails explore / This Cruel, this Inhospitable Shoar," unleashing his anger at all those living in Maryland (1031). For the failed factor, a lack of proper trade with Britain will ultimately doom the colonists to "turn Savage," becoming superstitious pagans. Exiled from "Trade, Converse, and Happiness" through their deserved abandonment by British ships, the lower-class planters and conniving businessmen and lawyers will finally go completely "Native" and be even less recognizably English. Aligning with the factor's theory of Native American origins, the factor's final Juvenalian rant against the Marylanders who abused him represents his belief that trade and commerce are what constitute civilized society; any Englishman that is cut off from trade with Britain will most likely turn savage.

Cooke, like Behn, places the English body into the foreign, colonial environment and distinctly separates American pipe smokers and tobacco planters from the Englishman (a nonsmoker) who sees planting as beneath him. Both satirists also recognize the ubiquity of tobacco within Anglo-American life and culture. However, unlike Behn's Hazard, who is of upper-class birth and carries with him all of the expectations constructed around that status, the factor's birth is intentionally obscured by the satirist, even as he attempts to judge those with whom he interacts according to the English class system. While the text was written for both English and American audiences, it is clear by the end that the satirical persona is meant to be read as suspect and unreliable. For Cooke, the English figure will never quite adjust to the colonial environment, due partially to the lack of a coherent, discernible class system; the English body, unused to American culture and economic practices, will be just as ill prepared for buying tobacco as it is for smoking it.

CONCLUSION

For Ward and Spooner, tobacco's role as a driver of trade was highly problematic, especially regarding moral behavior; to smoke tobacco, then, is to risk becoming Indian. Both Ward and Spooner see tobacco as invading England through trade, but ultimately Ward directs the blame more appropriately at the English government than at the colonies themselves. Behn and Cooke, however, seem to recognize more fully tobacco's importance both for the colonies and for Britain. Both satirists attempt to sidestep the problem of tobacco's Indigenous roots, with Behn ignoring it completely and Cooke's factor presenting the savagized cultivation of tobacco as distinct from the English act of trading tobacco. For Behn and Cooke, the colonial space offers a unique chance to experiment and play with views of Englishness within a foreign environment. For both writers, who spent at least parts of their lives in colonial settings, juxtaposing the English mindset with the seemingly wild, uncultivated space of British America allows them to satirize the ways in which English citizens attempt to map British cultural dynamics onto a different environment; rather than just mocking the American citizens, they use extremely class-conscious characters to play with social principles. The commercial aspects of tobacco in these texts provide a "way in" to the British citizen but both Hazard and Cooke's factor fail to use this material good properly to ingratiate themselves into the colony. However, whereas Behn shows how the traditional aspects of the culture (the class system and the English marriage market) finally enable Hazard to be successful, Cooke's factor fails in his business dealings and retreats to Britain defeated. For Behn, English cultural dynamics of class and gender still function as tools of advancement in the colonies, but for Cooke, these systems can easily be misapplied to the social environment, leading to utter ruin.

4

"THE CEREMONY OF THE SNUFF-BOX"

Snuff in British Satirical Essays and Poems, 1709–1732

IN *THE SPECTATOR*, NO. 275, PUBLISHED January 15, 1712, Joseph Addison presents his readers with a strange series of visual images. Attending an "Assembly of Virtuoso's [*sic*]" of the then-burgeoning field of science (clearly meant to be a Royal Society gathering), Addison watches a demonstration in which the audience hears "many curious Observations, which [one of the doctors] had lately made in the Anatomy of an Human Body."[1] The remarks of these virtuosos and the lengthy discussions at the meeting prompt in Addison's mind "so many new Ideas" that his imagination leads him to a "very wild Extravagant Dream" that night (*The Spectator*, no. 275, 2:570). In Addison's dream, he is attending another proto-scientific anatomical study, but this time the subjects being evaluated are the head of a beau and the heart of a coquette. This dream, whether an actual occurrence or a fictive event used as a rhetorical jumping-off point, depicts a scientific process for satirical purposes, allowing Addison to "cut apart" the elements of foolish, self-obsessed people.

The anatomy of the beau's head dominates the discussion of the dream. The brain smells of orange-flower water, a common type of male perfume. "Ribbons, Lace and Embroidery . . . invisible Billetdoux, Love-Letters, pricked Dances, and other Trumpery of the same nature"—items commonly appearing in satires of fops and beaus—are stuffed within one of his skull's cavities, while "In another we found a kind of Powder, which set the whole Company a Sneezing, and by the Scent discovered it self to be right *Spanish*. The several other Cells were stored with Commodities of the same kind, of which it would be tedious to give the Reader an exact Inventory" (571). Here, Addison mocks the beau's predilection for snuff tobacco, a plain or perfumed ground powder commonly inhaled through the nostrils, which became popular among the English middle and upper classes at the beginning of the eighteenth century. Although the powder itself is just one of the "Commodities" that fill the young man's head, it is the only one named outright and specifically labeled as an import, originating in Spain. That the beau has abused this drug becomes apparent three paragraphs later when Addison depicts its physiological effects on his nasal cavity. As Addison examines the cribriform plate, the bone that articulates with the nasal bone, he finds that the cavity beneath it is "exceedingly stuffed, and in some Places damaged with Snuff" (572).

This satirical autopsy of the beau's head is an early depiction of snuff in eighteenth-century British satire, and it sets a pattern for criticisms to follow. In his treatment of the tobacco product, Addison shows clearly its potentially negative effects on health, a judgment that would show up in satires of snuff throughout the next two decades. Through his open critique of the deceased beau's vanity, he also alludes to the use of snuff as a commodity to provide one with a fashionable air. Throughout this era of satire, snuff would often be connected to falsity and social facades. Whereas pipe tobacco tended to be treated alternately as a beneficial staple commodity of the Englishman or negatively as an Americanizing substance, as discussed in the previous chapter, snuff tended to be viewed as an invading, foreign substance, despite the fact that, as I discuss below, much of the snuff consumed in England was produced domestically and falsely presented as a foreign import.

The following chapter examines satirical texts that focus on and discuss snuff, investigating the ways in which the writers of this period treat snuff as a commercial product, while also looking at the depiction of snuffboxes and the rituals these ornate objects helped generate. It begins with a brief look at the origins of snuff's history and popularity in Britain before considering the ways in which it was treated in satirical texts published between 1709 and 1720. During these years, satirists tended to treat snuff as an invader of proper upper-class conversation and habits. Sir Richard Steele evaluates the commercial tobacco product according to ideals of conversation and decorum in *The Tatler* and *The Spectator*. While considering snuff's role in daily commerce, he illustrates its ability to damage discourse.

Steele's writing on snuff greatly influenced Alexander Pope's representation of the product in *The Rape of the Lock* (1717), which evaluates consumerism alongside upper-class masculinity. Pope represents snuff as a commodity that negatively affects male conversational habits in particular, using the character of Sir Plume to comment on the mannerisms and gestures of such men. This emasculating effect of snuff becomes vividly (and humorously) apparent when Belinda weaponizes it against the Baron.

The final section of the chapter discusses the more graphic and grotesque treatments of snuff in texts of the 1720s and early 1730s, considering how these satirists highlight snuff's harmful effects both on one's perception in public and on one's general health. The anonymously written and highly misogynistic *Whipping Tom* (1722) provides a striking example of snuff's prominent role in Juvenalian satire as part of a larger attack on luxurious spending, which the writer associated with the blurring of class and gender distinctions. I then juxtapose the use of snuff in Jonathan Swift's *The Lady's Dressing Room* (1732) and its use in the non-canonical poem, *The Gentleman's Study* (1732) to show the quite different ways in which this commodity could be deployed to attack each gender. These three texts represent a greater fear of the assimilation of snuff into British culture than Addison, Steele, and Pope, mocking the commercial roots of the practice through the realistic (and physically revolting) aspects of a snuff habit. These texts illustrate the impact that the invasion of commercial luxuries had on satirists. Thus, the gentle concern with snuff's effect on polite conversation early in the century gives way to graphic and scatological attacks on snuff as a physical and national pollutant.

NOTHING TO SNEEZE AT: FOREIGN SNUFF AND ITS CONVERSATIONAL CONSEQUENCES IN EARLY EIGHTEENTH-CENTURY PERIODICALS

In his 1720 text *The Humorist*, Thomas Gordon mocks the snuffbox, the ornate containers in which people kept their prized snuff tobacco, and the ways these ornamental pieces were being implemented in English conversation (see figure 4.1).

In his second essay on "Modern Conversation," he writes, "The Snuffbox is of infinite Use and Reputation to the fine Talkers of this Island, as well for the social Mein, and the familiar friendly Air that it gives the Speakers, as for affording by itself one intire Topick of Discourse, and for inserting several agreeable Parentheses, and many necessary and beautiful Pauses."[2] In the passage, Gordon addresses a kind of domineering use of snuff and snuffbox during conversation, problematic behavior that, as we shall see, originates in Steele's periodical writing. Throughout *The Tatler*, *The Spectator*, and (as discussed in the next section) Pope's *The Rape of the Lock*, popular satires fretted about the ability of snuff, both the powder itself and the ornate boxes that housed it, to influence and corrupt English identity. While setting an early precedent of his antipathy to overindulgence of snuff, Steele's treatment of the drug shifts following his interactions with the perfumer and snuff-maker, Charles Lillie; however, throughout his work in *The Tatler* and *The Spectator*, Steele establishes the foreign nature of this substance, while also evaluating the ways in which snuff-taking affects middle- and upper-class gender divides. Given the centrality of polite conversation to periodicals such as *The Tatler* and *The Spectator*, the use of snuff during conversation was extremely suspect; Steele's essays speak to the ways in which the product could have strange effects both on the subject of conversation—what is being said and how it is being rationally debated—and on the gestures and means of delivery—how the conversation is conducted and what manners are prioritized. His satirical writing, like Addison's, seeks to expose snuff's ability to invade British consciousness,

Figure 4.1 A snuffbox, featuring silver gilt and tortoiseshell inlaid in fine wire, with sprays of flowers with insects and birds. Made in England or France, ca. 1720–1740. © Victoria and Albert Museum, London.

both through the powder's bodily, pharmaceutical effects and through its ritual effects on British conversation.

Surprisingly, literary treatments of snuff have received very little scholarly consideration. Emily C. Friedman's book, *Reading Smell in Eighteenth-Century Fiction*, is one interesting exception.[3] In her book, Friedman evaluates the smellscape of the eighteenth century, and in the first chapter discusses both pipe tobacco and snuff. In her discussion of nasal tobacco, she examines the "sights, smells, gestures, and objects associated with the consumption of snuff" and argues that "In a period marked by the formation of British identity as set in contrast to French identity, the notion that 'French manners' might alter British identity is a continuing anxiety, and the cosmopolitan connotations of snuff were rendered further complex by its associated with the French" (38, 40). One particularly interesting aspect of Friedman's argument is the influence of snuff, not so much in its smell (which "Unlike pipe smoke, the smell of snuff did not need to be controlled through demarcating spaces or places as it did not create a large scent aura around the user," 38), but in its appearance and sound. She notes that "Instead of pipe smoke, unpracticed or excessive snuff-takers filled the air with noise" (41). While she discusses certain aspects of the "gestures and objects" of snuff, my reading of snuff satire looks more specifically at the conversational uses of snuff powders and the snuff-boxes that hold them.

Although snuff came to prominence in England in the first decade of the eighteenth century, it had been practiced there since the early seventeenth century. Lauren Working notes that Thomas Dekker described the process of snuff-taking as early as 1609.[4] Further, Stephen Coleman points out that snuff had long been practiced in Europe among the aristocracy, and it was very popular in Charles II's court, a fad taken from France; however, the trend did not extend much further than his courtiers and Englishmen who had picked up the habit while traveling.[5]

Charles Lillie—who is discussed more fully below due to his close connection to Steele—provides a brief history of how this substance first became popular in England in his 1740 treatise, *The British Perfumer, Snuff-Manufacturer, and Colourman's Guide*.[6] In this history, he describes the plundered goods from Sir George Rooke's highly successful peninsular campaign during the War of Spanish Succession (1701–1714). In the Battle of Vigo Bay, Rooke's forces plundered goods from Cadiz, Spain, including "some very rich merchandize [sic], plate, jewels, pictures, and a great quantity of chochineal [an expensive dye], several thousand barrels and casks of fine snuffs were taken, which had been manufactured in different parts of Spain. Each of these contained four tin canisters of snuff of the best growth, and the finest Spanish manufacture" (294–295). On top of this expensive cargo, the fleet also plundered Vigo, taking many containers of snuff, which the captains and sailors soon learned was highly regarded across Europe.

Once back in England, the sailors found a "very quick and cheap market," selling the product easily (*The British Perfumer*, 296). Lillie closes the anecdote by showing how fast a consumer product can find a commercial market: "Thus distributed throughout the kingdom, novelty being quickly embraced by us in England, arose the custom and fashion of snuff-taking" (297). Throughout his discussion, Lillie shows how English snuff manufacturers profited from the substance's foreign identity, chronicling the many ways in which they would attempt to produce—oftentimes in the cheapest, quickest, and most disgusting ways possible—a product that appeared like its foreign counterpart. Over the course of thirty pages, Lillie meticulously breaks down the qualities (color, texture, and smell) of the best types of snuff, and details the ways a buyer can determine if a product is genuine or not. He describes Havana snuff as bright yellow, Seville snuff as a light brownish red color with a very moist and oily texture, and Brazil snuff as green. While Lillie does praise some English imitations, he still notes the differences between them and the more expensive and higher-quality imported snuff. He also warns the reader that the worst types of English imitations use disgusting materials such as starch dust, brick dust, plain yellow sand, sweepings from tobacco shops, and even rotten wood (315). While many customers intentionally bought English-made snuff like the kind Lillie produced, no doubt others were duped into buying products that appeared to be a more expensive foreign brand. As we shall see, the perceived alien nature of snuff would be a consistent source of mockery.

During the first half of the eighteenth century, snuff became a highly ritualized custom for middle- and upper-class men and women as it increased in popularity. Friedman writes, "the more practiced and polished snuff-taker provided a more pleasing visual component [than those who were unused to snuff]: the placement of finger or wrist, the flourish of the snuffbox itself. Many of the images of the snuff-taker emphasize elegance, urbanity, and sophistication" (43). Unlike those smoking pipes, snuff-takers could consume in public while being less irritating to those around them (*Reading Smell*, 38). Snuff offered users the ability to demonstrate their kindness by sharing their tobacco with others, while also showcasing their disposable income with expensive imported brands. With the wide availability of personalized snuffboxes, consumers could also demonstrate their wealth, elegance, and even wit.[7] Additionally, female snuff-takers did not seem to be stigmatized, provided they did not use excessively (*Reading Smell*, 47). In his *A Letter of Genteel and Moral Advice to a Young Lady* (1740), Reverend Wetenhall Wilkes writes, "Snuff is taken by so many Ladies of refin'd Taste and unexceptional good Qualities, that I have nothing to offer in prejudice of its moderate Use."[8] Wilkes seems to imply that enough well-known fashionable women use snuff to make it a ritual that makes one appear more refined.

In 1709, one of the first satirical treatments of snuff in England appeared in the pages of Steele's periodical, *The Tatler*. In no. 35, Steele discusses the habit of taking snuff, which he sees as problematic to conversation.[9] In his opening line, he notes that he attempted to remain quiet regarding the product; however, because his "patience" has been pulled to "the utmost Stretch" and because his acquaintances' abuses of the product have grown so pervasive, he has chosen to air his grievances (*The Tatler*, no. 35, 1:255). He states that he will examine "the Humour of taking Snuff, and looking dirty about the Mouth by Way of Ornament" (255). Steele attacks snuff on two primary fronts, which show up in the double meaning of "looking dirty about the Mouth by Way of Ornament": On a surface level, one's face and body become dirty from the physical act of snuffing the powder; and figuratively, the snuff-taker looks and speaks foolishly as a result of snuff.

After alluding to the visual and conversational effects of a snuff habit, Steele relates a short anecdote as an example of snuff's negative effects. He writes, "I sat by an eminent story-teller and politician who takes half an ounce in five seconds, and has mortgaged a pretty tenement near the town, merely to improve and dung his brains with this prolific powder" (255). Steele's acquaintance is both a prodigious snuff-taker and a raconteur, but because he is constantly snuffing, his stories take even longer to tell. Steele's use of the verbs "improve and dung" signify that the storyteller attempts to use the act of taking snuff to advantage in his stories. In this instance, dung means "To enrich (land) with dung, manure, etc.; to apply dung or other fertilizing material to (earth, a crop, etc.); to manure, to fertilize," which suggests both the improvement of crops (no doubt alluding to snuff's origins) and fecal matter; additionally, Steele puns on "mundungus," which is a "tobacco of poor quality" or "bad-smelling."[10]

In addition to using the snuff to accentuate his story, the politician also seems to be obsessed with the powder itself. He constantly interrupts himself to take snuff, unable to get through any of his own long speeches without repeatedly reapplying it to his nose. Steele eventually hides the box from his friend, hoping to see how the man's conversation and demeanor will change without its assistance. The man is unable to finish his story without frantically asking about his snuffbox. The event provokes a realization: "This Observation easily led me into a Philosophick Reason for taking Snuff, which is done only to supply with Sensations the Want of Reflection" (256). The man, Steele tells us, uses snuff as a type of punctuation or dramatic pause that stands in for what a good, natural conversationalist would supply through carefully thought-out word choices. Thus, Steele sees snuff use as an artificial way of improving one's conversational faculties at the most superficial level; however, this deliberate use ultimately leads to a crippling physical and mental dependence.

The man's body language when looking for his snuffbox instigates Steele's epiphany. He realizes that his acquaintance is making a very particular gesture, pausing to take the snuff, but the temporary loss of his snuffbox makes the gesture somewhat more exaggerated. This interest in conversational gestures and the ability to read those gestures (along with the accompanying motivations behind them) is an important component of polite conversation for both Steele and Addison and would be a major element in *The Spectator*.[11] In *The Tatler*, no. 35, however, Steele is already showing an interest in gesture and its meaning within human speech.

This commentary on snuff as performative prop reinforces and builds on Michael G. Ketcham's work on conversation and rhetoric in *The Spectator*. There are three "nodes" or connecting points of gesturing that Ketcham discusses in his book: the "perception of gesture and to the related arts of physiognomy, painting, and theater," "the framework of moral judgments supported by this perception of gesture, including the endorsement of an urban retirement," and "a language of esthetics that spans both these accounts of social life" (29). Ketcham's description of the use of physiognomy—reading people's gestures in conversation and making moral judgments on the basis of observation—is particularly important here. Ketcham argues that "In this world of appearances other figures, like Mr. Spectator and Will Honeycomb, devote their attention to gesture" (30). These two personas, along with some of their acquaintances, examine others' conversational gestures and movements, which in turn inform their views of other people. Pointing to nos. 252 and 354, both written by Steele, Ketcham lists a few of Mr. Spectator's friends, one who reads "the language of the eyes" and another who claims expertise in interpreting glances. Regarding the role of gestures in the periodical, "The *Spectator* thus resolves itself into a succession of scenes, a shadow play of gestures in the theater of the world, where words may be spoken but where the drama is in the accompanying action" (30). However, this ability to read gestures necessitates the ability to understand internal motivations as well: "[all these essays] assume the same orientation toward social knowledge by attempting to correlate outward behavior with inward character. . . . The gesture or expression has no value when taken in isolation. It must be interpreted, both with reference to the actor and with reference to the situation in which the act occurs" (33). In the case of the storyteller in *The Tatler*, the gesture—the man using snuff to create a succinct but artificial pause in a story—must be "read" and interpreted by the onlooker. In this case, one should interpret the storyteller as a pompous, unskilled speaker who uses a product to enhance, unsuccessfully, his rhetorical power over his audience. By understanding the intent behind the gesture (the speaker keeping his audience spellbound) and how the gesture is truly understood (the perceptive audience sees through the gesture and will later mock it), the reader recognizes that the product actually works against the user's intent.

Steele's fears regarding snuff and its corrosive effects on social interaction underpin more specific concerns about gender. Speaking of female snuff-takers, he writes, "But of all Things, commend me to the Ladies who are got into this pretty Help to Discourse [the use of snuff to artificially improve conversation]. I have been this three Years persuading *Sagissa* to leave it off; but she talks so much, and is so learned, that she is above Contradiction" (no. 35, 1:256–257). Here, Steele's female friend, Sagissa, will not listen to suggestions that she should give up snuff, providing Steele with the opportunity to expose how her pride limits her ability to observe good conversational decorum. Her inability to accept this specific advice indicates her inability to learn from those around her, especially her male acquaintances who seek to curb her abuse of the powder. Seemingly, as her use of snuff has grown, so has her obstinate behavior toward those from whom she should learn.

As Steele continues his story about Sagissa, it is snuff that ultimately ruins her supposedly perfect and learned reputation. One day, she requests that one of her gallants hide from other visitors in her closet. Later, when she is forced to enter her closet to retrieve some item, her gallant kisses her suddenly, and because she has just taken snuff, a material that her lover does not, he accidentally inhales the dust and sneezes, alerting the guests to his presence. This moment of embarrassment, Steele tells us, brings about a change in Sagissa that all his own "Eloquence never could accomplish"; the discovery of her lover proves "that profound Reading, very much Intelligence, and a general knowledge of who and who's together, cannot fill up her vacant Hours so much, but that she is sometimes oblig'd to descend to Entertainments less intellectual" (257). Sagissa's desire to appear intelligent and witty, represented through her use of snuff, ultimately reveals her to be less perfect than she had initially let on. Her humiliation dovetails nicely with Steele's discussion of the male storyteller, reflecting snuff's ability to build up an intelligent, witty persona before undoing it. As we shall see, however, Steele's representation of femininity and snuff in this early essay is much more benign than other representations (including his own) that would be produced in the next two decades.

Several months after the publication of this essay, Lillie, a man relying on snuff as a cornerstone of his profits, began writing letters to Steele. In no. 92, written on Wednesday, but published as part of Thursday, November 10's entry, Steele reprints Lillie's most recent letter for his audience (*The Tatler*, no. 92, 2:77–78). In the letter, Lillie asks to be "advantageously exposed in [Steele's] paper, chiefly for the Reputation of Snuff" (78). As a businessman, Lillie acknowledges the importance of advertisement and asks (more than once, it seems) for Steele's help. Indeed, Steele appears somewhat apologetic for not returning Lillie's correspondence sooner, as well as the potentially negative effects *The Tatler*, no. 35 may have had on Lillie's profits. Out of respect for Lillie, Steele takes a more relaxed stance on snuff: "Taking Snuff is what I have declar'd against; but as his Holiness the Pope allows Whoring for the Taxes rais'd by the Ladies of Pleasure, so I, to repair the Loss of an unhappy Trader, indulge all Persons in that Custom who buy of *Charles*" (78). While seeing much wrong with an excessive snuff habit, especially regarding its effects on conversation, Steele sees the ingenuity of a man of business, and he chooses to alter his earlier invectives against snuff-taking. If one chooses to take snuff, Steele declares, they should only do so after purchasing it from Lillie.

Notably, Steele compares his own backtracking in this regard to the embracing of prostitution by the pope, showing how the immorality of certain commodities can be pushed aside in the name of domestic commerce. Ever interested in trade, Steele reasons that he can lighten his criticism of snuff if it will assist this perfumer. He even argues that he may license such "baubles"—here, "A small ornament, piece of jewellery, decorative accessory, etc., that is showy or attractive but typically inexpensive or of little value"[12]—as a cane or telescope for Lillie, and no other vendors, to sell. In fact, Steele would later include Lillie as a character in *The Tatler*, nos. 103, 110, 256, 259, and 265, in which the perfumer is represented as a stenographer for Isaac Bickerstaff, who holds court as the judge of British society. Ultimately, Steele's consideration for Lillie's business was financially lucrative, as Lillie would go on to publish his work and sell his writing in the shop.

In his next acknowledgment of Lillie, in no. 94 dated November 14, Steele notes that he has received a present and a kind letter from the perfumer, thanking him for his advertisement (1:84–88). The letter, Steele tells us, reveals that many have visited Lillie's shop "upon my recommendation." After suggesting again that his readers only purchase snuff from Lillie, stating that he sells "the best Barcelona" snuff, Steele again, somewhat snarkily, points to snuff's effects on conversation, this time by also advertising other commodities to be found at Lillie's establishment. He writes,

> He has several helps to discourse besides snuff (which is the best Barcelona), and sells an orange-flower water, which seems to me to have in it the right spirit of brains; and I am informed, he extracts it according to the manner used in Gresham College [the meeting place of the Royal Society]. I recommend it to the handkerchiefs of all young pleaders: it cures or supplies all pauses and hesitations in speech, and creates a general alacrity of the spirit. When it is used as a gargle, it gives volubility to the tongue, and never fails of that necessary step towards pleasing others, making a man pleased with himself. (87)

Although he claims in no. 92 that he will discontinue some of his critiques of snuff, he somewhat indirectly mocks its use as a means of promoting oneself during conversation. While he refers to snuff as a "help to discourse," Steele focuses most prominently on Lillie's perfume, alluding to the foppish practice of using it too liberally before socializing. Thus, he shows a willingness to attack snuff less directly in an attempt to assist Lillie with his sales. While he may not be attacking snuff as directly in no. 95 as in no. 35, he still associates an overindulgence of snuff with the excessive, foppish use of perfume, aligning these practices with a lack of proper English control and articulation.

Not quite two years later, Steele would provide an even more direct (but more biting) promotion of snuff, this time as part of his collaboration with Addison on *The Spectator*. An advertisement appeared as part of *The Spectator*, no. 138, published August 8, 1711, which touted a robust school taught at Lillie's shop, instructing those interested in "The Exercise of the Snuffbox, according to the most fashionable Airs and Motions." Donald F. Bond, in his footnote on this advertisement, tells us that it was a genuine advertisement that helped make Lillie a great deal of money, and both Bond and Cynthia Wall point to the advertisement's impact on Pope's *A Rape of the Lock*.[13] However, while it did help generate business for Lillie, the piece has a clear satirical bent. In the advertisement, snuffboxes and their usage signal a type of foppishness that is the male equivalent of coquetry. Mocking this foppishness, and commercial luxury more broadly, the advertisement mentions that the school would be held at a Lillie's shop at the corner of Beaufort Buildings near the Strand, as well as at a toy shop near the coffeehouses of the Exchange. By listing these specific locations, the writer takes a satirical jab at the types of locations at which young men spend their time and money. By pointing out the importance of having a secondary location near the Exchange for "young Merchants," the satirist mocks the heavy usage of snuff by those involved in trade and commerce. Indeed, the frequency of the fake classes illustrates Steele's belief that they would be extremely popular and lucrative, drawing on a clientele intimately familiar with the product as consumers, merchants, and potential investors.

As in *The Tatler*, no. 35, Steele represents snuff usage as deeply connected to forms of conversation; however, while the essay in *The Tatler* openly mocks snuff's detrimental effects on people's ability to communicate with each other, this advertisement hyperbolizes the strange but complex conventions that were beginning to form around the ritual of taking snuff. Describing the so-called curriculum of the class, the advertisement notes:

> The Exercise of the Snuff-box, according to the most fashionable airs and motions, in opposition to the Exercise of the Fan, will be taught with the best plain or perfumed snuff, at Charles Lilie's, perfumer, at the corner of Beaufort-buildings on the Strand, and attendance given for the benefit of the young merchants about the Exchange for two hours every day at noon, except Saturdays, at a toy-shop near Garraway's coffee-house. There will likewise be taught the Ceremony of the Snuff-Box, or rules for offering snuff to a stranger, a friend, or a mistress, according to the degrees of familiarity or distance; with an explanation of the careless, the scornful, the politic, and the surly pinch, and the gestures proper to each of them. (*The Spectator*, no. 138, 2:225–226)

This "Ceremony" is connected to specific social rules that Steele mockingly insinuates are developing in the world. Not only are there different rules for offering snuff to acquaintances and strangers, but there is a growing language of word and gesture surrounding the consumption of the product. One would learn when to employ a "careless Pinch" or a "surly Pinch." Notably, these gestures are each connected to negative behaviors, ones that can easily be read by conversational partners.

While *The Spectator* usually encourages trade and commerce, it tends to push back against luxuriousness. In his article, "Commerce, Conversation and Politeness in the Early Eighteenth-Century Periodical," Stephen Copley notes that "Shaftesbury's aristocratic dismissals of commerce as beneath the concern of 'gentleman' are not replicated in the periodicals, in which trade is by no means disparaged, and in which justifications of 'commerce' constitute an important strand of argument alongside discussions of 'conversation.'"[14] Engaging with the ideas of trade and commerce in their project of polite conversation, Addison and Steele treat these systems kindly, while mocking the overly luxurious. Copley also points out that Addison and Steele are themselves dealing in a medium—the periodical—

that is itself a commodity. The final lines of the advertisement constitute a significant and hyperbolic break from the first stanza, as a note explains that a local maker of snuffboxes, metaphorically referred to as an undertaker, has been working to build up "a Body of Regular Snuffboxes" "to meet and make head against [all] the Regiment of Fans" (363). Here, Steele restructures the excessive consumption of luxuries, such as snuff, snuffboxes, and fans, and presents them in a military metaphor, mockingly connecting the loss of British manhood with socially constructed, foppish habits and luxuries.

Steele's discussion of female snuff-taking in *The Spectator*, no. 344 focuses much more directly on traditional ideals of femininity than his earlier work, while drawing more attention to the commercial qualities of the product (3:277–279). In the trademark style of *The Spectator*, the issues presented in the essay, supposedly raised by one of the periodical's readers, focus on propriety and decorum. In the first line, Steele's persona states their reason for contacting Mr. Spectator: "I HAVE writ to you three or four Times, to desire you would take Notice of an impertinent Custom the Women, the fine Women, have lately fallen into, of taking Snuff" (278). The speaker—presumably the speaker is a man, given that he discusses these "fine Women" as a third party—goes on to explain what they believe to be two very different problems of femininity created by snuff: "This silly trick [of snuff-taking] is attended with such a Coquet Air in some Ladies, and such a sedate Masculine one in others, that I cannot tell which most to complain of; but they are to me equally disagreeable" (278–279). The speaker is troubled by an inability to see how snuff affects women on a broad scale, given that it makes some women more flirtatious and vapid with a "Coquet Air" while making others more masculine.

Unlike in his previous essays in *The Tatler*, Steele is more descriptive regarding the ways in which snuff is used non-decorously during social gatherings.[15] Mrs. Saunter and her niece, archetypal characters standing in for female snuff-takers who lack propriety, exhibit the kinds of behavior that make snuff particularly problematic. Mrs. Saunter takes snuff while eating, causing her to open her mouth and expose her mouthful of food to others. Mrs. Saunter's niece is ruder. Steele's speaker notes that if the niece "is not as offensive to the Eye, she is quite as much to the Ear, and makes up all she Wants in a confident Air, by a nauseous Rattle of the Nose when the Snuff is delivered, and the Fingers make the Stops and Closes on the Nostrils" (279). Her loud snuffing and snorting sounds disrupt conversation and annoy others.

Unlike *The Tatler*, no. 35, this essay is much more prescriptive, describing the very small circumstances in which snuff-taking would be acceptable. The speaker notes, "As to those who take it for no other end but to give themselves Occasion for pretty Action, or to fill up little Intervals of Discourse, I can bear with them; but then they must not use it when another is speaking, who ought to be heard with too much Respect, to admit of offering at that Time from Hand to Hand the Snuffbox" (279). While the speaker does not like the thought of women taking snuff, the women who take it to appear more attractive or to fill a short pause in discourse are not as bothersome as those who pressure others to consume it as well. As in Steele's previous essay, he emphasizes snuff's usage as a kind of conversational "filler"; however, for this usage to be proper and polite, the snuff-taker must appear to be listening rather than fixating on her snuffbox, and she must not interrupt someone who is speaking by offering them snuff or taking it herself.

Steele thus questions the supposedly polite attempts of snuff-takers to provide others with the product, and by addressing this problem, he reminds his reader of the commercial implications of snuff. When discussing Flavilla, another negative archetype of the female snuff-taker, the speaker describes her assertive nature in offering snuff to others. As the speaker points out, this desire to provide others with snuff may at first appear polite, but in actuality, it is absolutely absurd: "But *Flavilla* is so far taken with her Behaviour in this Kind, that she pulls out her Box (which is indeed full of good *Brazile*) in the middle of the Sermon; and to shew she has the Audacity of a well-bred Woman, she offers it the Men as well as the Women who sit near her" (279). Steele straddles the line of hyperbole in this description; Flavilla is so unaware of her surroundings that she offers even the churchwarden a pinch of her snuff.

At the same time, Steele is subtly critical of the consumer market surrounding snuff. By interrupting the flow of the sentence with a parenthetical aside that describes the type of snuff in her box—"(which is indeed full of good *Brazile*)"—the speaker parrots Flavilla's consumer pride in the imported, and presumably expensive, tobacco product. Readers are asked to visualize the unaware, self-important Flavilla offering in whispers to surprised male and female onlookers an expensive type of snuff she believes will impress them. Discussing polite conversation and commerce in these periodicals, Copley states: "Instruction in polite taste is, in large part, instruction in cultivating standards of discriminating consumption, and expressing those standards in appropriate social exchanges" (67). Flavilla has flouted all of these standards of polite taste: she has not been careful and unobtrusive in her consumption of snuff; she has certainly not chosen the correct social environment (a church would never have been viewed as a place for two-way exchange); she stresses the economic reality of snuff in boasting its origin; and she is not being leisurely about her use. Steele, mocking female snuff-takers' lack of propriety, shows the extreme pride connected to the origins of one's snuff. Not only does snuff interrupt polite conversation, it forces its way into situations in which conversation should not exist.

Throughout his essays, Steele shows that nasal tobacco, while perhaps harmless in itself, has fundamentally altered polite conversation in a negative way.

Because of the sheer importance of polite conversation to Addison and Steele's overarching project of developing a better class of English citizens, Steele combats the use of snuff in conversation, calling into question its effects on the way people use commercial products in polite company.

"THE PUNGENT GRAINS OF TITILLATING DUST": SNUFF AND EMASCULATION IN *THE RAPE OF THE LOCK*

Pope's mock epic, *The Rape of the Lock*, constitutes by far the most famous eighteenth-century satire to feature snuff; surprisingly, however, there has been little said regarding its use. In his essay "'Hairs less in sight': Meteors, Sneezes, and the Problem of Meaning in *The Rape of the Lock*," Dwight Codr discusses the sneeze caused by snuff but does not focus on contemporary views of snuff-taking, and Richard Kroll briefly alludes to snuff in his pharmacological study of the poem.[16] Providing important context to snuff usage and its effect on the characters of the poem, Geoffery Tillotson, Cynthia Wall, and Julian Ferraro and Paul Baine point to the influence of the advertisement in *The Spectator*, no. 138 on Pope's treatment of snuff, snuffboxes, and fans, providing some excellent notes regarding Sir Plume's snuff use.[17] Wall also more directly connects these elements to Sir Plume's behavior to traditional satires of fops and how Pope's use of punctuation gestures toward snuff-taking (363), which I address more fully below. This lack of scholarly attention is doubly strange, given near-ubiquitous discussion of commodities in scholarly evaluations of the poem, such as those by Laura Brown, Stewart Crehan, and Colin Nicholson.[18] Pope uses snuff in a twofold way, mocking both snuff's invasion into polite conversation and upper-class social interactions and its effects on upper-class masculinity more broadly. Pope clearly shares with Steele a satirical interest in how snuff has become woven into the rhythms of polite conversation. However, in comparison to Steele, Pope particularly targets upper-class masculinity when satirizing snuff, and he relegates the excessive use of the product to just one character, Sir Plume. Pope to a greater extent than Steele uses snuff's invasion of the body to symbolize the effects of commerce on British identity.

Pope's poem has received much critical attention for its presentation of luxury and commodities, as well as its early evaluation of economic principles. From the first moment that snuff is mentioned in the second stanza of canto III, readers are asked to question its effects on conversation, in a way similar to what appears in Steele's essays. After Belinda's journey by boat to Hampton Court, the speaker provides a description of the nighttime activities that occur as the aristocracy begin to enjoy themselves. As with much of *The Rape of the Lock*, the first and second stanza of this canto frequently juxtapose serious, national matters with more mundane concerns. At Hampton Court, Queen Anne considers state affairs while enjoying tea: "Here Thou, Great Anna! Whom three Realms obey. / Dost sometimes Counsel take—and sometimes *Tea*."[19] The second stanza continues this juxtaposition as one partygoer "speaks the Glory of the *British Queen*" while another "describes a charming *Indian Screen*" (ll. 13–14). The serious affairs of the nation, an obvious source of polite conversation, will almost instantly segue to discussions of popular commercial items. This emphasis on consumer products shows up again only two lines later in the final couplet of the stanza as Pope describes more aspects of the conversation occurring at Hampton Court: "*Snuff*, or the *Fan*, supply each pause of chat, / With singing, laughing, ogling, and all that" (ll. 17–18). Like Steele, Pope satirizes contemporary conversation and the centrality of consumer products such as snuff, more commonly associated with men in the poem, and ornate fans, associated with women. While much of the poem evaluates the use of foreign commodities to target women specifically, the use of snuff mocks men in particular. The use of "supply" in line 17 ironically implies that these pauses in conversation are absolutely necessary to the "chat," while also punning on the term's relevance to commodities. Thus, for Pope's speaker, conversation—taken daily by the aristocracy—is akin to tea, Indian screens, snuff, and fans: things to be constantly used up before buying new.

Pope satirizes the effects of snuff on upper-class conversation most significantly through his character of Sir Plume, who appears first in canto IV. After the lock is cut in canto III and Umbriel the Gnome returns from Spleen in canto IV, Thalestris attempts to rouse Belinda from her shock, and after her speech fails, Thalestris asks her beau, Sir Plume, to intervene, hoping he can intimidate the Baron and to "demand the precious Hairs," a physical manifestation of Belinda's honor (l. 122). Sir Plume, who we are told is of his "*Amber Snuffbox* justly vain," demonstrates the exact type of speech patterns mocked in Steele's essays in *The Tatler* (l. 123). Leading up to Sir Plume's speech, Pope writes, "With earnest Eyes, and round unthinking Face, / He first the Snuffbox open'd, then the Case," (ll. 125–126). The poet's use of zeugma powerfully displays Sir Plume's simplistic way of thinking and speaking. Pope uses this syntactical arrangement to satirize the ways in which Sir Plume equates polite conversation with the use of snuff. He opens the snuffbox in a deliberate manner before speaking, and it is clear to the reader that taking snuff is more important to him than conversation, as he opens the snuffbox *before* opening "the case," or the discussion of the stolen lock of hair.

Sir Plume's treatment of object (snuff and snuffbox) and conversation is fitting within the commodity-centered aspect of Pope's satirical world. Discussing commodity culture in the poem, Colin Nicholson writes:

> In a creative display of pre-Marxian perceptions of modern economics, an object-dominated consciousness begins to reveal itself, with practically every couplet inferring connections between a personal and social life and the world of traded artefacts. Patterns of imagery and metaphor

ingeniously propose ways in which human life is 'lived' by means of an extension into the purchasable possessions that significantly animate the narrative. "Trivial things" operate powerfully in the world Pope constructs and human determinations are correspondingly adapted. (31)

In this case, the "traded artefacts" of snuff and snuffbox are imbued, at least in the mind of Sir Plume, with rhetorical power; however, unlike many of the commodities used in the poem, snuff will not "operate powerfully" for Sir Plume, and the supposed rhetorical power of snuff in conversation is proven nonexistent. As Wall points out, "Sir Plume is rendered nearly inarticulate by the practice" of snuff-taking (65n17). Thus, the commodity has the power to undo speech itself.

When Sir Plume first speaks, Pope uses punctuation—here dashes, but also through the multiple caesuras created in each line—to stress Sir Plume's inability to articulate his thoughts. Pope writes:

> And thus broke out—"My Lord, why, what the Devil?
> Z—ds! damn the Lock! 'fore Gad, you must be civil!
> Plague on't! 'tis past a jest—nay prithee, Pox!
> Give her the Hair"—he spoke, and rapp'd his Box. (ll. 127–130)

The speech itself comes as a form of interruption, given the long dashes used in lines 127 and 130. The frequent pauses allow the reader to hear Sir Plume's lack of coherent thought. As pointed out by Wall, these lines could also signify the use of snuff during conversation. Connecting Sir Plume to Pope's satirization of French-style foppery, Wall notes, "Although we don't know whether Sir Plume's amber snuffbox had any particularly French association, the practice of taking snuff between words . . . was associated with the 'effeminizing' French customs so popular among upper-class fops" (363).[20] Further, annotating lines 123–124, she notes that he is a "fop, a beau, a spark, proud of his clothes and accessories, full of mannerisms and little ceremonies" (77). These mannerisms fit with the types of behaviors mocked in Steele's advertisement for Lillie in *The Spectator*, no. 138, discussed above, which Wall includes in her section on the cultural context of the poem.[21]

Despite Wall's insightful reading of the mid-speech dash, which I also read as Plume's excessive, foppish snuff use, we are also meant to connect the dash directly before and after the speech as symbolizing part of his conversational snuff ritual. Not only do these dashes represent the physical act of inhaling snuff, but this punctuation also represents the opening of the snuffbox case/discussion of Belinda's hair ("then the Case, / And thus broke out—"), and the closing of the box with the closing of his rambling speech desiring the Baron's returning of the lock ("—he spoke, and rapp'd his Box"). Indeed, Ferraro and Baine refer to the rapping of the snuffbox lid as a "ridiculous gesture of Challenge" to the Baron.[22] Further, Pope may be using the dash punctuation before, during, and after the speech to connect these behaviors with the "fashionable slang" that Sir Plume spits out when cursing ("Z—ds!").[23] Like Steele's storyteller in *The Tatler*, no. 35, Sir Plume believes his delicate mannerisms of opening the case, the taking of the powder, the snapping closed of the box, and the rapping of its lid, along with his foul language, will grant him rhetorical power.

As Steele establishes in *The Tatler* essay, the use of snuff is meant to replicate dramatic pauses in conversation. As with canto III, line 17 of his poem, Pope is illustrating the ways in which high society attempts to use snuff as a signifier of a conversational pause. Like Steele's storyteller in *The Tatler* essay, Sir Plume replaces a natural, rhetorically significant conversational pause with an artificial one that is generated by his use of snuff. When Sir Plume raps the snuffbox lid at the end of his speech, this action functions as a kind of exclamatory gesture, meant to add emphasis to the words of someone whose language is already plagued with oaths.

Given this rhetorical use of the snuffbox, we can read the snuffing of the tobacco powder in line 129 as a similar sort of punctuated gesture. Noticeably, the caesura in line 129 matches the content of the line. Up to this caesura, Sir Plume has only stated that the joke has been taken too far ("Plague on't!' 'tis past a jest"), but after the caesura, he is (slightly) more demanding, telling the Baron to give back the lock ("nay prithee, pox! / Give her the hair"). Snuff's physiological effects are spurring on Sir Plume's accusatory nature, not unlike the sexualized feelings of the Baron and Belinda that occur due to the scent of coffee. In "Death and the Object: The Abuse of Things in The Rape of the Lock," Barbara M. Benedict writes,

> Pope's poem . . . suggests that the things that inhabit the human world endanger both objects' function and humans' morality. As objects are carried away by people, people are carried away by objects, and in return, objects carry away value.
>
> Objects in the poem represent, arouse, and confound passions in people that threaten moral standards; they stir mortals to desires they fail to fulfil.[24]

In this situation, Sir Plume's powder and snuffbox seem to offer elevated speech and boldness. However, given the emasculating effects that Pope instills in snuff, especially later in the poem, the punctuated acts of snuffing and of closing the snuffbox lid bestow only slightly emboldening effects on Sir Plume, especially since his demands are packed into just half a line. Snuff and snuffbox provide a bump in courage, but only a momentary one.

The Baron, of course, is unconvinced and refuses to return the hair, and in a rare instance of Pope's sarcasm coming through the voice of the poem's antagonist, the Baron mockingly replies, "It grieves me much . . . / Who speaks so well should ever speak in vain" (ll. 131–132). Here, the audience sees how unsuccessful Sir Plume and the supposed rhetorical power of snuff are in actual discourse. When considering that commodities in the poem almost always have a supernatural ability to affect change in the world, the scene is doubly significant as the snuff is found wanting. Through the Baron's reply, Pope creates a clear divide between the person who believes himself to be conversationally empowered by snuff and his actual inability to persuade those listening. Discussing pharmacology in *The Rape of the Lock*, Richard Kroll notes that Sir Plume and his snuff clearly show, through his lack of articulation, the impotency of the poem's male figures. Kroll writes, "Sir Plume—whose original, Sir George Brown, had cause to be offended by the representation—appears, with his 'round unthinking Face' (*R*, 4.125), stupified, rendered incoherent, desexualized by the snuff with which he is synecdochically associated" (129–130). That Sir Plume's attempts to use snuff to assert dominance actually fail alludes to a problem of masculinity within the poem and its connection to such consumable items.

In addition to showing how snuff and snuffboxes (as well as the social cues associated with them) are used in polite and contentious conversation, Pope also deploys snuff as a very literal weapon within the final battle scene of the poem. In a technique similar to the advertisement printed in *The Spectator*, Pope's characters use many different abstract and corporeal objects as weapons: clever metaphors, the men's wit, the women's hair, frowns, glances, the aforementioned snuff, and a bodkin pin. Importantly, snuff is the only object used to assault another person physically, as Belinda's bodkin, treated in the mock epic like an ancestral sword, is only ever used to threaten the Baron. Describing in detail the scene of Belinda's martial use of the snuff, Pope writes,

> But this bold Lord, with manly strength indu'd,
> She with one Finger and a Thumb subdu'd:
> Just where the Breath of Life his Nostrils drew,
> A Charge of *Snuff* the wily Virgin threw;
> The *Gnomes* direct, to ev'ry Atome just,
> The pungent Grains of titillating Dust.
> Sudden, with starting Tears each Eye o'erflows,
> And the high Dome re-ecchoes to his Nose. (ll. 79–86)

In these four couplets, Pope characterizes snuff in a similar way to Addison and Steele. For all three writers snuff is an unnatural powder that invades the body. As with Sagissa's lover in *The Tatler*, no. 35 and Addison's group of "Virtuosos" in *The Spectator*, no. 275, Pope shows that those not used to snuff respond poorly to the substance and the body rejects it in the form of a mighty sneeze.

Despite Belinda's military prowess, Pope quickly changes the portrayal of snuff from a weapon of righteousness to an invading, foreign substance, as the focal point moves from Belinda (expertly throwing the powder, which is guided by the gnomes) to the Baron (receiving the snuff and succumbing to the sneeze). The entrance of the snuff into the place "Just where the Breath of Life his Nostrils drew" implies that this invasion goes against the natural act of breathing. The fact that the gnomes, the patron sprites of the now-more-prudish Belinda, are helping direct the earthy powder reinforces the idea that the substance cannot find its way without the help of supernatural, guiding spirits; snuff-taking goes against nature itself. The addition of the couplet referencing the gnomes also allows Pope to include a clever description of the pharmacological nature of the tobacco product. While it is largely ineffective in improving Sir Plume's conversational skills, its physical effects are very real. The snuff, a "titillating Dust," provides a brief, but powerful, comment on the alluring, and therefore problematic, nature of consumable and habit-forming substances.

The snuff and the sneeze it elicits play an important role in emasculating the Baron, emphasizing snuff's metaphorical role as an invader of the British body. In his interesting, almost forensic evaluation of the scene in which Belinda's lock is lost, Codr remarks that because "the eighteenth-century reader . . . was routinely exposed to satires on snuff and the sneezing it often provoked," the contemporary audience would have taken the public sneeze as "a violation of social propriety and, thus, as comical in its own right" (177); however, while Pope is no doubt playing on the strangeness of such a mighty sneeze—after which the entire environment "re-echoes to [the Baron's] nose," (l. 86)—the sneeze also indicates that the Baron is probably not a usual partaker of snuff.

Here, it is important to consider the snuff rituals of this period. Initially, in the seventeenth century, "sneezing was considered beneficial, within the snuff ritual . . . even the sneeze became part of the scene, and the trappings of the tobacco consumer now included a delicate handkerchief."[25] However, Lillie points out that this brief fashion was no longer followed by the eighteenth century (294). Discussing users' desires to sneeze, Friedman notes that "inhaled snuff immediately irritates the nasal lining, leading the user to sneeze, spreading the fine powdered product all over his or her clothes. While the most practiced of snuff-takers were able to suppress this response, not all were successful" (42). However, as discussed with *The Tatler* and *The Spectator* essays above, satirists of this period tend to divide habitual snuff-takers from those who do not use it by their ability to control their sneezes.

Just as snuff debilitates Sir Plume's masculine discourse, the invading, unnatural substance robs the Baron of his manliness, allowing him to be overpowered by the female warrior. Despite the Baron being a "bold Lord with manly strength endu'd," a wave of just "one finger and thumb" on the part of Belinda, armed with a mere pinch of snuff, subdues the Baron. Even as he is defeated in battle, the snuff forces tears from his eyes, further robbing him of his manhood.

Given the popularity of *The Rape of the Lock*, it is unsurprising that snuff, with its increasing popularity among men and especially women, would continue to be evaluated, especially for its effects on upper-class interactions. Addison, Steele, and Pope each use the material effects and gestures connected to this substance to consider how commercial luxury invades and weakens British social circles; however, because snuff was a relatively new social phenomenon, these satirists reject this new invading substance, symbolically representing the English body politic through the physical reactions of individual English bodies: the snuff-induced sneezing of Sagissa's lover, of Addison's sneezing scientists, and of Pope's conniving Baron. As we shall see, the satirical use of snuff and its effect on the physical body would change drastically starting in the 1720s, presenting vivid, and much viler, imagery for readers.

SNUFF, SNOT, AND STAINS: THE RISE OF GROTESQUERY IN SATIRES ON SNUFF

Starting in the 1720s, satirists began to fixate on the bodily consequences of snuff, showing the lasting (and disgusting) effects of prolonged and excessive usage. Rather than looking briefly at the sneeze of an infrequent user, these more Juvenalian writers—two anonymous authors and Jonathan Swift—instead foreground grotesque and scatological images, attempting to curb snuff's popularity through shame. As with the writers responding to the Gin Craze in the next chapter, these satirists would consider the adverse effects of a consumable product on one's body. Whereas the periodicals and poem discussed above expressed worry about the invasion of snuff-taking into polite conversation and its immediate effects on the unaccustomed body, these writers consider more fully the problems of what happens after snuff has been repeatedly taken into the body through heavy usage. The poets invade the reader's mind with this bodily imagery, rendering the fashion for snuff disgusting and disturbing, and arguing that the habit of taking snuff creates problems of hygiene along with health. Within their works, the anonymous writer of *Whipping Tom*, Swift, and an anonymous female poet portray snuff as a vile habit. Their criticism is more than visceral, however, for they also criticize the ability of snuff to complicate distinctions between the classes and genders. Furthermore, by presenting snuff-taking in a grosser light, these satirists seek to reconstruct as disgusting a habit that, as they viewed it, had become commonplace and thus far too ingrained in the culture.

Whipping Tom: Or, a Rod for a Proud Lady, a highly misogynistic pamphlet first published in 1722,[26] is one of the first satirical pieces to take a more grotesque, bodily approach to snuff and its effects. If the writer is to be believed, the pamphlet was popular, and it appears to have run through six editions and resulted in an expanded version in 1723. The pamphlet derives its name from the strange serial attacks on women that occurred first in 1681 and again in 1712. During the string in 1712, which lasted from October through December, Thomas Wallis and his accomplice attacked as many as seventy women, beating them with birch rods.[27] Emulating Wallis's misogynist attacks in print, the writer of *Whipping Tom* seeks to correct what he sees as proud behavior in women. This anonymous satirist views excessive luxury as a social evil, and throughout his pamphlet, he attacks women, and occasionally effeminate men, by mocking the pride and vanity associated with the commercial luxuries they enjoy. Between the two pamphlets the writer examines different perceived problems of the female consumer, including tea drinking, the fashionable practice of wearing scarlet cloaks, the use of hooped petticoats, and most importantly here, snuff-taking.

Whipping Tom's essay on the product, "The Foppish Mode of Taking Snuff," begins with a lengthy digression, focusing primarily on female pride. The anonymous writer then turns specifically to the idea of snuff as an unnecessary luxury. Describing his first interaction with snuff, the author tells his audience that he saw a fop behind the Strand and near the Exchange, who, due to all the black powder on his nose, looked as though he were an African monkey (7). Given that he finds the fop near the coffeehouses and the Exchange, both sites of commerce, the satirist associates snuff with money and commercial activity. The satirist illustrates this connection more forcefully by reviewing the history of snuff-taking techniques: "In the primitive Times of taking this exotick, or outlandish Commodity, it was sparingly taken out of a Spring-Pipe fixt to a wooden Box in the Shape of a pair; but now the Mob is as difficult in the Shapes of their Boxes, as in the manner of taking what they contain" (7–8). Discussing the specific fad for using a "Spring-Pipe," a fad Lillie corroborates (294), the satirist argues that the pipe initially allowed the user to inhale only a small amount of tobacco. Now, he implies, people go through even more tobacco than they did originally. The designs of the snuff-boxes, the writer implies, are themselves causing women and fops to spend ever more money on the material, while the containers also allow for other sinful adornments, including mirrors.

These elements of foppishness lead the writer to discuss what he sees as even more significant issues: the extension of this vice to the lower classes and the importation of the substance itself. As I discuss in chapter 5, the Gin Craze, which began in the 1720s, caused many English citizens to become unsettled by the idea of a consuming lower class. As we shall see in anti-gin writing, this pamphlet exposes a similar fear toward the lower class, whose habits of consumption are modeled on those of their social betters. *Whipping Tom* shows that the trend of snuffing had started to catch on among the lower orders. In the first version of the pamphlet, the satirist writes: "But here ends not the Foppishness of our modern Snuff Takers; for when now even Carmen and Porters, Chairmen and Hackney Coachmen, Skipkennels, and others of our Sham-Gentry get together, the little Eloquence their illiterateness allows them, is display'd in nonsensical Harangues on the Goodness and Virtues of *Burgomot, Spanish, Bologn,* or *Scotch* Snuff, which last generally among the among the inferior Fops" (8). According to the anonymous pamphleteer, snuff's popularity destabilizes class divides, creating in the lower classes a problematic desire to match the extreme luxury of the elite. Mocking these members of the lower and middle classes and referring to them as "Sham-Gentry," the writer satirizes their attempts to present themselves in conversation as eloquent and refined, despite in fact being illiterate. As Friedman notes, this polemic pamphlet not only shows the "effects of snuff on the brain" but also exposes the "foppish, 'sham-gentry' pretension" of those non-aristocratic people with access to what originally was an upper-class commodity (45). The facade of refinement does not hold up to scrutiny—as the illiteracy of these lower-class figures attests—but it nonetheless exposes the ability of consumer culture to affect class distinctions negatively.

Disruptions of class and gender dynamics do not remain separate but instead coalesce, as the satirist argues that snuff contaminates not only middle- and upper-class status but especially that of high-society femininity. Examining female snuff-takers, he argues that women begin to take on the physical characteristics of men when they use snuff. He writes, "Our *English* Women . . . do so transform the Physiognomy with this nasty Snuff, that Foreigners take them to be young Soldiers, with long Mustachoes or Whiskers, especially too when they see the Variety of Postures, they use in handling a Snuffbox" (9). According to the satirist, not only do women appear to have male facial hair due to the dark snuff collecting on their upper lips and cheeks, but they also take on physical mannerisms usually considered masculine and potentially lower class. If the satirist has portrayed snuff as making men more foppish, and thus more feminine, he argues that it causes women to "exceed all the motions an Adjutant [military officer's assistant] shews, in the Exercise of a Battalion of Foot" (9). Thus, snuff greatly imperils gender identification alongside class distinctions.

Given that the essay is a deeply vicious (and misogynistic) satire, it also employs disturbing, grotesque bodily imagery common to more bitter, Juvenalian satires; in comparison to the more urbane, witty Horatian style of Addison and Steele's essays and Pope's poem, this essay includes graphic imagery of snuff's long-term effects on the body to emphasize its problematic qualities. The writer details various techniques people use when taking snuff: Some people merely dip a single finger in to get a very small dab of powder and then "this Nostrils play'd, then t'other"; others take a "pinch" between their thumb and forefingers, alternatively employing a palms-upward motion for one nostril and a back-of-the-hand motion for the other; and still others, mainly women, take a pinch between their thumb and fingers and hold it "perhaps a quarter or half an Hour, not snuffing it, but daubing it with such unbecoming Airs" (9). The satirist ridicules the rituals associated with this luxury product, and then he emphasizes bodily reactions (on the part of both the onlooker and the snuff-taker) to the powder: "'tis enough to make one spew, to see the excrementitious Matter of the Head, mingled with Snuff hanging under their Snot-Gauls" (9). Angela McShane notes that while male snuff-takers were mocked for their adoption of "feminized interests in decorative dress and social gossip . . . women were rebuked for the unwomanly filthiness and unwonted independence that the habit engendered."[28] Here, the satirist creates a disgusting image, meant to offset the pompous behavior of the women who dab snuff to their noses over long periods of time. Describing the scene as something that would make an onlooker vomit, the satirist describes the snuff that "mingled with" the snot, or "exrementitious Matter of the Head," as it drips and hangs down. The excremental, scatological imagery is increased by the use of kenning ("Snot-Gauls") at the end of the sentence. Gall, "An excrescence produced on trees, especially the oak, by the action of insects, chiefly of the genus Cynips," provides a disturbingly vivid image of a bead of nasal drip.[29] From the eighteenth-century perspective of health, tobacco, when used minimally as a purgative, provided an important function; however, when overused, especially to serve one's vanity, the healthful effects became problematic and disgusting, especially in public.

Furthermore, the anonymous satirist connects these disturbing, bodily images directly to medical issues. Near the end of the pamphlet, he demonstrates that excessive snuff-taking constitutes not just an overindulgence based on excessive pride but also a risking of one's physical health: "But besides the taking of Snuff out of Pride, a too frequent Use of it, whether plain or scented, is very prejudicial to the Health" (11). On top of citing colds, general respiratory issues, and asthma, he provides grotesque medical examples to horrify his audience. He tells us that within the "Lungs and Brains" of many snuff users there "have been found Clods or Lumps of Snuff, bigger than Walnuts, or Pidgeons Eggs, which have been the sole Cause of their Death" (11). Discussing both strange (lumps the size of birds' eggs and walnuts) and common medical ailments, the writer shows that snuff-taking is unnatural for the body and that it constitutes a widespread public health issue in Britain. These specific examples expose a broader problem for England: in addition to undercutting the supposed refinement of snuff-taking, the satirist of *Whipping Tom* shows that snuff damages every aspect of the English body, attempting to horrify men and women of all classes into giving up the habit.

Like *Whipping Tom*, Swift's famously disgusting poem, *The Lady's Dressing Room*, and *The Gentleman's Study*, a reaction poem written anonymously by a Dublin woman in 1732, also contain this more bitter and bodily-focused satire of snuff.[30] Swift's poem contains perhaps the most famous example of scatological imagery in Augustan satire. In the poem, Strephon sneaks into the dressing room of Celia, a woman with whom he is infatuated, and catalogs, in disgusting and horrifying detail, the dirty objects that fill the space, including particularly nasty eighteenth-century beauty products, piles of soiled laundry and pieces of cloth (used for personal hygiene), gummed-up combs, and the dirty water bowl of Celia's pet. The poem ends famously with Strephon discovering Celia's chamber pot and having the epiphany that Celia, like all human beings, must defecate.

Although the use of snuff in the poem is minimal, by looking briefly at how snuff is employed, and then turning to the reaction poem *The Gentleman's Study*, I hope to make a larger argument that both Swift and the anonymous female writer are evaluating the ways in which class and gender fit with the use of a commercial, luxury product like snuff. In Swift's poem, snuff appears only in one line. Lines 11–58 describe various cloths that are heaped up in piles, including towels, petticoats, handkerchiefs, stockings, and the caps that women wore at night when sleeping. Examining the dirty handkerchiefs, Swift writes, "Nor be the Handkerchiefs forgot / All varnish'd o'er with Snuff and Snot" (ll. 49–50). As in the rest of the poem, Swift breaks down the illusionary aspects of a woman's public persona by revealing to his audience what external agents—be they clothes, makeup, a cute pet dog, or a popularly consumed tobacco product—actually look like behind closed doors. In the case of snuff, we see the grotesque truth of its effects on the body. Further, Swift also plays on the medicinal associations of snuff with the scatological. As Marcy Norton notes, the fact that tobacco was used extensively in early modern medicine connected the drug to its role as a purgative, a role alluded to in treatments of snuff: "In keeping with the material detritus that snuffing exacted, along with the medical characterization of tobacco's work as one of evacuation, snuffing was often likened to defecation, and the resultant snot, to shit."[31] No matter how elegant a woman may look when artfully taking snuff, Swift implies, it will cause her to create more snot, reminding her of her biological functions. The excessive snot produced by snuff-taking ultimately ends up on a handkerchief on the floor of Celia's chamber. The handkerchief, "varnished o'er with snuff and snot," seems to have been abandoned, presumably because the residue of the snuff has discolored it. Since snuff came in a variety of different kinds and colors, one would imagine it would easily stain a (presumably) white handkerchief. Swift thus shows that snuff not only is highly consumable and habit-forming, but it also forces other forms of consumption; Celia goes through more handkerchiefs because of the product. Like the anonymous author of *Whipping Tom*, Swift uses grotesque, scatological imagery to render snuff-taking disgusting rather than a polished, fashionable ritual. In this way, he destabilizes the pedestal on which upper-class men placed upper-class women, exposing that—like the makeup they use to adorn their faces and bodies—the snuff they take to appear refined is actually grotesque when viewed more closely.

The anonymous female poet of *The Gentleman's Study* examines these same gendered constructs from a different angle, while also considering, to a more significant degree than Swift, class distinctions. Published the same year as Swift's poem and providing a gender-swapped inversion of the original, *The Gentleman's Study* does not follow its predecessor in having an upper-class figure invade the space of another aristocratic character. Instead, the main figure of the story is a working-class woman, Mrs. South, a milliner hoping to settle her bill with Strephon, the same character featured in Swift's piece. While in Swift's poem, Strephon sneaks into Celia's room when her servant Betty is busy, *The Gentleman's Study* features a jesting moment in which Tom, Strephon's servant, tricks Mrs. South into waiting in Strephon's room, saying that his master will be there soon. Given that Tom convinces Mrs. South to remain there "with an odd, but friendly Grin" on his face, it is clear that he wishes to expose the gross, drunken, sexually licentious behavior of his master to an outside party. Thus, before even beginning her catalog of Strephon's disgusting study, the anonymous satirist has begun to set up both gendered and class-based contentions.

The use of tobacco and snuff in the poem illustrates issues of luxury and commerce, sexual immorality, cleanliness, and obsession with consumption. One particularly effective aspect of the poem is its ability to mix the dirty elements together through its use of metaphor, confusing the reader to a greater extent than Swift's poem as to where one smell or sight ends and another begins. After discussing a pile of stockings, shoes, and other clothes, the speaker notes that "A Close-stool helpt to make the Fume, / Tobacco-spits about the Room; / With Flegm and Vomit on the Walls" (5). As readers, we have already been told two stanzas prior that "Four different Stinks" lay together of "Sweat, Turd, and Piss, and Leather," meaning that the use of different grotesque, bodily smells and sensations unite to confuse. Discussing the chamber pot, the writer notes that it "helpt," not solely, "to make the Fume." Here, the satirist could be using "Fume" in two different capacities: the most obvious definition is an "Odorous smoke (e.g. that of incense, tobacco)," but it can also mean any general, unpleasant smell excreted from the body.[32] The writer implies that the Fume could be either the fecal smell of the chamber pot, the type of tobacco smell that would come from the liquid of the "Tobacco-spits" covering the floor and walls, or, as is more likely, a combination of the two. The speaker shows that men—in comparison to most women—are often enthralled to three specific tobacco products: chewing tobacco (a habit not as common in England), pipe tobacco, and snuff. These habits unite to make phlegm and mucus a greater problem than we see in Swift's poem, and clearly its effects on the male English body are devastating. Indeed, a few moments later, the speaker juxtaposes two types of tobacco against the clothing they stain: "Pig-tail and Snuff, and dirty Gloves, / Some plain, some fring'd, which most he loves" (5). "Pig-tail" refers to a type of rope-shaped bit of chewing tobacco, which, along with the snuff, ends up dirtying his gloves, even though they may be his favorite pair. The tobacco spit, the smell of the dirty chamber pot, and the gloves dirty from chewing tobacco and snuff imply that men, not women, have more substantial problems with hygiene, health, and consumerism.

Whereas Swift fixates on the disgusting aspects of eighteenth-century makeup and beautifying products, this female satirist examines more specifically the grotesque and consumeristic aspects of tobacco in general. After discussing chewing tobacco and its effects on the room, she turns to pipe tobacco and snuff:

> Of Pipes a Heap, some whole, some broke,
> some Cut and Dry for him to smoke;
> And Papers that his A—se has clean'd,
> And Handkerchiefs with Snuff all stain'd. (5)

Here, the pipes themselves are piled in a "heap," representing the easily replaced clay tobacco pipes discussed in the previous chapter. While many of the pipes are unusable, many are essentially ready to smoke, showing the complete lack of control Strephon has over his habit. Furthermore, mingled among the papers that Strephon uses to clean himself are the very same stained handkerchiefs that Swift uses to shame Celia. However, given the sheer number of tobacco products and the amount of stains and filth they create, the writer argues that male consumption of tobacco constitutes more of a problem than female.

When Strephon finally makes it back to his study, we see the effects of a long night of debauchery, spending, and consuming. The grotesque imagery shows how consumer luxury can negatively affect one's appearance:

> Then in came *Strephon*, lovely Sight!
> Who had not slept a wink all Night,
> He staggers in, he swears, he blows,
> With Eyes like Fire, and snotty Nose;
> A mixture glaz'd his Cheeks and Chin,
> Of Claret, Snuff and odious Flegm. (7)

If Swift's poem tells us in the first stanza that Celia is gorgeous, a "goddess . . . Arrayed in lace, brocades and tissues," a direct description of Strephon is not supplied until the latter half of this poem. After Strephon stumbles around, cursing and breathing hard, the writer describes his red eyes, a result of his heavy drinking and lack of sleep, along with the "snotty Nose" that signals the overuse of snuff. However, most disgustingly, Strephon's face is layered over with a mixture of wine, snuff, and mucus or "odious Flegm," which of course would have been viewed as a problematic imbalance in the health of the body. Unlike the Strephon of Swift's poem, the disgusted milliner sees the gentleman and witnesses his revolting nature in person. By emphasizing the commodities' effects on Strephon's face, the female satirist shows how expensive habits such as snuff and wine could affect one's health and social standing.

Furthermore, the ways in which Strephon's extreme consumerism relate to class are key to understanding the poet's goal. Given that Mrs. South is a milliner, a member of the middle class seeking payment for her services, it comes as a shock to her when in a moment of morbid curiosity she looks through the gentleman's pockets and finds signs that she may never be repaid. She finds letters from Strephon's debtors, long tavern bills, and a very nice snuffbox that, behind its mirror, holds a "bawdy picture" (6). As McShane notes, snuffboxes containing personal images were extremely common, and it was undoubtedly likely that men would hide pornographic pictures in them as well ("The New World of Tobacco," 44–47). Whereas for Swift disgust is mingled with sexual desire, the female satirist uses the snuffbox to connect sexual desires with commercial ones. The ornate box holds both a commercial luxury in the form of fine snuff tobacco and a picture that encodes sexually deviant aristocratic male desire, an element that reoccurs several times within the poem. In the penultimate stanza of the poem, Mrs. South, realizing that Strephon has passed out after a night of hard drinking, and no doubt also sickened by all that she has witnessed, chooses to leave without being paid. In her poem, the satirist examines the differences between men and women and their perceptions of one another, and as a female satirist, chooses to provide a female response that instructs her own gender as to what men are truly like; further, this female satirist focuses more attention on class dynamics, grafting these critiques of upper-class behavior onto her exploration of gender. As a working woman of the middle class, Mrs. South is forced to confront the realities not only of what men are like at the hygienic level but also how they behave as consumers, ultimately realizing that she will find payment from such a man extremely elusive.

In *Whipping Tom*, Swift's *The Lady's Dressing Room*, and *The Gentleman's Study*, snuff is investigated not just as a product that invades the body of the polite speaker, but also as a corrupting agent that makes the human body (more) disgusting and grotesque. Investigating snuff as a consumer product, these writers argue that the substance is not only part of a facade but also a substantial indicator of one's lack of intelligence and good breeding. Rather than being merely a false means to mimic intellectual superiority, it reveals one's slavish, animalistic desire for sensory experience.

CONCLUSION

In these satires, we see an increasing fear of snuff as a luxury product. From 1709 through 1714, Steele, Addison, and Pope primarily treated snuff as a luxury product invading polite conversation and interactions. By the 1720s and 1730s, it was being frequently criticized for its significant effect on the physical body, and thus scatological imagery plays an increasingly important role in the mockery of the product. Throughout this period, the invasion of luxury goods into eighteenth-century life created unique opportunities and problems for satirists interested in discussing the practical elements of an increasingly commercial world. As satirists, these writers recognized that the popularity of products within a consumer culture was changing the ways people interacted with one another. By criticizing snuff's effects on polite conversation, on British masculinity, on the human body, and on foreign and domestic commerce, satirists from the first half of the eighteenth century sought to curb the influence of a product that, unlike wine, ale, beer, gin, or pipe tobacco, could easily be used within most social circles.

5

ENGLISH SATIRICAL WRITING IN THE AGE OF MOTHER GIN, 1723–1751

"THE DISTILLING OF MALT," WROTE Daniel Defoe in 1713, the last year of his periodical *The Review*, "has so great a Concern in [the economy of England], That it must for ever pass with me for a Trade as Profitable to the Public as Necessary to be Supported."[1] Throughout his journalistic career, Defoe consistently championed English liquors as a substitute for French brandy, an import from one of England's chief rivals on the global stage. He was a long-standing proponent of distilling spirituous liquors, publishing an adamant defense of the trade in *A Brief Case of the Distillers, and of the Distilling Trade in England, Shewing how Far it Is the Interest of England to Encourage the Said Trade* (1726).[2] However, as Jessica Warner notes, Defoe, only two years later, would blame many of the nation's problems on gin, the most popular of these spirituous liquors, in his 1728 pamphlet *Augusta Triumphans: Or, the Way to Make London the Most Flourishing City in the Universe*.[3] In his pamphlet, Defoe blames gin drinking among the "lower sort" for disrupting English manufacturing. He writes, "Now so far are our common People so infatuated with *Geneva* [gin], that Half the Work is not done now as formerly."[4] Furthermore, these critiques of gin show up in his fiction as his 1722 novel, *The History and Remarkable Life of the Truly Honourable Col. Jacque* in which the eponymous Colonel Jack's wife bankrupts him due to her gin drinking.[5]

While Defoe is known for changing his stance in his political writings, this shift from pro-distilling to anti-gin reads as particularly dramatic. To understand this change, one must understand the economic fervor that drove the production of English spirits. "Gin" is a shortened version of "Geneva," the English word derived from the original Dutch "Jenever/Genever"; "jenever" itself comes from the Latin word "juniperus," which refers to the juniper berries from which it is distilled.[6] Originating in the Netherlands during the 1650s, the spirit eventually found its way to England during the reign of William III, most likely through England's involvement with the Nine Years' War (1688–1697).[7] Alcohol taxes, of course, provided important funds for William's wars. In fact, in the minds of many writers, William himself introduced the Dutch beverage to England (*Gin*, 5–6). Because of these expensive wars, the king needed funds, which were easily raised by increasing excise taxes on expensive, imported commodities; eventually William sought to undercut Louis XIV economically, and French brandies were banned (*Craze*, 32). Warner writes, "the landowners sitting in Parliament nonetheless had a vested interest in finding new markets for their surplus grain, and to this end they were prepared to support legislation designed to protect English distillers from foreign competition" (32).

Likewise, Patrick Dillon notes that while William may not have drunk gin or personally introduced it to England, "it was William of Orange whose Acts of Parliament opened the floodgates to the cheap spirits that were soon being sold in cellars and garrets all over London" (6). William simultaneously challenged the French in war, disrupted their export trade, created a market for his country's lesser surplus grains, and greatly developed the domestic enterprise of distilling liquor. Coinciding with England's financial needs was a general desire among the populace to find a good, cheaply produced domestic liquor to substitute for French brandy that was rendered too expensive, having to be smuggled into the British Isles (*Gin*, 6). Then, English gin appeared to fill the market gap, using juniper berries and fruit additives to mask the taste of the very potent liquor.

Part of Defoe's long-standing defense of distilled liquors derives from the principles of mercantilism, which was the main economic policy in Europe from the Renaissance period through the first half of the eighteenth century. In his earlier *Some Thoughts upon the Subject of Commerce with France* (1713), Defoe argues that over his years of writing, many of his views on trade had changed, but that one element had not: his stance on whether or not to trade with France during times of war.[8] He points to the problems with past trade exchanges between France and England:

> I have nothing to do here with the question so much Canvass'd . . . Whether the Trade to *France* was always to our Advantage or no? I acknowledge I was always of an opinion that it was not: I mean as to the *Ballance of Trade* [my emphasis]. I was bred to the *French* Trade from a Youth, and have known my share of the Particulars of it, and I know their Import was always very Heavy when our Duties upon them were Low, our Gust to their Wines, Brandy, Silks and Fashions High, and the Number of sorts of Goods Great, which we dealt with them. (14)

He goes on to explain that French wines and brandy, among other trade goods, had created, and would continue to expand, a major trade deficit. As a system, mercantilism centered on the concept of "the balance of trade," the belief that "the fundamental purpose of trade was not to increase the general assets of the country but to maximise the quantity of bullion [precious metals, such as silver and gold] that flowed in from abroad."[9] Under this system, an individual country's wealth was viewed as the total amount of these bullion reserves, without considering more complex metrics, such as gross domestic product, which factors in the amount of goods and services a sovereign nation can generate.

Over the course of the eighteenth century, the mercantilism system would fall out of favor as international trade became increasingly pivotal and complex. Throughout the century there would be three competing schools of European economic theory: the vestiges of mercantilism; physiocracy, a French theory developed by François Quesnay, Victor de Riqueti, Marquis de Mirabeau, and Anne-Robert-Jacques Turgot, that stressed agricultural production's role in economic expansion and that produced the concept of laissez-faire; and early capitalism as developed by David Hume, John Millar, and Adam Smith, who incorporated ideas from both mercantilism and physiocracy. These developments ultimately culminated in the capitalistic concepts expounded by Adam Smith in *An Inquiry into the Nature and Causes of the Wealth of Nations* (1776), which is traditionally thought of as the beginning of modern economic theory.

Coinciding with this change in economic thought was the rise of Mother Gin and the resulting Gin Craze. This period, lasting from the 1720s through 1751, was marked by an explosion in gin's popularity, a rise in lower-class gin consumption, a resulting moral panic on the part of the middle and upper classes, and numerous laws seeking to halt gin distribution. During this craze, which is often considered one of the first modern drug epidemics, lower-class intoxication was viewed as a plague that was upsetting established social orders; indeed, Warner compares the period to the crack cocaine explosion of the 1980s, citing both the harmful overindulgence of gin among the lower orders and the fear sweeping through the middle and upper classes.[10] During the period, gin was combated legally in a way unprecedented for British alcohol consumption, resulting in eight individual acts over the course of the period: the Gin Acts of 1729, 1733, 1736, 1737, 1738, 1743, 1747, and 1751. Writers with an interest in economics, including Defoe, Bernard Mandeville, and Henry Fielding, examined the problem of lower-class gin consumption, and their problematization of this beverage coincided with the slow movement away from mercantilism.

Traditional mercantilist thought during the seventeenth and eighteenth centuries was that luxury was damaging England, and the idea that the working classes might be able to overindulge was a source of major concern. As Jonathan White points out, "the issue of laboring-class gin drinking, like that of laboring-class consumption more generally, was bound up with the concerns animating debates about luxury and, more broadly, with the historical emergence of 'the economic' as a separate sphere of knowledge and social practice."[11] Regarding the idea of "luxury," modern readers often infer an economist interpretation of this word, as Maxine Berg makes clear: "Economists associate luxury with elite consumption; they define luxury in terms of income, social division, and social exclusion. Luxury goods, in this analysis, are those goods to which most people do not have access. They feature in current consumer society as designer and branded goods connected with lifestyle choices of distinction, diversity, and individuality."[12] However, as Berg points out, early modern views of what constituted a luxury were not stable. She writes, "Economic and social theorists from the late seventeenth century to the eighteenth century debated the meaning of luxury and its social and economic implications.... Contemporaries were deeply interested in the changing characteristics of luxury goods, and in the problems of separating these from necessaries" (31).

This lack of stability on what constituted a luxury means that economic writers like Defoe, Mandeville, and Fielding were more likely to conceptualize and stylize lower-class overindulgence in gin as a type of luxuriousness that was highly problematic for their social station. In this way, luxury should also be considered according to the broader seventeenth- and eighteenth-century definition of the term: "The habitual use of, or indulgence in what is choice or costly, whether food, dress, furniture, or appliances of any kind."[13] Further, as Berg contends, "Restriction to the elites is not an essential element in the idea of a luxury. Any community or family may have symbolic days, persons, or occasions that need to be celebrated with especially rare consumption" (30). While the word "luxury" was still strongly associated with the upper class, as in Joseph Addison's *Spectator*, no. 55, writers like Mandeville and Fielding treat lower-class gin drinking as relatively "costly" to the impoverished worker.[14]

In his philosophical treatise *The Fable of the Bees* (1723), Mandeville goes against the grain of traditional mercantilist views, stressing the economic benefits of consumerism, luxury, and extravagant spending. Despite his praise of luxuriousness in the middle and upper classes, Mandeville largely condemns gin medically, morally, and economically. Trained as a physician, Mandeville problematizes the drinking of gin and other potent liquors due to their effects on bodily health, and as a writer interested in the social and economic health of the nation, he stresses that gin will likely lead to social decay. While entertaining the possibility of the financial possibilities of the drink, he rejects the idea that the laboring classes should have access to an indulgence he believes will only stop them from fulfilling their economic role. Throughout his writing, Mandeville styles gin as a type of lower-class luxury—a luxury that does not fit within the proto-capitalistic, but still ultimately mercantilist system he champions. This treatment of gin, I argue, becomes a consistent feature in the economic, ethical, political, and satirical writings of the period.

After evaluating Mandeville's shaping of anti-gin narratives, I then turn to John Gay's *The Beggar's Opera* (1728), showing how Gay plays with this narrative through his complex, satirical structuring of class in the play. In addition to mocking gin, Gay also uses the liquor to satirize the proto-capitalist policies of Sir Robert Walpole. Representing gin from a multitude of angles, Gay provides a more nuanced understanding of gin, problematizing Mandeville's narrative of gin as lower-class beverage.

Looking at the laws, policies, and events that shaped the turbulent Gin Craze, I then examine three little-known satirical pieces, printed from 1729 to 1738, that mock and question the various Gin Acts and the misconceptions of those seeking reform. These writers consider more fully those who gin legislation will most greatly impact: the lower-class drinkers themselves and the business owners who must deal with impractical legislative measures. The seldom-studied poems by Elias Bockett and Stephen Buck expose the ways in which gin was also seen by many as a key to lower-class productivity and to the happiness of the non-elite, while the noncanonical drama *The Informers Outwitted: A Tragi-Comical Farce* (1738) seeks to mock the social chaos and disruption of trade caused by the Gin Acts.

The chapter ends by looking at the gin policies of the 1740s and early 1750s, examining the mercantilist principles expounded by Henry Fielding in *An Enquiry into the Late Increase in Robbers* (1751), published the same year that England passed its final Gin Act. Helping bring an end to the Gin Craze, Fielding's text pulls from the many cultural threads surrounding the gin debate, showing the dangers of a society in which consumerism had finally reached the working classes.

BEEHIVES AND BOTTLES: GIN AS A LOWER-CLASS LUXURY IN MANDEVILLE'S *THE FABLE OF THE BEES*

It did not take long for Londoners to recognize that gin, with its high alcohol content and heavy rates of consumption, might be negatively affecting the lower classes. With the rise of Mother Gin, English writers and reformers recognized that an unprecedented social phenomenon was occurring around them. In 1724, Edward Chandler, Bishop of Lichfield and Coventry, preached a scathing condemnation of spirit shops before the Society for the Reformation of Manners, referring specifically to the gin shops Middlesex magistrates were investigating at the time:

> It is thus the Patrons of debauchery do cater for the pleasures of the unenterprizing sinners ... Among the many complaints of this sort, that of Strong-Water-Shops, is none of the least, by reason, that they are multiplied into such Numbers, and distributed into such convenient distances for the destruction of the lives, and corruption of the manners of the lower people, in all parts of the town. One can't but be touch'd out of meer humanity, with the havock these liquors make of so many of our fellow-creatures. Strong liquors are now become the Epidemick distemper of this great City.[15]

Here, Chandler exhibits the type of moral panic generated by religious groups when confronted with the realities of a beverage that was as strong as brandy and cheaper than beer.[16] Bernard Mandeville, however, recognized that gin was not just a moral problem but an economic one as well. In his writing, Mandeville establishes the idea that gin is a lower-class luxury, a perspective that greatly influenced the viewpoints of later writers and reformers working during the Gin Craze; unlike many of these writers, he is less interested in gin consumption as a moral behavior and more interested in its consequences for physical and economic health.

In 1705, Mandeville published a 423-line satirical poem called *The Grumbling Hive; or, Knaves Turn'd Honest*, in which the Holland-born physician mocks the English for their inability to acknowledge the vice that leads to the successes of their country.[17] Envisioning the English as disaffected bees, Mandeville develops the hive as a microcosm of the English social order, and he examines the ways in which varying social behaviors and occupations affect different social strata. The speaker informs us that the bees are unhappy with their hive, despite having "Luxury and Ease," despite having a hive that is stable because of its "Laws and Arms," and despite living under a "better Government" than any other community. In the third stanza, the speaker explains why these bees are so well off: "Vast Numbers throng'd the fruitful Hive; / Yet those vast Numbers made 'em thrive" (1). The bees are constantly producing, creating commodities for their fellow bees, which serve to "to supply / Each other's Lust and Vanity" through consumable goods (1). It is the sheer number of worker bees—constantly providing goods and services to the others—that creates enough jobs to keep them busy and thriving. Throughout the poem, Mandeville looks at many social positions, institutions, and occupations, arguing poetically that these essential aspects of society are ultimately created through the self-centered vices of the bees themselves.

Despite its interesting conceit, the poem did not initially attract much attention. However, when Mandeville published an expansion of the poem in 1714, supplementing it with prose sections (referred to as "Remarks" in the text) and developing his ideas as a more detailed philosophical treatise, the public took notice. In this version of the text, entitled *The Fable of the Bees: Or, Private Vices, Public Benefits*, and in the subsequent editions that came over the next two decades (I deal primarily with the 1714 and the 1723 editions in this chapter), Mandeville outlines his central paradox: "private vice, public benefit," by which he means that the individual, sinful behaviors that people exhibit, such as avarice, greed, and gluttony, ultimately lead to broader economic good for Britain.[18]

Within *The Fable*, Mandeville brushes aside traditional ethics and instead sketches the importance of private vices for economic growth in England. While Mandeville should still be considered a mercantilist, his text goes against traditional, hardline mercantilism by glorifying luxuries and especially those that come from other countries. In Remark F, Mandeville argues that "Virtue is made Friends with Vice, when industrious good People . . . get a livelyhood by something that chiefly depends on, or is very much influenc'd by the Vices of others, without being themselves guilty of, or accessary to them, any otherwise than by way of Trade" (117). These "industrious good People" are not subject to the vice themselves but are merely profiting from it monetarily, which will in turn allow them to purchase other goods from their fellow citizens.

After setting up his argument in Remark F, Mandeville takes alcohol as an example to prove his point, first considering the initial international trade that brings in imported wine or brandy: "Thus the Merchant, that sends Corn or Cloth into Foreign Parts to purchase Wines and Brandies, encourages the Growth or Manufactury of his own Country; he is a Benefactor to Navigation, encreases the Customs, and is many ways beneficial to the Publick" (117). Mandeville shows the complexities of international trade and how it brings in public moneys such as customs duties; however, he quickly shifts to the larger effect alcohol has on economics: "Yet it is not to be denied but that his [the Merchant's] greatest dependence is Lavishness and Drunkenness: For if none were to drink Wine but such only as stand in need of it, nor any body more than his Health requir'd, that multitude of Wine-Merchants, Vintners, Coopers, &c. that make such a considerable Shew in this flourishing City [London], would be in a miserable Condition" (117–118). Merchants, Mandeville reminds us, are not the only ones thriving off drinking and merry making; indeed, there is a whole host of businesses that make their money off these morally questionable habits.

For Mandeville, pride, vanity, and even drunkenness cause people to purchase luxury goods, and while these luxuries may lead to immoral behavior, the items are necessary for domestic production and tranquility. A healthy economy is built on the desire for material commodities, objects individuals use to distinguish themselves from others. The desires for the very luxury items condemned by not only traditional morality but also by traditional mercantilists actually sustain a healthy economy. As Kathryn Sutherland notes, Mandeville argues "for the economic necessity of . . . Britain's foreign trade" but "nevertheless diverges sharply from the extreme mercantilist condemnation of luxury as economically and morally enervating. For him, morality and economics are separate. People are naturally attracted to luxury, and foreign imports stimulate the domestic economy."[19] Unlike traditional mercantilists, Mandeville sees foreign importation as key to a nation's survival.

The complexity of Mandeville's paradox, "private vices, public benefits," fits very well with his varied treatment of alcohol. It is worthy of note that in the 1714 edition of this text, Mandeville discusses alcohol minimally. For instance, in 1714's Remark Q, he expounds on the many complex forms of honor in the world, comparing strong liquors' ability to instill artificial feelings of courage to traditional bravery itself; notably, Mandeville does not discuss gin or alcohol extensively in this version of his text, nor does he examine alcohol as a commodity. However, when writing his 1723 edition of the treatise, he must have felt the need to address gin, for its effects on both the body, as well as the national economy. Throughout his writing, Mandeville claims that gin wreaks havoc on the body. After condemning gin in Remark G of *The Fable*, referring to it as a "Fiery Lake that sets the Brain in Flame, Burns up the Entrails, and scorches every part within; and at the same time [is] a Lethe of Oblivion," he draws on his medical background to point out the many horrible bodily illnesses that can result from its use (121–122).

Mandeville frequently approaches problems from the perspective of a physician, his lifelong career; many of his publications address medical topics. Indeed, Roy Porter notes that much of Mandeville's pragmatic "realism" comes from his experiences in the profession. He writes, "It is, of course, hardly an accident that this man who loved playing the no-nonsense realist was a practicing physician and medical author, professionally inured to the blunt truths of the flesh. He gloried in strutting around in the persona of a hardbitten dissector of human nature."[20] In the 1711 edition of his medical essay, *A Treatise of the Hypochondriack and Hysterick Passions*, Mandeville argues that wine can be an effective medicinal treatment, but that those people who drink even "two to three glasses" with their usual dinner will lose all the positive medicinal effects that wine could yield them when they are in poor health.[21]

While he points to wine's positive effects on health (when not drunk to excess) and points to its stimulation of the English economy, Mandeville draws a much stricter line when addressing gin consumption, which harms both the individual body and the national one. Remark G of the 1723 edition of *The Fable* offers a nuanced evaluation of gin as a consumable material. In his 1723 edition, Mandeville's evaluation of gin evolves into a clear disdain for the lower-class beverage, and he condemns it over the course of several pages. Mandeville writes,
Nothing is more destructive, either in regard to the Health or the Vigilance and Industry of the Poor than the infamous Liquor, the name of which deriv'd from Juniper-Berries in Dutch is now . . . shrunk into a Monosyllabble, Intoxicating Gin, that charms the Unactive, the desperate and crafty of either Sex, and makes the starving Sot behold his Rags and Nakedness with stupid Indolence, or banter both in Senseless Laughter, and more insipid Jests (121). Here, Mandeville shows his antipathy to the liquor, exposing the lower-class gin drinker's lack of drive (and inability) to contribute to society through labor.

Mandeville then considers gin from an economic perspective more fully, highlighting the problems with the type of commercial exchanges to be expected with gin distribution. According to Mandeville, sellers of gin tend to be extremely heavy drinkers of the product. He notes, "Among the doating Admirers of this Liquid Poyson, many of the meanest rank, from a sincere affection to the Commodity it self, become Dealers in it . . . But as these Starvlings commonly drink more than their Gains, they seldom by selling mend the wretchedness of Condition they labour'd under whilst they were only Buyers" (122). Because gin is inexpensive to produce and because it is a domestic product without a high markup, it is necessarily cheap when sold, meaning there is little monetary benefit to the seller. Furthermore, in Mandeville's version of mercantilism, this situation poses a larger problem because the person selling the gin is also indulging in it, rather than merely catering to "the [particular] Vices of others" (117). These people, constantly consuming their own stock, cannot properly engage in commercial exchanges, impeding the constant, flowing monetary exchange that characterizes Mandeville's ideal system. After pointing out the amount of "Want and Misery" caused by gin, Mandeville notes that the retail sellers of the beverage (i.e., those who obtain the product from a larger distributor and do not produce the gin themselves) are mostly "broke and ruin'd" if they consume the beverage, and those who do not "are their whole Life-time obliged to take the uncommon Pains, endure the Hardships, and swallow all the ungrateful and shocking [scenes of squalor], for little or nothing beyond a bare sustenance, and their daily Bread" (123). To Mandeville, gin is too public a vice, and it produces little economic benefit. Gin, Mandeville argues, has the potential to rob England of an important renewable resource, its lower-class manual laborers, and thus it impoverishes the country to the point that the cycle of trade is halted.

Despite his professional hatred of and moral opposition to gin, Mandeville plays devil's advocate with himself when discussing its economic effects. He notes, "The Money that arises from the Duties upon Malt, is a considerable Part of the National Revenue, and should no Spirits be distill'd from it, the *Publick* Treasure would prodigiously suffer on that Head." He also lists the many jobs the trade necessarily produces (123). To explore these ideas, Mandeville fashions a "sharp-sighted good humour'd Man," a hypothetical defender of gin's potential benefits, who sees the possible economic potential of gin that Mandeville ignores (124). Mandeville spends the rest of Remark G discussing the many ways in which gin might be a boon to England. Mandeville's "good humour'd Man" argues, for instance, that while gin may cause domestic crime, this problem may be "over-paid in the Advantage we receiv'd from it abroad, by upholding the Courage of Soldiers, and animating the Sailors to the Combat; and that in the two last Wars no considerable Victory had been obtain'd without" (124). Here, the writer, considering the broad scope of gin and its effects on people, suggests it may cause English soldiers and sailors to fight more fiercely and bravely for their country; the topic of alcohol's effect on England's military would return repeatedly over the next three decades, playing a pivotal role in pro- and anti-alcohol tracts.[22]

Mandeville, via his hypothetical gin defender, argues that if even one person could profit enough from gin to sustain himself and to impact British commerce positively, it may be worth it to allow gin distillation to continue. However, his willingness to explore these pro-gin sentiments also serves his larger goals within the treatise. James Nicholls contends, "Mandeville's purpose was not to condemn gin but to show that even this most diabolical commodity had a role to play in promoting the common good.... Most importantly, even if the majority of gin-sellers were rank topers only a small number had to become rich through the trade to have a disproportionately beneficial social impact."[23] While Mandeville does describe gin as detrimental to lower-class health and productivity, he also understands that an argument could be made for its economic benefits to society.

Mandeville sees class distinctions as integral to maintaining economic prosperity in England, and as alluded to above, he believed that keeping the laboring poor from laziness was essential to British productivity. Like traditional mercantilists, Mandeville believed that class distinctions were crucial, and his belief in the importance of luxury and avarice is specifically connected with his view of the middle and upper classes. In Remark Q of *The Fable*, he states directly that the lower classes must not be paid very much so they keep working and retain their lower social standing:

> The chief and most pressing use there is for Money in a Nation, is to pay the Labour of the Poor . . . whatever procures Plenty makes Labourers cheap, where the Poor are well managed; who as they ought to be kept from starving, so they should receive nothing worth saving. . . . but it is the Interest of all rich Nations, that the greatest part of the Poor should almost never be idle, and yet continually spend what they get. (209)

Here, we find that Mandeville equates the number of laborers, the lower class, with the economic health of the country, a common belief in mercantilism. Using political arithmetic, a concept I discuss more fully below, many mercantilist writers theorized that by estimating the possibility of high death rates among the working classes of England one could enact policies to avoid labor shortages—losses that inevitably lead to financial hardship for the country. According to this type of thinking something as simple as the poor being paid too high of wages could destabilize such a system.

Exhibiting a key difference from laissez-faire forms of capitalism that would start to develop later in the century, Mandeville believed that having a strong central government oversee financial matters would maintain these important social divides and lead to wider economic prosperity. Sutherland notes that "it was an article of mercantilist faith that the subordination of ranks within a closed economy served national security," and considering Mandeville's impressions, we can see how gin would jeopardize the stability of these ranks (474). Thus, Mandeville treats gin as not only an unhealthy, poisonous substance to the individual, lower-class body but also as a dangerous corruptor of the body (the laboring people) of the nation. However, as we shall see, writers reacting to Mandeville's ideas about gin and class would question gin's ability to destabilize class distinctions and, in some cases, would posit that it ensured British commercial success.

A CURIOUS LIQUOR: GIN AND BETRAYAL IN GAY'S *THE BEGGAR'S OPERA*

The year 1720 saw one of the world's first economic bubbles burst, the South Sea Event, a major historical moment that facilitated Sir Robert Walpole's rise to power. It is not surprising that during a decade in which luxury was coming under extreme scrutiny—many reformers, such as members of the Society for the Reformation of Manners, saw the bubble bursting as divine punishment for middle- and upper-class greed and corruption (*Gin*, 47–51)—gin would also be targeted, given the patterns of overindulgence that were becoming steadily more noticeable. It would be near the end of the decade that John Gay's *The Beggar's Opera* (1728), one of the most complex and rich satirical pieces of the eighteenth century, would arrive on stage to mock Walpole and the types of monetary systems he manipulated to accumulate wealth and political power, including those created during the South Sea fallout.[24] In his text Gay transposes the lowly London underworld onto the high operatic stage, burlesquing the current sociopolitical arena in his treatment of London's seedy underbelly, and from its very first performance, audiences recognized the ballad opera as an attack on Walpole's political realm.

Much has been said regarding *The Beggar's Opera* as a product of the eighteenth-century's skepticism of complex systems of finance, shifts in economic thought, and increasing consumerism. J. Douglas Canfield, for instance, comments, "The play is specifically a satire against the new system that has taken over Gay's world: incipient capitalism," and Pat Rogers and David Nokes each illustrate the importance of writers such as Defoe and Mandeville on the play.[25] Rogers argues that Peachum is "an embodiment of the [Defoe's] English tradesman," arguing that Peachum's businesslike manner adds "force to the critique of public mores which suffuses *The Beggar's Opera*" and "sharply reinforces the satiric equivalence of Walpole and [Jonathan] Wild" (100–101). While also stressing Defoe's importance to the text, Nokes points to Mandeville's *The Fable* as the "single [most important] literary source for the commercial ethics which Gay satirizes in the opera" (145), and quips that it might be more appropriately titled *The Business Man's Opera* (138). As these scholars indicate, the economic systems of the eighteenth century, the writers discussing such systems, and the political figures corruptly manipulating them all had a major impact on the world Gay presents. This informed and cynical view of economics would shape his treatment of the characters of the play, as well as the liquor they enjoy.

Given the criminals and reprobates that make up the cast of characters, it seems obvious that Gay would feature an infamous liquor like gin, a beverage very much in the public consciousness when the play was first acted. Despite the huge role of commerce and economics in the play, alcohol has been for the most part neglected by scholars, and specifically, the presence of gin—in a time when the beverage was quickly becoming a major social problem in London—has been almost completely ignored.[26] Gay's presentation of gin and of alcoholic beverages, like so many other aspects of the play, is frustratingly difficult to pin down and resists one single identifiable treatment, which, I argue, is due partially to the complex, satirical arrangement of class in the play, as well as Gay's multivalent staging of consumable materials. Throughout the play, Gay uses alcohol as a signifier of betrayal, a human behavior that flourishes in a world in which money and luxury are pursued above all else, and he characterizes gin in myriad, and seemingly contradictory, ways: as a lower-class luxury; as a more refined liquor that has differing levels of quality for those with a good palate or, in language of the play, are "curious in [their] liquors" (55); as just another commodity serving proto-capitalist bourgeois desires for monetary and political gain; and finally as a dangerous poison. While in certain scenes, he configures gin as a drink of the lower class, similar to what we see in Mandeville and Defoe, he also styles it as a middle- and upper-class beverage in others. Treating gin in this way and showcasing it along with other alcohols, Gay considers the fate of Britain as it begins to transform into a more capitalistic society where class structures have less significance.

In the tavern scenes in the first half of the play, Gay sets up the relationship between alcohol, economics, and class through Macheath's treatment of gin and other alcohols. In act 2, we find Macheath at a tavern near Newgate Prison with his gang of highwaymen, discussing their recent successes and enjoying "*Wine, Brandy, and Tobacco*" (25). All three of these items are necessarily imports, with tobacco coming from the British colonies of America and wine and brandy most likely coming from France. There were of course British-distilled brandies, which were often referred to as "Parliament brandy," an early alternative name for gin; given that "gin," "strong water," and "cordial" are the specific names used by the characters for gin, it is safe to presume that Macheath and his men are drinking French brandy, which would have been a more expensive and would likely have been smuggled into the country. Gay uses wine to connect Macheath and his men to the aristocratic Cavalier and libertine traditions (as discussed in chapter 1), emphasizing throughout the play Macheath's rapacious desire for drink, his frivolity with money, his voracious libido, and his inability to remain faithful to the women he loves. Like the Royalist Cavalier or the Restoration rake, Macheath drinks imported wine, establishing his wealth, his bravery, and his sexually consuming nature.

Furthermore, this drinking of wine—due both to its expensiveness and the ways in which it establishes Macheath as a descendant of the Cavalier and Restoration libertine—connects to the complex nature of Gay's class structuring in the play. In his seminal chapter on the text, "The Beggar's Opera: Mock-Pastoral as the Cult of Independence," William Empson contends that Macheath's social status represents much more than the surface-level, highwaymen station to which he is assigned by the plot. Empson argues that Macheath is the "hero" of the play with Peachum and Lockit, members of the newer, bourgeoisie class and representing the villains of the story. Empson argues that "Gay dislikes [Peachum] as a successful member of the shopkeeping middle class, whereas Macheath is either from a high class or a low one" (203). Expanding on Macheath's upper-class attitudes, he writes,

> One cannot go far into the play without insisting on the distinction between the two sorts of rogues, which is made very clearly and gives a rich material for irony. The thieves and whores parody the aristocratic ideal, the dishonest prison-keeper and thief-catcher and their families parody the bourgeois ideal . . . ; these two ideals are naturally at war, and the rise to power of the bourgeois had made the war important. (217–218)

Since the publication of his essay, most critics have tended to agree with Empson's evaluation of the play's class dynamics. Gay's Macheath—with his merry making and sexual promiscuity, combined with his views of honor and innate nobility—exposes a world in which the aristocracy has been shamefully pushed out of its traditional position in favor of capitalistic wealth; thus, choosing wine and brandy in this instance shows a clear divide from an alcohol like gin that was most commonly associated with the lower classes.

While using wine and brandy to represent Macheath as an aristocratic stand-in, Gay blurs the lines of gin's lower-class status in the tavern scenes of act 2, presenting gin first as a lower-class beverage (much like Defoe and Mandeville), and then as one often drunk by middle- and upper-class women. In scene 4, after Macheath's men leave, eight prostitutes arrive to drink and keep him company. Macheath addresses them individually in a long opening speech. Speaking directly to one of the prostitutes, Betty Doxy, Macheath mocks her drinking habits: "Do you drink as hard as ever? You had better stick to good wholesome Beer; for in troth, Betty, Strong-Waters will in time ruin your Constitution. You should leave those to your Betters" (29). In his statement, Macheath shows a clear distrust of the highly alcoholic drink or "strong water" (most likely a cheaper brandy), which he believes could cause long-term physical repercussions to Betty's body, her main source of revenue.[27] Although Macheath is willing to spend money on an expensive brandy for himself, he suggests that the lower-class prostitute drink "wholesome Beer," which would be both cheaper and more befitting her class station.

Throughout the rest of the tavern scene, Macheath treats gin as a lower-class luxury, one that he is more than willing to provide for his guests. Through his "aristocratic" highwayman, Gay presents gin as a beverage that is new enough to the tavern that it might be presented as a more expensive beverage than it would be when hawked on the streets, as seen in Mandeville and in moral pamphlets. After singing a drinking song together, Macheath calls for more wine, and then, attempting to show off his wealth, he tells the group of women that "If any of the Ladies chuse Ginn, I hope they will be so free to call for it" (30). As Judith Hunter points out, most taverns would have had many more options available for hard alcohols other than gin.[28] Despite his attempts to impress the women with the supposed frivolity of his offer, Macheath's gesture exposes his understanding of their class positions. His willingness to supply the prostitutes with whatever gin they can consume illustrates his desire to buy their attention, but he undercuts his attempt to show that he spares no expense by the fact that gin is very cheap. The women may "indulge" themselves with lower-class drinks like gin but not those associated with the upper class—such as brandy and other expensive liquors—for which Betty was lightly reprimanded. By pushing the women to drink cheap gin, Macheath shows his awareness of the fact that the more gin he buys them, the less wine, the more expensive luxury item, he has to pay for.

In addition to showing off his ability to afford gin, Macheath also posits that gin is a woman's drink. After his open offer of gin to the group, Jenny Diver—seeking Macheath's attention so she can more easily betray him to Peachum—assumes that Macheath must be speaking directly to her: "You look as if you meant me. Wine is strong enough for me. Indeed, Sir, I never drink Strong-Waters, but when I have the Cholic" (31). Here, Jenny is perhaps acting a little haughty about her more developed palate, or she may also be annoyed with Macheath's insinuation that she, as a lower-class prostitute, will not see through his attempt to push cheap liquor. Instead, she declares her own preference for an expensive beverage, wine, before claiming that she only uses gin, which had often been used in cordials, medicinally for a stomachache.[29]

To her pert response, Macheath jests that this is "Just the Excuse of the fine Ladies! Why, a Lady of Quality is never without the Cholic" (31). As with his reference to Betty's social "betters," Macheath stresses Jenny's lower-class status, not quite allowing her to be one "of the fine ladies." Not only does he ignore Jenny's claimed preference for wine, but Macheath also mocks middle- and upper-class women using feigned, omnipresent stomachaches as an excuse to drink gin. Here, Gay may be contributing to or mocking a misogynistic social critique of female gin drinking, which seems to have already been gaining popularity in the late 1720s, but that would show up in major anti-gin pamphlets of the 1730s and 1740s, such as Thomas Wilson's *Spirituous Liquors the Bane of the Nation* (1736) and David Hall's *An Essay on Intemperance, Particularly Hard Drinking* (1742).[30] In this moment, Gay presents Macheath as blurring gin's cultural status since he treats it as a luxury for women to enjoy, while inadvertently illustrating the drink's (and his own) cheapness. Throughout the tavern scene, we see Macheath, much like the Royalist Cavalier or the Restoration libertine, appreciating and drinking wine; however, he subtly figures gin as a lower-class drink when asking the women to enjoy as much of it as they want, while also positing that it is something constantly enjoyed by "fine ladies." While subtly alluding to the lower-class status of gin, Gay also treats it as a luxury in these scenes, not quite showing the social mistrust of gin that was already developing during the 1720s.

It is fittingly ironic, then, after his condescending, sexist comment, that Macheath is ultimately betrayed by wine. Emulating Judas Iscariot, Jenny pairs her wine with a kiss as she betrays Macheath to Peachum: "I must and will have a Kiss to give my Wine a zest" (33). Jenny seems to enjoy her betrayal of Macheath, sweetening her wine by ensuring the highwayman's capture. This theme of personal betrayal for monetary benefit, a defining conceit of the play, continues in the next scene, and through these moments, alcohol is subtly linked to nefarious plots, as communal drinking seems to be linked to communal scheming. After Macheath is taken away to Newgate Prison and as Peachum offers to pick up the tavern bill, the prostitutes are left on stage by themselves, bickering about the money that Suky Tawdry and Jenny have been rewarded for Macheath's capture. Despite jockeying for the captain's attention in the earlier scene, the prostitutes are now only concerned with getting a cut of the reward money. Jenny quickly silences their protests, offering them a share in a "Bowl of Punch"—most likely a cheap rum or brandy punch—to be drunk by all the women together (34). Just as alcohol helps undo Macheath, it is also used to christen Jenny and Tawdry's act of betrayal.

Gay adds another layer to his representation of gin as he shows the most troubling example of communal scheming, representing the callous nature of the British underworld through the characters most connected to proto-capitalist economics: Peachum, Lockit, and Mrs. Trapes. In act 3, scene 6, their business meetings, which are facilitated by brandy and gin, expose poignantly Gay's burlesque of complex systems of finance. Because Mrs. Trapes appears at only one point in the play, scholars have tended to examine Peachum and Lockit more extensively; and although Gay seeks to fool his audience into believing otherwise, Mrs. Trapes is very much on equal footing with her male colleagues. Like Peachum and Lockit, Mrs. Trapes is uncannily good at manipulating the less enterprising members of the London underworld. All three have legitimate jobs that supplement their criminal enterprises, a concept Peachum refers to a "double capacity" in the second line of the play (5). Peachum is a thief-taker and a fence, allowing him to make money off those criminals who are no longer of use to him; Lockit is a jailor who arranges the advantageous release of certain criminals for a fee, while also being bribed for better accommodations by the criminals themselves; and Mrs. Trapes makes money as a bawd, while also leasing clothes to prostitutes to retain more of their profits. Discussing Mrs. Trapes's dual roles as buyer of goods and sexual procuress, Colin Nicholson states, "For Mrs. Trapes there is no difference between the running of a brothel and any other investment and management programme."[31]

A criminal conspiracy with loose connections, Peachum, Lockit, and Mrs. Trapes form a kind of triumvirate in the London underworld. The use of alcohol will end up signaling this equality, but Gay first uses contemporary cultural distinctions between brandy and gin to mislead his audience regarding Mrs. Trapes's business acumen. In act 3, scene 5, before Mrs. Trapes joins Peachum and Lockit on stage, the two men are drinking brandy, which signifies the wealth these two bourgeoisie figures have amassed through their deft manipulation of the underworld. While Peachum and Lockit drink and peruse their account books, Mrs. Trapes arrives at Peachum's warehouse to conduct business. Before entering, the men discuss her, describing Mrs. Trapes as "a Woman who drinks" and who "will enliven the Conversation" (55). As she enters at the start of scene 6, Peachum compliments her in a strange way: "Dear Mrs. Dye, your Servant—One may know by your Kiss that your Ginn is excellent" (55). Lockit, smitten with his former lover and undoubtedly a bit drunk, attempts to flirt with her, stating "There is no perfum'd Breath like it—I have been long acquainted with the Flavour of those Lips—Han't I, Mrs. *Dye*?" (55). As with Macheath and the zest added to Jenny's wine, Gay connects the materiality of alcohol, the smells and tastes, with sexual desire; however, by mentioning the smell of gin on her breath, a contemporary audience may have been persuaded to see Mrs. Trapes as a step below the two men, who have been drinking expensive, imported brandy. Gay seeks to mislead his audience through her choice of lower-class gin.

However, despite reeking of gin, Mrs. Trapes proves to be a competent, single-minded businesswoman. Mrs. Trapes replies casually to Lockit's flirtatious comments, stating that she is "curious" in her selection of the liquor (55), meaning she is "Careful as to the standard of excellence; difficult to satisfy . . . esp. in food, clothing, matters of taste."[32] In addition to illustrating Mrs. Trapes's connoisseurship of (supposedly) lower-class items, the fact that she is "curious" regarding her gin and that Peachum compliments the gin's quality allows Gay to once again play with gin's status and imply that it could also be a middle-class beverage enjoyed and used by the moneyed, power-wresting bourgeoisie.

Peachum, Lockit, and Mrs. Trapes have long been read as satirical stand-ins for scheming, middle-class proto-capitalists, and scholars often view these characters as direct attacks on Walpole and the immoral systems of finance he represented.[33] Just as Macheath represents the declining aristocracy, Gay ironically represents Mrs. Trapes, a bawd and high-ranking London criminal, as a more sophisticated middle-class figure than she actually is at the play's most literal level. Thus, Gay treats this liquor in two different but equally important ways. First, gin is treated as the lower-class luxury, à la Mandeville and Defoe, a cheap product that seedy, criminal members of society abuse. Second, Gay shows that gin is a liquor that the middle class enjoys as a luxury beverage and that may have varying levels of quality, asking the audience to see the ways in which the middle class may reject the materials of social sophistication set up by the once dominant class, the landed gentry.

However, considering the play's mockery of Walpole, we can also read this scene as critiquing the very proto-capitalist system that the corrupt prime minister used to make money and to sustain power. Just as Macheath—an amalgam of the lower class and the aristocracy, the two classes being subjugated and exploited by the power-hungry middle class—is a drinker of expensive imported goods, so are Peachum and Lockit, who can now afford such materials; however, Mrs. Trapes, also a stand-in for the bourgeoisie, is associated with gin, a domestic substance that played an important part in Walpole's own fiscal policies. This scene—perhaps the most critical of Walpolean finance and economics in the entire play—presents gin in a strikingly different fashion than what we see in the other scenes featuring alcohol, and indeed in most literary treatments of the liquor. By 1726, the first legislative reactions to gin were in the works, and Walpole did his best to block such endeavors, hoping to keep gin distillation going for his own personal and political gain (*Craze*, 94–95). As with the excise duties on beer and wine discussed in chapters 1 and 2, the taxes on gin were crucial to the British government, and the distillation of gin supplied an important market for the surplus grains of the landed gentry, a group that Walpole, above all else, sought to keep on his side. Discussing the initial, failing attempts of the Royal College of Physicians, who were seeking to introduce a gin reform bill in 1726, Warner writes,

> The physicians had, moreover, chosen the worst possible time to present their petition. The nation was for all intents and purposes at war with Spain, forcing Walpole to raid the Sinking Fund [the financial fund that had helped Britain out of the devastation of the South Sea Event] . . . Under the circumstances Walpole was in no mood to tamper with one of the Crown's most important sources of revenue, especially since a small portion of those revenues was by now being used for the construction of his new manor at Houghton Hall. (95)

Walpole would continue to resist anti-gin policies, but in 1729, only a year after *The Beggar's Opera* debuted, the first Gin Act passed Parliament. As I discuss below, literary writers were well aware of Walpole's pro-gin position, with Elias Bockett praising "Bob" in his dedication to his satirical poem, *Geneva: A Poem* (1729).

Given Walpole's policy toward gin, and the fact that *The Beggar's Opera* was a satirical attack on Walpole and his administration, Gay seems to be manipulating gin in this scene as a symbol of the type of callous financial maneuvering for which the corrupt politician was already infamous. Furthermore, as with Jenny's wine, Mrs. Trapes's gin is instilled with the type of betrayal common in the wealth-obsessed world of his play. It comes as no surprise that the shrewd businesswoman Mrs. Trapes just happens to mention Macheath and his whereabouts so that she can barter a more advantageous deal with Peachum and Lockit. The gin itself is thus connected with betrayal and scheming and the type of moneymaking systems that advance Walpole and people like him.

However, as with many aspects of eighteenth-century London society presented in his play, Gay does not favor one representation of its cultural artifacts but instead supplies almost contradictory, opposing perspectives that at first seem to undercut his satirical stances. Rather than merely countering the view of gin as a dangerous, lower-class beverage, asking his audience to reinterpret the drink, Gay chooses to reinforce gin's hazardously cheap reputation near the end of the play. Seeking instead to present the many different public perceptions of the beverage, Gay shows that gin drinking is far more complex and nuanced (especially with the socioeconomic classes that drink the liquor) than we see in the writing of Defoe and Mandeville. After disrupting the common anti-gin narrative, he then mocks gin as a beverage in a more traditional way, highlighting its destructive nature in a way similar to many anti-gin reformers.

This final treatment of the liquor comes when Lucy attempts to poison her rival with a cordial made of gin. Once again, Gay features gin in a scene examining betrayal. In act 3, scene 7, Lucy, now furious over Macheath's abandonment, states, "Jealousy, Rage, Love and Fear are at once tearing me to pieces" (57). After a short song, in which she announces that she will revenge herself on Polly, she declares that she has her "Rats-bane ready" (58). Showcasing the dangerous nature of the liquor, Lucy believes that she "run[s] no Risque" of being caught poisoning Polly because she "can lay [Polly's] death upon the Ginn, and so many dye of that naturally that I shall never be call'd in Question" (58). While gin seemed to help with stomachaches and other minor health issues, many people also died from drinking it. Gay plays on the irony that a beverage used medically by all strata of society was often produced in lower-class establishments with very unhealthy ingredients and under unsafe conditions.

Adding to Gay's mockery of gin in this part of the play, Polly is highly suspicious of Lucy when the latter attempts to get her to take a gin cordial. She replies, "Strong-Waters are apt to give me the Headache—I hope, Madam, you will excuse me" (59). Attempting to reassure her rival of the gin's good quality, Lucy responds, "Not the greatest Lady in the Land could have better in her Closet, for her own private drinking" (59). Here, Gay seems to mix his jokes intentionally, as Lucy presents her gin as a luxury item—it is as good as the gin drunk by "the greatest Lady in the Land"—while also showing the irony of gin being so infamous for its toxicity that Lucy believes she could, literally, get away with murder.

As the scene continues, Lucy tries to coax Polly into drinking the poison; however, by scene 9, Polly is suspicious: "All this wheedling of Lucy cannot be for nothing . . . By pouring Strong-Waters down my Throat, she thinks to pump some Secrets out of me" (61). Although she realizes the cordial is intended to weaken her in some way, Polly, the only truly moral character in the play, does not assume the worst of her romantic rival. After the women see that Macheath has once again been caught by Peachum and Lockit, Polly drops the glass in shock. This candid moment ultimately causes Lucy to relent, forgiving Polly who clearly "was not happy enough to deserve to be poison'd" (61). In the scenes with Polly, Lucy, and the poisoned cordial, Gay makes several jokes at gin's expense, borrowing much from middle- and upper-class condemnations of the drink. First, eighteenth-century British gin was highly intoxicating, especially given the health and size of the people ingesting it. Regarding the many (undoubtedly true) stories regarding what we would now recognize as alcohol poisoning, Lesley Jacobs Solmonson points out that this very potent liquor would have affected people of the eighteenth century to a much more dangerous extent as early modern Londoners were on average several inches shorter; further, she indicates that the low nutritional value of their food would have also caused the gin to affect their bodies differently; further, because of the way the alcohol was distilled, this gin would have been, Solmonson argues, around 160 proof, making it twice the potency of today's gin and putting it on equal footing with modern moonshine.[34] Second, Gay's audience would have be aware of the types of people hawking gin on the streets, alluded to by Mandeville in Remark G, most of whom could not be trusted to distribute alcohol that was safe to consume. Any gin could be tainted by whoever distilled or distributed it. Finally, given that Lucy plans to serve Polly the drink as a type of medicine, there is presumably a joke at work here at the expense of apothecaries, who would have provided both medicines and poisons to the general public.

In *The Beggar's Opera*, Gay provides myriad treatments of gin. Through this varied representation, Gay presents not just one viewpoint but actively seeks to show how differing views can exist simultaneously within a society as complex (and corrupt) as London's. Indeed, he seems to imply that all these views, as seemingly contradictory as they are, are true at once. Considering Gay's interest in the type of betrayal that occurs in the London underworld, the type that is rewarded by a proto-capitalist, Walpolean system that advances the most cunning, backstabbing, and corrupt behavior, one can see Gay's ironic, distant sort of anxiety over the direction in which his country was headed. He questions a world in which the economic power of the most corrupt members of the rising middle class could supplant traditional, aristocratic power. Furthermore, Gay critiques a system like proto-capitalism that drives people, and especially women, to betray others for personal wealth and luxury, especially when those figures are operating under the influence of a highly intoxicating spirit like gin.

LOWER-CLASS NECESSITY AND UPPER-CLASS EXCESS: SATIRICAL RESPONSES TO GIN REFORM

England's first Gin Act was passed in 1729, one of eight that Parliament enacted from 1729 to 1751. These laws and policies were created to combat the abuse of gin, especially by England's lower classes. The rise of this extreme alcohol abuse coincided with the slow dismantling of the mercantilist line of thinking, and many thinkers saw extreme luxury, even among the upper class, as highly problematic. As lawmakers, religious figures, and economists looked around at the luxuries provided by the movement toward capitalism, they condemned gin as the result of vanity. Ideas regarding luxury were changing, but the belief that the lower classes might start to obtain their own form of luxury still seemed greatly taboo, with even the more nontraditional Mandeville condemning gin and configuring it as a lower-class luxury. However, from the passage of the first Gin Act and up through the passage of the Gin Act of 1738, much of the satirical writing of the period questioned the demonization of gin in the unpopular laws being passed. This section examines three such texts by seldom-studied authors pushing back against gin reform: Elias Bockett's poem *Blunt to Walpole: A Familiar Epistle in behalf of the British Distillery* (1730), Stephen Buck's mock panegyric poem, *Geneva. A Poem in Blank Verse* (1734), and the anonymously written *The Informers Outwitted: A Tragi-Comical Farce* (1738), all of which respond critically to the Gin Acts.[35] In the case of Bockett's and Buck's poems, the writers argue that gin is not a lower-class luxury but is in fact crucial to the productivity of the lower orders; further, these satirical poets engage with anti-gin narratives concentrated on class and gender dynamics. However, the anonymous satirist behind *The Informers Outwitted*, despite mocking gin drinking and overindulgence, attacks reform by highlighting the acts' negative effects on commerce and social order. Investigating and satirizing parliamentary efforts at gin reform, these texts seek to present the voices of those most impacted by the laws.

Before turning to these satirical texts, however, it is crucial to understand the social moment in which the Gin Craze occurred and the ways in which trade facilitated it. By 1725, gin was garnering a bad reputation in London. While supplying jobs, avenues to profit from surplus grains, and the benefits of excise taxes, it was also recognized as a very real social epidemic. During the Middlesex Quarter Sessions of 1725, Sir Daniel Dolins noted that the "Wickedness," "the excessive drinking [of] Gin, and other pernicious Spirits; is become so great, so loud, so importunate; and the growing Mischiefs from it so many, so great, so destructive to the Lives, Families, Trades and Business of such Multitudes, *especially of the lower, poorer Sort of People*; that I can no longer doubt, but it must soon reach the Ears of our Legislators in Parliament assembled."[36] Unsurprisingly, people of the middle and upper classes condemned the social disruption they saw as a direct result of the heavy production, distribution, and consumption of gin. As predicted by Dolins, it did not take long before members of Parliament took notice of gin's effects on the lower class.

As noted above, Walpole was a staunch proponent of the distilling trade, which helped keep the landed aristocracy on his side. Walpole resisted gin reform to ensure their continued support. Throughout the period, the prime minister would repeatedly attempt to halt legislation on the matter. White comments, "Once it became clear that Walpole's government intended to make spirits a milk cow for the state, the gin bill became socially divisive and politically contentious" (42). However, by 1729, the first Gin Act was passed. Because the law targeted publicans who sold gin by imposing a very high, £20 annual licensing fee to serve the liquor, which was later raised to a staggering £50 in 1736, rather than slowing down gin distribution, unlicensed sales of the beverage on the city streets skyrocketed. Since these sales were more difficult to police, gin selling became a common occupation for those who were desperately poor, increasing the stereotype of gin as the beverage of lower-class criminals.

With the Gin Act of 1733, British lawmakers sought the aid of paid informers to combat the illegal sale of gin, passing three subsequent acts (in 1736, 1737, and 1738) that offered informers monetary rewards for the names of apothecaries, storeowners, tavern owners, and publicans who sold gin illegally; however, these "eyewitness" informers were often outright liars. In the Gin Act of 1733, for instance, informers were paid half of the £10 fine issued to those on whom they informed, a sum that equated to a livable wage for a year's worth of work. Unsurprisingly, this system was extremely unpopular as informers were known for using many tricks and lies, oftentimes feigning illness, to convince their prey to sell them gin for medicinal purposes. These informers were often beaten, threatened with violence, and, at points, murdered during riots; indeed, in the wake of the many riots of 1738, the Gin Act of the same year made attacking informers a felony (*Craze*, 222–224).

These Gin Acts were in large part a result of three primary cultural narratives that dominated the reform movements of the Gin Craze. The first, as discussed above, was Mandeville's configuration of gin as a type of lower-class luxury. The other two narratives pushed by gin reformers concerned the disruption of social hierarchies and the dissolution of traditional gender dynamics. One major reason gin seems to have gained so much attention in this period is that many people, especially among the upper class, believed that gin robbed the lower class of not just their drive and ability to perform manual labor but also their respect and admiration of class distinctions. Speaking at a session of Parliament in 1743 that ultimately led to the Gin Act of 1743, Lord Hervey shows the clear class anxiety surrounding the gin debate:

We live, my Lords, in a Nation, where the Effects of strong Liquors have been for a long Time too well known; we know that they produce in almost every one a high opinion of his own Merit; that they blow the latent Sparks of Pride into Flame, and, therefore, destroy all voluntary Submission, they put an End to Subordination, and raise every man to an Equality with his Master, or his Governour. They repress all that Awe by which Men are restrained within the Limits of their proper Spheres, and incite every Man to press upon him that stands before him.[37]

Hervey's comments expose elite male fears of the beverage. Enough gin renders innate nobility invisible to the drinker, this argument goes, a consequence that ultimately leads to insubordination and possibly to outright violence.

Another commonly circulated cultural narrative was the idea that gin disrupted female and male roles. The fact that women both commonly sold and imbibed gin caused reformers to believe the liquor jeopardized heteronormative femininity. As a product, gin offered work opportunities to women that were customarily reserved for men. Peter Clark indicates that from 1735 to 1751 the numbers of female spirit sellers in Middlesex County increased substantially from about 23 percent to almost one-third of unlicensed sellers by 1751.[38] Additionally, Warner notes, "There were three reasons why selling gin appealed to so many women: it required little or no capital; it did not require membership in a professional organization; and it was one of the few occupations from which women were not effectively or explicitly excluded" (51). The economic freedom that gin selling provided would, of course, be considered a problem due to its ability to take women away from their domestic role.

On top of providing a means to make money for themselves and their families, gin also gave women the chance to enjoy alcohol in a way that had oftentimes been barred to them. As alluded to with Macheath's joke in *The Beggar's Opera*, women could buy gin as a medicinal beverage, but presumably many drank it for its intoxicating effects. Reformers worried that a middle-class woman who drank gin threatened to destabilize her home, as she would become too familiar with servants, who would in turn spread "the secrets of the household around the neighborhood" (*Gin*, 215). If gin could cause men to neglect their duties outside the home, gin could cause women to forget their position within it.

The greatest moral panic, however, was reserved for female gin drinkers and their ability to be mothers. For reformers throughout the Gin Craze, drinking among lower- and middle-class women constituted a major social problem as it caused health problems for both mother and child. In his famous pamphlet, *Distilled Spirituous Liquors the Bane of the Nation* (1736), the famous gin reformer Thomas Wilson considers the ramifications of gin drinking on English mothers, arguing that gin's corrupting influence would shrink the working-class labor pool. Wilson presents his argument using political arithmetic—an early form of statistical analysis developed by economic thinkers, such as John Graunt, William Petty, George King, and Charles Davenant, in the late seventeenth and early eighteenth centuries. This early economic practice employs various types of metrics to inform policy decisions; as Julian Hoppit notes, these thinkers, developing the use of statistical analysis to make decisions, saw numerical data as "literally statistical-that is state-thinking."[39] Hoppit addresses Davenant's definition of the term and how it shaped eighteenth-century understandings of this revolutionary step toward political economy:

> To Davenant, "By Political Arithmetic, we mean the art of reasoning by figures, upon things relating to government." This often repeated definition neatly summarizes the discipline's thematic and methodological peculiarities. The breadth of the definition, including within political arithmetic's remit anything of interest to government, is most important. Political arithmetic was not, it is worth stressing, confined to estimates of national income and population, for it might also explore public finances, economic performance, poor relief, military matters, religious affiliation, social order, and so on. (517)

Pulling from Dr. Stephen Hales's tract, *Friendly Admonition to the Drinkers of Brandy* (1734), Wilson applies political arithmetic to the gin epidemic, using statistics to show that the working-class population would likely decrease due to English mothers drinking gin.[40] On page 35, Wilson writes, "If therefore *Childbearing Women* are habituated to strong inflaming Liquors, the little *Embrios* must and will have a Share . . . we may concluded certainly, that *Hot Spirituous Liquors* must greatly prejudice them before they are born. Accordingly we might have observed formerly, that the Children of poor labouring women, that seldom if ever drank any such liquors, were generally more strong and hearty and throve better, than those of Persons who eat and drank to Excess." In this section of his writing, Wilson fears in particular what we would call fetal alcohol syndrome. He believes that English women drinking highly intoxicating gin will "prejudice" the babies while they are in the womb, meaning "To injure materially; to damage."[41]

In addition to appealing to his audience's emotions, Wilson is also making an economic point. In a sentiment that would be echoed later by Henry Fielding, Wilson highlights the contemporary view of gin's unnatural consequences on femininity. Lower-class women's primary economic role, according to contemporary views, was birthing strong children to ensure that Britain never suffered labor shortages. After elaborating on the negative impact gin has on unborn and nursing children, he considers its impact on the British economy:

> The Bodies of Men, as I have prov'd before, are without doubt the most valuable Treasure of a Country, and in their Sphere the ordinary People are as serviceable to the Commonwealth as the Rich, if they are able to work . . .

> Whatever therefore hinders the Increase or weakens the laborious Hands, is an Evil of the most pernicious and dangerous Nature, and ought by all means to be immediately suppressed, and totally prohibited (43).

Employing his political arithmetic argument in which the availability of the workers is greatly diminished, Wilson argues that gin drinking among women in particular constitutes a major social problem. While he would go on to discuss the effects of gin on Britain's military prowess, through the insolent nature of soldiers overindulging in gin, the ability of women to have access to such a potent liquor constitutes the greatest problem.[42]

Just as gin reformers employed specific cultural narratives to combat the drinking of gin, pro-gin satirists responded with their own narratives, seeking to revise broader cultural views of the liquor. One of the first poets to respond to these anti-gin narratives was Elias Bockett. Writing under the pseudonym Alexander Blunt, Bockett published two pro-gin poems, one in 1729 and the other in 1730. In his first poem, *Geneva: A Poem*, which directly addresses Sir Robert Walpole, Bockett worked to counter many of the arguments that were beginning to surface in the war on gin.[43] In particular, he sought to reframe gin not as a type of lower-class luxury but as a necessity for the working classes. In the second half of the poem, Bockett illustrates the importance of gin in the daily life of a hardworking Londoner:

> . . . The market-woman,
> With basket on her head, can take a glass,
> Preservative from all th' inclemencies
> of weather. (24)

Written in mock-grandiose blank verse, the poem functions as a structured defense of lower-class gin consumption, and Clara—a personification of gin and a mouthpiece of Bockett's pro-gin views—refutes the logic of the anti-gin beer-brewing figure, Feculdo, within a courtroom setting. While this poem helped outline Bockett's own views in favor of gin distillation, his second poem, *Blunt to Walpole: A Familiar Epistle in behalf of the British Distillery*, uses more fully economic arguments to assert gin's benefit to English society.[44]

As with his first poem, Bockett addresses the poem to the de facto prime minister; however, while he had used a mock-Miltonic voice in his earlier piece, here he speaks more directly to the political figure. Throughout this second poem, he shows the positive role gin plays in the daily commerce of England, and he arranges the front matter of his pamphlet to amplify the voice of the working classes. Seeking to rebut narratives of lower-class excess, Bockett explores gin as a kind of lower-class necessity that keeps the English economy going.

Before dealing directly with the specific polices of the Gin Act of 1729, Bockett provides the voice of one of the very people who would be negatively affected by gin prohibition. Quoting a paper from the Middlesex Quarter Sessions of 1725, the very sessions in which Sir Daniel Dolins had stressed the importance of Parliament addressing gin abuse, the title page of this quotes a market woman directly: "We *market-women* are up early and late, and work hard for what we have. We stand all weathers, and go thro' thick and thin . . . for if it was not for something to chear my spirits between whiles, and keep out the wet and cold; alack-aday! it would never do! we should never be able to hold it; we should never go thorowstitch with it, so as to keep body and soul together" (1). This woman would have to get up very early in grueling weather conditions to sell to her customers. Providing this note from a session of court, Bockett shows how gin prohibition could negatively affect the lower class, putting a face on the people who use gin in a responsible manner.

With the quote, Bockett gives voice to one of the people most affected daily by these laws, setting a tone for the poem that follows. This poem, like his previous one, is addressed to Walpole, whom Bockett sees as an ally against gin reform, and he again uses the persona of Alexander Blunt, a gin distiller. Addressing "Sir Robert," the speaker notes that while Walpole is surrounded by people advising him on gin policy, his own perspective is the most important as it comes from an economic- and commerce-focused viewpoint. Before revealing himself to be a distiller, he emphasizes the magnitude of the decisions that Walpole is making. Bockett writes,

> . . . The life of *trade*,
> The *revenue* of the royal house, and
> The fate of *families* many a thousand,
> Are all concern'd in what's before us,
> And join with my address in chorus. (6)

Here, Bockett seems to be hedging his bets by not only providing emotional evidence for his claim, but also by using practical economic evidence, describing the effects of these laws on trade and on the wealth of the monarchy.

Furthermore, after chronicling his own loss of money over the course of several pages, he blames the "Geneva Act," the Gin Act of 1729, for these financial woes. While this act failed miserably to decrease lower-class consumption, it did significant damage to the respectable side of gin production and distribution, while not really affecting those who hawked gin illegally on the street (*Craze*, 221). In addition to being nearly impossible to police, the act was inherently flawed as it set a steep price on the annual licensing fee respectable establishments had to pay to serve gin. On page 17, Bockett examines the problem of licensing in detail. He notes that every year one must pay £20, a considerable sum, to sell gin legally, even though it was very cheap to distill. Since gin was not as popular among the middle and upper classes, one could not simply mark up the alcohol and transfer the burden of payment to the consumer. Thus, few people could ever make much money off gin distillation, so purchasing such a license was never worth the investment. In fact, he writes that

> The only men, if there are any,
> Who can by a *license* make a penny
> Are those who, in such manner use it,
> As if their study was, to abuse it;
> Who rules and orders never mind. (18)

As Bockett rightly points out, the extreme measures of the law excluded those who wanted to sell gin in safe, law-abiding establishments, putting more selling power into the hands of the people that were willing to sell it on the streets without a license (*Craze*, 44). As a distiller, the speaker shows that not only has his livelihood been damaged beyond repair, but also that criminals, people unconcerned with "rules and orders," are benefiting from the law, rather than being hindered by it.

Examining the Gin Act of 1729 from a consumer's perspective, Bockett suggests that gin should be considered a necessary product for the livelihood of the poor, countering the view of gin as a luxury. On page 25, Bockett brings up the idea that the lower classes often need gin to improve their lives. He writes,

> Mean while, the *poor*, whose way of living
> Makes requisite a *dram* reviving,
> Half naked, must without it go
> Thro' wind and rain, thro' frost and snow.
> Could these (as seldom can they) spare,
> Three half-pence, for gut-starving beer;
> Like cordials, wou'd it warm the heart,
> And joy and sprightliness impart?
> Colds, agues, rheumatisms, and death
> Prevent,—at least retard?—No, 'faith.

As with the epigram at the beginning of the poem, Bockett provides a very effective visual of the way the Gin Act affects the working classes. Not only do they end up spending too much money buying beer, they also do not receive the benefits of drinking gin. Drinking a small amount like a dram (one-eighth of a fluid ounce), manual laborers and tradespeople are more prepared for harsh, cold environments. Thus, Bockett combats the narrative of gin causing laziness, instead positioning it as crucial to Britain's work force.

In addition to reexamining gin's effects on productivity, Bockett also suggests that upper-class luxury ultimately leads to lower-class overindulgence. He ridicules the "Pamper'd and proud" who do not understand the type of unhealthy and exhausting conditions the poor face on a daily basis (26), arguing that the root cause of lower-class overindulgence is a desire to imitate those at the highest levels of society. Bockett writes,

> The *little vulgar* imitate
> The manners of the *vulgar great*;
> Like *courtiers*, *pedlers*, keep their words,
> And *tinkerers* will b' as drunk as *lords*. (30)

Using juxtaposition and antithesis, Bockett shows how the behavior of these seeming opposites, ("*little vulgar*" and "*vulgar great*," "*courtiers*" and "*pedlers*," "*tinkerers*" and "*lords*"), are essentially the same, but he stresses how differently their sins are perceived.

However, Bockett also considers the problem at a higher economic level, showing how the new law will affect international trade. On page 23, he argues that France will ultimately be the beneficiary of the Gin Act. He asks Walpole, and the rest of his audience, to "Judge, if the *general good*'s augmented. / Judge, if its fit, that BRITAIN's *trade* / Should sink, or be to *France* convey'd" (23). He expands this critique, showing how much money would be taken out of England through the purchase of French imports. Bockett argues that the people who want to destroy their lives with English gin would do so with French brandy if that was all that was available to them. Bockett believes that if laws are put in place to "advance" or raise the British brandy price to the price of the imported French, it will just cause them to spend more money on alcohol—one not distilled in England. Here, Bockett employs a mercantilist mindset to bolster his argument against the Gin Act of 1729. He suggests that protecting British distilling will boost the economy; if the law is kept in place, however, France will reap the rewards when their brandies become more popular. Such a sizable disruption of domestic trade, Bockett argues, will cause money to be pulled from England and redistributed to France.

In his poetry, Bockett argues that gin should not be considered a luxury for the lower orders, but a necessity to their continued productivity. While luxurious consumption can create problems, Bockett points to the elite as the root cause of such overindulgence in the lower orders. Despite the panic over lower-class gin drinking, Bockett represents gin as a type of necessity, not unlike the libertine treatment of wine in chapter 1; however, whereas libertine wine drinking was associated more with identity and privilege, Bockett stresses gin's importance to Britain's economic stability.

Employing similar arguments to Bockett's but focusing more on ideals of lower-class femininity and masculinity, Stephen Buck's *Geneva. A Poem in Blank Verse* (1734) provides a panegyric treatment of gin and a celebration of the reversal of the Gin Act of 1733. The Gin Act of 1733 had been a complete failure, much like the previous one, due to its use of paid informers to police the sale of gin; these informers seldom got their promised fees, since many of the people they targeted were people who were unable to pay the fine (*Craze*, 102). In his preface, Buck argues that some readers will think the poem "may be taken in an Ironic or Sarcastic Sense, and is rather a Satire than a Panegyric," but that the poem is in fact genuine in its high praise of gin. Buck's fears that his readers will misread the poem as a mock panegyric, causing his audience to misinterpret the poem's grandiose treatment of its lower-class topic as ironic. However, while Buck underscores his approval of gin, his work also ridicules the Gin Acts, highlighting their destructive nature.

In the opening lines of the poem, the speaker announces his clear happiness with the politician responsible for ridding Britain of the most recent Gin Act. He writes,

> Bless'd be the Man! for ever bless'd his Name!
> Whose patriot Zeal excited him to move
> The British Senate to reverse the Law,
> So baneful, as its Force all Compound Drams,
> And Gin; the best, destroy'd . . . (9)

The speaker thinks Parliament has much more fairly considered gin's good qualities, which he expounds on throughout the poem. While not as technically proficient as Bockett, Buck provides similar defenses of gin in his text. Like Bockett, Buck criticizes the way these laws put undue strain on lower-class workers, and as with Bockett's writing, Buck specifically uses female workers to show the importance of gin to lower-class livelihood.

In pages 12–13, Buck provides a detailed vignette of a group of market women taking gin to fortify themselves for the day. As these women prepare for their busy day, Buck states that they "Proceed to purchase those Supplies of Life," including a trip to their local dram shop, another name for a gin shop. Gin shops in particular were a lightning rod for gin reformers, being popularly represented as squalid, dangerous shacks where lower-class drinkers became stupid with drink and where violent criminals waited for prey.[45] In Buck, however, we get a more mundane glimpse into the shop:

> For Oh what Joy! when their keen Eyes explore
> Some hospitable Shop with open Doors,
> Whose Guardian vigilant, has shook off Sleep,
> To deal his Drams to this Itin'rant Tribe. (12)

Rather than housing a predatory man, ready to attack the women at the first opportunity, Buck's dram-shop owner is a "Guardian" who is both vigilant to ensure a safe environment for the women, but also tired due to the earliness of his morning. While admitting that "there is an absence of direct evidence" of whether gin shops were especially filthy and dangerous, Clark notes that "in the few cases where we have the rental value of dram-shops, were not especially low, and no doubt the grocers and apothecaries engaged in the trade had substantial premises" (70). There were no doubt examples of squalor and extreme abuse in the many gin shops of London, but these examples were likely outliers within the general gin-drinking population.

In Buck, the gin shop is presented as a reputable business rather than a frightening place that threatens the women's safety. It is clear that the shop's proprietor has "shook off sleep" to sell specifically to the early-rising market women and is a trustworthy man (12). After taking their drams, the women purchase "Slices of Bread, replete with Spices strong," which serve as a "Concomitant of [the] Gin" that they drank. The women, then, have spent their money in a careful, thoughtful fashion that will prepare them for a busy day of work. Rather than the scenes of people wasting all their money on gin as we hear about in Mandeville, the women are fastidious and use the gin as a boost to purposeful labor, rather than a means of escapism.

Buck juxtaposes this scene of hardworking femininity with the masculine enterprise of war. Like Mandeville, who admits that gin may yield soldiers the courage they need to fight, Buck shows scenes both of an older veteran and a younger soldier remembering and recounting their battles while drinking gin. In the case of the veteran, the gin allows him to warm up his sleeping "vital Spirits" of war and discuss the horrible battles he saw, providing a therapeutic effect (13). Meanwhile, when drinking gin, the younger soldier is capable of remembering his battle and the importance of what he fought for: "Thus Conquest is renew'd; all painful Wounds, / The Limbs which from their Trunks robust were torn, / And Age itself, are in Oblivion lost" (14). Despite having lost limbs for England, the soldier recalls more easily why he lost those limbs, "renewing" the memory of the glorious battles in which he participated. For Buck, gin factors into both male and female lower-class pursuits, deconstructing the narratives that the drink is only consumed by those who abuse it to a dangerous degree.

Like Bockett's defense of gin, Buck's poem evaluates the Mandevillean representation of gin as a lower-class luxury, and while Mandeville sees this luxury as a danger to England, Buck sees it in a positive light. If Bockett argues that lower-class luxury is no worse than that of the upper class, Buck seems to embrace gin's luxury status, especially considering that it can help make members of the lower orders more industrious. He addresses even more directly the topic of one's social station by examining gin's ability to remove class distinctions within the drinker's mind. He writes,

> What can impart such Solace to Mankind,
> As this most pow'rful Dram, which levels all
> The diff'rent Ranks in this unequal World?
> The poor Plebeian, elevate by Gin,
> Fancies himself a King, or happy more;
> Crowns, Maces, Stars, with Garters azure, red,
> Or verdant, he condemns. . . . (14)

Just as Lord Hervey feared, the gin drinker, a "poor Plebeian," can transcend in his mind the limits of his societal station. Yet Buck's gin drinker ultimately realizes that he is much happier than a king, given his lack of responsibility. In the lines that follow, the gin drinker dismisses "the Miser's avaricious Cares, [as a result of] Amassing Wealth" that they will never enjoy (14). Buck, like Hervey, argues that the gin drinker temporarily lacks class consciousness; however, unlike Hervey, Buck sees this inability to recognize their station as both admirable and temporal. Rather than chasing vain luxuries that bring no true joy, Buck believes that gin provides every need, stating in the conclusion that gin's "Votaries prefer thine easy Charms, / To those of Grandeur, Wealth, or empty Fame: / Meat, Drink, and Raiment are compriz'd in thee" (14). While Buck hyperbolizes gin's ability to provide for the drinker, he also satirizes the upper class's pursuit of luxuries that never fulfill their desires. For Buck, the gin drinker's lack of recognition of class station does not seem to be connected to a potential for violence so much as an apathetic, temporary escape from the class system; furthermore, by showing the industrious nature of the market women above, Buck seems to imply that gin provides a needed relief after the grueling labor of lower-class life.

Like Bockett's and Buck's poetry, the anonymously written *The Informers Outwitted: A Tragi-Comical Farce* (1738) seeks to push back against the gin reform of the 1730s, using economic- and commerce-based ideas to show gin's importance to England. However, unlike these earlier works, the play's primary goal is not to counter anti-gin narratives of overindulgence; indeed, at moments in the text, it seems to reinforce them. Instead, the anonymous playwright—writing from a point where the many legislative experiments to halt gin production have mostly brought about chaos—mocks the impracticality of the Gin Acts. Looking at the real-world effects of gin reform, the play shows the devastation the laws have had on England, and rather than working to prove that gin is a lower-class necessity, the writer instead shows how it affects middle-class shop owners, arguing that daily commerce and trade are disrupted by the application of such reform measures.

The primary joke developed in the first half of the play comes at the expense of the informers, those who were paid a fee for supplying information on establishments where gin has been illegally sold. These informers were particularly hated as they often lied to convince businesspeople to sell them gin—a beverage many shop owners would only have for private, legal consumption. As noted above, the use of informers had been a component in gin legislation since the Gin Act of 1733. As Warner points out, these informers were deeply unpopular, as their success often required local constables to arrest their own neighbors (and at times, relatives) for a law they saw as ridiculous (168–169). Stories abound of corrupt informers, and between 1737 and 1738, a number of violent mobs caught and brutally punished men and women who had acted as informers. By the Gin Act of 1738, the year the play was published, legislators had amended the law to protect informers from mob retribution.

Against this backdrop, the satirist presents the informers as vile and ridiculous. The play itself, which is dedicated to distillers, druggists, apothecaries, chemists, and keepers of public houses and chandler shops, offers a comic scene in which Trueblue, a pub keeper, gets revenge on an informer, allowing the middle-class audience the chance to laugh at what they would have seen as proper comeuppance for the hated informer. Before Trueblue is avenged, he explains the ruin that the informer, Halfpace, brought on him:

> I am resolved to learn *Phisiognomy* before I let go another Dram. What a wicked age do we live in? No man is at the bottom what he appears to be in outward Shew. Here comes one Rogue [Halfpace] holding his Belly, and crying out with the Gripes: Why, I let him have perhaps a Three-half-penny Dram, and that more out of good Nature and Charity than Profit: And what is the Effect of this? This same fellow goes immediately to a Magistrate, and informs against me for retailing Spiritous Liquors; I am taken out of my House, carried before his Worship, the Rogue swears, and I must pay ten Pounds, or go to the Hourse of Correction. (9)

Gin, it is important to remember, was considered a medical treatment for stomachaches, meaning that well-meaning shop owners (and especially chemists and apothecaries) were uniquely vulnerable to those informers feigning illness or pain. After hearing Trueblue's story, one that would have been horribly familiar to the early modern audience, they are rewarded with Trueblue's successful revenge: he poisons his informer with a corrosive liquid, and then the community tells the local constable that Halfpace was swearing against the king. The informer is then taken away to stand trial. For the satirist, laws that rely on (and enrich) such immoral people will never truly work, and ultimately such policies will only create chaos and financial ruin.

Despite mocking the unscrupulous informers, the writer treats the argument that gin is a lower-class necessity ironically, showing that such claims are seldom true. On pages 15–17, the two lower-class women, Killquartern, a market woman, and her friend Mrs. Bung-your-Eye, a wheelbarrow woman, discuss current events, drinking gin as they take a break. Their dialogue first reveals the impracticality of gin legislation, as Killquartern points out to her friend that the recent laws have actually led to an explosion of gin sellers on the streets. She tells her companion: "Altho' a thousand Distillers are broke since the late Act, yet ten thousand Dramsellers are started up in their Places" (15). This huge influx of sellers of gin on the street manages to make gin more available for them as they are constantly meeting sellers of gin everywhere. Bung-your-Eye notes, "If I go to Market, I have no sooner bargain'd for my Goods, but I am ask'd to bung my Eye [take a dram of gin]: Their Stock lies in a small Compass in their Pockets, and sometimes under their Petticoats, for Conveniency" (15). As is alluded to here, many of the people selling gin on the street are women, a fact revealed by the playwright through a reference to the woman's undergarments. Not only does this clue in the audience to the seller's gender, but it also raises concerns of sexually licentious acts being tied to gin selling on the street.

In addition to showing that Killquarten and Bung-your-Eye enjoy the increased availability of gin, the satirist also problematizes the idea that gin leads to lower-class productivity. The women, clearly worried and angry that gin might disappear due to more changes to the gin laws, begin drinking it in excess, while alluding to the same kinds of arguments used by Bockett and Buck. Taking a dram of gin, Killquartern states, "Ah! If the Members o'th' House knew but the Worth on't in a cold Morning, they would ne'er part with it so easily" (16). Like Buck and Bockett, the writer illustrates gin's ability to warm the drinker on a cold day; however, the long drunken conversation that follows and the women's behavior show that gin is in fact interfering with their ability to get anything constructive done. Indeed, rather than completing their work for the day, Killquartern begins to pretend that her father was a wealthy country gentleman. Through these fantasies, the satirist seems to show that class lines may indeed become invisible to the person overindulging in gin. These problems are compounded as the scene ends with Bung-your-Eye declaring her desire to drink herself to death should Parliament take away her liquor.

While the writer of *The Informers Outwitted* is most concerned with investigating the problem of informers and the social disruption resulting from this practice, he also shows that tavern and shop owners must be careful to use only proper, legal business practices in their daily lives. While stressing the legislative flaws of the Gin Acts, the play also satirizes the illegal business practice of those who sell gin in their shops and drinking establishments, promoting sound, legal business methods. The play censures the shopkeeper's illegal practices, such as dram selling and the buying of smuggled merchandise, that yield quick profits but can irreparably ruin businesses. Throughout the course of the play, three of the men endanger their businesses through their rash decisions. Provender, a publican, agrees to buy stolen brandy, Scammon, a druggist, purchases smuggled goods, and Gameright illegally serves a bowl of gin punch. After several of the men discuss the times they have gambled their livelihoods on such schemes, the group agrees that henceforth they shall push for only legal dealings to be done in their neighborhood, building a united front against corrupt practices.

In this moment, the men broaden their discussions to the changes in the ways in which business is conducted in Britain. Rather than being able to be an honest person in trade, Scammon claims that one must have "a Project, or a Puff to sell his goods" (52), implying that you must have a devious plan or ready lies, shown metaphorically in a "Puff" of hot air, to make it in business. Given the rampant, illegal but unpoliced selling of gin in the streets, the operation of the Gin Act is itself to blame. Responding to Scammon's belief that a "Fair Trader" cannot become rich in England's current economic climate, Provender states, "True, Sir. Publick Spirit hath took its Departure from this Island a many Years, and Great Men do as they please" (52–53). Here, the satirist puns on the nickname of Sir Robert Walpole, commonly referred to as a "great man" due to his prodigious weight. This treatment of trade signifies a fear of changing business practices that occurred during the seventeenth and eighteenth centuries. In *The Origin of Economic Ideas*, Guy Routh points out how different views of such practices were prior to the advent of capitalism: "The search for profit, which we regard and applaud as the main-spring of capitalism, was held to be immoral. A man was entitled to charge for his goods and services neither more nor less than what was needed to enable him to pursue his calling in the state appropriate to that calling . . . So to take advantage of the need of a buyer or seller when determining price would be a species of theft."[46] As the anonymous satirist of this text sees it, these "Projects"—practices that allow one to get ahead through cunning and that gesture toward a proto-capitalist view that "search[es] for profit"—should be avoided; however, because of the economic practices of Walpolean Britain, Provender believes, these methods must be used if one ever wants to be successful.

The scene in which these characters discuss their own improper methods leads them into an evaluation of upper-class luxury, providing a defense of gin that is similar to what we see in Bockett's and Buck's writing. As the men decide they will form a coalition of forthright businessmen, they begin to blame luxury for many of the ills of their world. Trueblue, a master of a public house, states, "If our Betters did as they ought to do, we should follow their Examples, and mend likewise" (54). Using Trueblue to examine upper-class morality, the satirist suggests that people of the lower and middle classes should recognize the disparities between the way the lower orders are meant to conduct themselves and the way the aristocracy behaves.

In response, Dew, a former distiller, asks if the others are aware of the many "Fashions [that] are made at court?" before stating that ultimately, "the lower sort will follow" their lead (54). However, Provender, another pub owner, points out that there are few differences between the middle and upper classes now: "Ay, Pox take their Fashions . . . The World is coming towards a Level, I believe. Where is the difference between a Tradesman and a Man of Quality? The Man of Quality keeps his Footmen in Livery, so does the Tradesman" (54). After listing additional examples of how the tradesman and the aristocrat (as well as their spouses) exhibit the same behavior, Provender blames "French *luxury*," meaning that the luxury of the aristocrat ultimately leads the middle-class tradesman to follow suit. In this context, the satirist shows that, given the druggists' and publicans' stations in life, luxury can lead people of the middle class to make poor decisions in the name of money. While the play makes much of mocking the Gin Acts and even gin drinking, it also critiques the effects of luxury on the non-elite.

Taken together, these three satirical pieces investigate gin's impact on British commerce, employing mercantilist arguments to complicate calls for gin reform. While Bockett and Buck seek to reconfigure gin as a lower-class necessity and to highlight its positive role in commercial activity, the playwright behind *The Informers Outwitted* instead shows how legislative attempts to restrain gin drinking only create more problems, especially for business owners. In this latter work, we see a stronger adherence to mercantilism, through the questioning of changing business practices associated with Walpole and with proto-capitalistic impulses. However, these satirical responses to reform would, ultimately, prove ineffective as more Gin Acts were on the horizon—legislation that would finally manage to slow the drinking of gin in Britain.

"... THAT POISON CALLED *GIN*": THE THOUGHTS OF A MAGISTRATE AND A CONCLUSION TO THE GIN CRAZE

The Gin Acts of 1743 and 1747 did their job well. These acts removed the unpopular informers from the equation, and set the price for licenses at a reasonable rate, making it more manageable for those wishing to sell the drink legally. Warner writes, "The fact that so many publicans took out licenses goes a long way toward explaining why the Gin Act of 1743 succeeded where its predecessors had failed. In effect, the new act placed the onus of policing customers on licensed publicans. This was a sensible step, given the fact that metropolitan magistrates had neither the manpower nor the inclination to do so themselves; publicans, by contrast, now had a stake in keeping their licenses, and the best way to do this was to turn away customers whose activities or behavior might bring their establishments into disrepute" (191). The act was also successful in that it placed heavy excises taxes on the liquor—a parliamentary push to raise money for the War of the Austrian Succession (1740–1748)—making it less lucrative for those selling on the street and thus less available to the lower orders (*Craze*, 223).

However, while from a modern perspective, we can now see that these acts were gradually succeeding, contemporary thinkers still saw gin as a dangerous social evil, illustrated most famously in William Hogarth's 1751 prints, *Beer Street* (see figure 5.1) and *Gin Lane* (see figure 5.2).

ENGLISH SATIRICAL WRITING IN THE AGE OF MOTHER GIN

Figure 5.1 *Beer Street*, etching and engraving by William Hogarth, 1751. Gift of Sarah Lazarus, 1891, the Metropolitan Museum of Art.

Together these prints highlight the differences between the two alcoholic beverages. While *Beer Street* pictures booming commercial activity, showing market women taking a well-deserved break and a beer barrel, fitted to a pully system, just arriving or perhaps being prepared for shipment, *Gin Lane* features instead a solitary businessman reaping the rewards of his trade, the pawnbroker. Whereas *Beer Street* has the industrious market women reading a ballad before returning to work, *Gin Lane* stresses the drunken, unfit mother unwittingly

[171]

Figure 5.2 *Gin Lane*, etching and engraving by William Hogarth, 1751. Harris Brisbane Dick Fund, 1932, the Metropolitan Museum of Art.

dropping her baby, a baby who had been nursing at a breast tainted by gin. Further, the characters of *Beer Street* enjoy plenty and sport the weight gain associated with beer drinking, and the latter picture shows instead emaciated men and women and a starving man sharing a gnarled bone with a dog. The differences between Hogarth's 1751 prints *Beer Street* and *Gin Lane* show the corrosive effects of gin and the continued degradation of British society. Given the close working relationship between Hogarth and Henry Fielding, the graphic satirist likely read Fielding's social tract, *An Enquiry into the Late Increase in Robbers*,[47] which was published a few weeks before Hogarth's prints were issued.[48] Indeed, Martin C. Battestin and Ruthe R. Battestin suggests that the two friends may have "agreed to employ their different talents in making a concerted attack" on the evils of gin.[49]

Fielding's text is an interesting discussion of pre-Smithian economics, as it evaluates the "Constitution" of a country (its general construction and organization based on its history) and its economic climate, while also attempting to deal with an important moral problem, that is, the increase of robbery throughout Britain. This social tract evaluates the many factors to which Fielding attributed the increase in highwaymen and gangs of robbers. In a manner similar to Bockett, Buck, and the writer of *The Informers Outwitted*, Fielding felt that the vast wealth that trade had yielded England inevitably led to excessive upper-class luxury, and that members of the lower orders, seeking to emulate the aristocracy, had adopted gin as their "diversion." Fielding argues that, because gin is a cheap luxury item, those in the lower class inevitably spend what little money they have to be distracted from their troubles—referring to this distraction through luxury as "voluptuousness"—rather than accepting their position in the social order. Eventually, their pursuit of diversion results in financial ruin, leading them to a life of crime.

While Mandeville championed luxury and spending for the upper classes, Fielding sees elite luxuriousness as both an important source of revenue and a corrupting model for the lower classes. Like the satirists who pushed against reform, Fielding is bothered by the excessive luxury of the upper class; however, whereas these earlier writers justify lower-class behavior because of upper-class luxury, Fielding instead allows that "Luxury [among the upper class] is probably rather a moral than a political Evil," meaning that it is personally sinful but does not lead to major social problems (77). Fielding states, "Let the Great therefore answer for the Employment of their Time, to themselves, or to their spiritual Governors. The Society will receive some Temporal Advantage from their Luxury. The more Toys children of all Ages consume, the brisker will be the Circulation of Money, and the greater the Increase in Trade" (83). The vanity, or prideful spending of the aristocracy, benefits England with a "Circulation of Money." Arguing in a vein similar to Mandeville, Fielding admits that at least upper-class excess leads to economic good. However, Fielding argues that, ultimately, lower-class gin drinkers achieve no economic good through the excessive and idle spending of their money. While the impulse for luxury may originate among the elite, lower-class voluptuousness has led England into its current crime wave.

Preemptively rebutting economic arguments in favor of gin distillation, Fielding, like Wilson, uses political arithmetic to stress that the long-term effects of lower-class gin drinking will harm Britain's economy. Using a mercantilist argument, he points to the corruption of motherhood as particularly damaging to the British work force. In his text, Fielding considers the "Infant who is conceived in

Gin" and "the poisonous Distillations of which it is nourished in the Womb and at the Brest" (90). Presenting a pseudoscientific rendering of fetal alcohol syndrome, Fielding considers the impact gin could have on infants as they grow. Building on Wilson's arguments, he stresses that these weak, malformed children will be the source of not only Britain's labor pool but also its military. Whereas Wilson alludes more directly to military insubordination due to gin drinking, Fielding stresses the inability of future, gin-born soldiers to protect their country: "Are these wretched Infants (if such can be supposed capable of arriving at the Age of Maturity) to become our future Sailors, and our future Grenadiers? Is it by the Labour of such as these, that all the Emoluments of Peace are to be procured us, and all the Dangers of War averted from us?" (90). In addition to creating unruly soldiers, gin, Fielding argues, will cause the next crop of British soldiers to be weak and ineffectual. How likely is it that such fighters could batter their enemy into peace? What will become of Britain's supremacy at sea when men born of gin cannot protect her ships?

Perhaps Fielding's greatest contribution to the fight against gin is the credibility his position as magistrate lends to his treatment of the liquor as a mind-altering substance. Fielding had served Westminster as a magistrate, quite successfully, from 1749 to 1754 (*Henry Fielding*, 457). In addition to creating one of the first modern police forces, the Bow Street Runners, Fielding tried cases and showed a particular aptitude to the job. As he discusses in his treatise, this position put him in daily contact with lower-class criminals who clearly committed their crimes while under the influence of gin. Discussing previous legal approaches to alcohol and the legislative role of suppressing vice among the poor, he stresses that a new type of inebriation has begun to occur, which was "unknown to our ancestors" (88), and he condemns "the strongest intoxicating Liquors, and particularly by that Poison called *Gin*" as root cause (89). Seeking to illustrate the mind-altering effects of such a potent liquor, Fielding writes,

> Many of these Wretches there are, who swallow Pints of this Poison within the Twenty-four Hours; the dreadful effects of which I have the Misfortune every Day to see, and to smell too. . . . Many Instances of this I see daily: Wretches are often brought before me, charged with Theft and Robbery, whom I am forced to confine before they are in a Condition to be examined; and when they have afterwards become sober, I have plainly perceived, from the State of the Case, that the Gin alone was the Cause of the Transgression, and have been sometimes sorry that I was obliged to commit them to Prison. (89)

Highlighting his extensive interactions with lower-class gin drinkers, Fielding illustrates the dangers caused by the lower class's unfettered access to gin. Observing gin drinkers, and smelling them, gives him a firsthand knowledge that seems to justify the moral panic to which British citizens had committed themselves.

Fielding's credibility as an observer of these instances cannot be doubted. Indeed, the Gin Craze was a time of dangerous consumption as the lower class enjoyed access to a more potent drink. However, for Fielding and other gin reformers, these views were also deeply rooted in their belief that the lower orders should only be paid enough to survive from day to day. Whereas modern proponents of capitalist systems stress upward mobility through industrious labor and saving, mercantilist writers, such as Defoe, Mandeville, and Fielding, do not believe that the lower classes should ever be able to rise above their current station. As Martin C. Battestin notes, Fielding was very "conservative in his social thought. He shared with his contemporaries in Britain . . . a conviction that the stratified structure of the social order was divinely ordained."[50] For Fielding, the ability of the lower classes to purchase such a luxury endangered the very systems on which society was built, and through his treatise, Fielding helped bring an end to the Gin Craze, as the very same year, the final Gin Act of 1751 effectively ended lower-class access to the beverage by making it prohibitively expensive, an approach for which both Wilson and Fielding had called. Fielding's writing on the subject, and the impact it had on Hogarth's prints, helped loosen the grasp Mother Gin had on Britain.

Studying such reactions to the Gin Craze exposes the sheer impact of the increase of nonessential items—whether they be wigs, carriages, imported clothing, wines, or a cheaply distilled spirit—had on the British consciousness. Seeing for the first time a lower class with a diversion other than a cheap alehouse, citizens of the middle and upper classes unsurprisingly became fearful of a consumable material—one that was easily produced, distributed, and purchased—that seemed beyond their control. However, the working classes seemed already to be forming answers to these questions. Despite having no legislative power to combat the morally driven narratives of anti-gin crusaders, many saw a prohibition of this alcohol as damaging to their ability to work, pushing back on middle- and upper-class critiques by asserting that these supposed luxuries were needed to help them contribute meaningfully to their developing economic world.

The Gin Craze, its many legislative responses, and the many texts it produced all expose a major step from the early modern era to our modern one as British anxieties regarding mass consumer culture came to a head. This period saw extreme fears of class destabilization as figures like Mandeville and Fielding point to the middle and upper classes' consumerism shaping the spending habits of those at the bottom. Gender dynamics too seemed affected at all levels. Fears of unfit mothers and weakened malnourished boys—sure to fail Britain's military and economic needs—abounded, and middle-class women's desire for gin, even when supposedly called on for medical purposes, was not going unnoticed. From this period would arise new questions about the nature of alcohol and other substances' effect on the mind and body, helping shift thinking toward a modern understanding of addiction, even as British merchants' involvement in the opium trade was on the horizon. Britain's interaction in a global market would continue to increase and as its economy moved closer to capitalism and further from mercantilism, English citizens wondered, anxiously, how consumable materials, made increasingly affordable for the lower orders, might reframe the very idea of Britishness itself.

EPILOGUE

The Smoke of War and the Imperial Thirst

Dr. Johnson observed, that our drinking less than our ancestors was owing to the change from ale to wine. "I remember," said he, "when all the decent people in Lichfield got drunk every night, and were not the worse thought of. Ale was cheap, so you pressed strongly. When a man must bring a bottle of wine, he is not in such haste. Smoking has gone out. To be sure, it is a shocking thing, blowing smoke out of our mouths into other people's mouths, eyes, and noses, and having the same thing done to us. Yet I cannot account, why a thing which requires so little exertion, and yet preserves the mind from total vacuity, should have gone out."[1]

DURING JAMES BOSWELL AND SAMUEL JOHNSON'S trip to Scotland—recounted in Boswell's *The Journal of a Tour to the Hebrides with Samuel Johnson, LL.D.* (1785)—the famous biographer recounts this quote from Johnson. As Boswell and Johnson "talked of manners," Johnson shows a strong awareness of the ways in which different products, whether ale, beer, wine, or types of tobacco, fluctuate in popularity. He points to the number of people who drank ale to excess prior to the explosion of wine's popularity among the non-elite in the late seventeenth to early eighteenth centuries. Furthermore, as he discusses pipe smoking, he considers its effects on those around the smoker, both as being problematic to social propriety and as an intellectual stimulus; although he does not specifically mention snuff, he alludes to it as a product that has a lesser effect on the surrounding company.[2] In his customary, wry fashion, Johnson highlights the rude nature of a now quite conventional ritual within public spaces.

What follows in the rest of Boswell's paragraph is a shift from a discussion of drinking and smoking to other ways in which customs have changed over the course of the eighteenth century. Addressing these changes, Johnson recounts, "I remember when people in England changed a shirt only once a week: a Pandour, when he gets a shirt, greases it to make it last. Formerly, good tradesmen had no fire but in the kitchen; never in the parlour, except on Sunday. My father, who was a magistrate of Lichfield, lived thus" (188). Specifically, Johnson points out that lower- and middle-class people more frequently change their clothing, rather than wearing just one outfit, and that more members of the lower orders build fires outside of their kitchens than formerly. This topic transitions into a short debate between Dr. Watson and Dr. Johnson over whether money was becoming more plentiful or whether one could just afford more luxuries with less money than in prior eras. We can see from this discussion that Johnson perceived vital connections between public consumption, the distribution of wealth that allowed for luxury, and the effects of political changes on what people consumed.

During the second half of the eighteenth century and throughout the nineteenth century, British tastes for tobacco and alcohol would change dramatically, shaped (as was often true of the time period discussed in this book) by war and imperial expansion. Snuff, of course, would continue to be popular during the period and up to the twentieth century, especially among women, and during this time, the association between snuff and effeminate men would grow. During the Regency period of the Prince of Wales (1811–1820), Beau Brummell—male sex symbol, fashion icon, and friend of the prince regent—began refining snuffing rituals to place more "emphasis on cleanliness." Brummell's use of snuff led to a greater association between foppery and snuff.[3]

Tobacco would also occupy a special place in British Romanticism. Both William Wordsworth and Samuel Taylor Coleridge smoked traditional British pipe tobacco, which no doubt fit with their lyrical jaunts into nature where their pipe smoke would dissipate into the air (*Tobacco*, 154). During the second wave of Romanticism, Lord Byron would be commonly associated with tobacco, often taking snuff and smoking both pipes and cigars (*Tobacco*, 154–155); he would present both pipes and tobacco throughout *Don Juan* (1819–1824), and cigars, a way of consuming tobacco that was not popular in Britain until the nineteenth century, would have a minor place in *The Island; or, The Adventures of Christian and his Comrades* (1824). It was during the Napoleonic Wars, and particularly during the British campaigns against the French in Spain (1808–1814), that British forces began smoking cigars, which as Iain Gately notes, were particularly effective for the daily life of the poorly outfitted British soldier: "[These] troops suffered extreme privations of hunger, and the utility of tobacco as an appetite suppressant was in part the impulse behind its popularity" (151). Additionally, cigars were more easily smoked during military marches than the easily broken clay pipes commonly used in Britain. Thus, after the first defeat and exile of Napoleon in 1815, the British army returned to a triumphant England, and cigar smoking quickly became a fashion for all levels of society (*Tobacco*, 152).

Like cigars, many aspects of British alcohol consumption during the nineteenth century would be tied closely to military engagements in foreign lands, and specifically to the British Empire's desire for colonial expansion. The gin and tonic first became popular during this period because quinine, an antimalarial drug, was a major component of tonic water.[4] Even ale production, a part of English his-

EPILOGUE

tory for hundreds of years, was shaped by British imperialism. During the voyage to British troops stationed in India, traditional ales and porters would spoil from both the extreme heat and the lengthy six-month trip. Eventually, however, a brewer, George Hodgson, began experimenting with a traditional type of pale beer called barleywine (or "October beer") that, because it used an almost excessive amount of hops and was strong enough that it needed to "mellow out" for a period of time, would survive the trip to India and fit the tastes of people living in warmer climates.[5] Because George Hodgson's sons were difficult business partners, representatives of the East India Trading Company eventually commissioned a separate brewer, Sam Allsopp, to replicate the beer, eventually becoming known as an India pale ale (IPA) due to the changes made by Allsopp. Meanwhile, as in the seventeenth century, wine consumption would continue to be intrinsically connected to customary trade restrictions based on international financial competition and war. For instance, in the second half of the eighteenth century, port would become the most popular wine in England, due in part to the high prices of French claret that the product had sustained since the 1690s.[6]

Situating the increased consumption of alcohol and tobacco within a specific historical period and contextualizing the ways in which people responded to consumption within the cultural, sociopolitical, and financial environments of Europe during the seventeenth and eighteenth centuries, this book ultimately exposes the ways in which the satire of this period sought to investigate changes in commerce and consumption occurring in an increasingly complex global market. Witnessing the ripple effects created by the fluctuations in an international marketplace and seeking to understand them without the benefit of significant hindsight, these writers illustrate many of the same anxieties we feel in the modern world. Just like us, the citizens of seventeenth- and eighteenth-century Britain saw the benefits of new products, bringing needed commerce, economic booms, and jobs, even as they feared the social ramifications of such items.

ACKNOWLEDGMENTS

I would like to begin by thanking Jennifer Airey, who read countless drafts of this project over the years. From the dissertation process through my efforts to complete this book, she continuously offered her time, humor, and thoughtful guidance. I also wish to express my gratitude to Laura Stevens who, in addition to advising me during my dissertation, provided feedback and encouragement that was paramount as I reshaped parts of this book. I am thankful to Lars Engle, who not only provided sage advice but also pushed me to reconsider constantly texts I thought I knew. I am also grateful to Paul McCallum, who first introduced me to literary satire and who directed me to books and sources so important to this project.

This book would never have been possible if it were not for the many opportunities and resources offered by the University of Tulsa. My project benefited greatly from funding provided by the university, which enabled me to attend conferences where I connected with other scholars and developed my ideas. Additionally, I am grateful to Nieta Pinkerton, who provided the grant funding that allowed me to travel to England. I also want to thank the staff of the University of Oxford's Bodleian Library, the London Metropolitan Archives, the British Library, and the University of Tulsa's McFarlin Library, whose work enabled my research. I am also grateful to Gilcrease Museum's Helmerich Center for American Research, where I participated in the Works-in-Progress Seminar; this seminar was immensely valuable as I worked to refine my ideas.

I want to offer my thanks to the readers at Bucknell University Press, who treated my work with such careful attention; their feedback was invaluable and helped me develop a stronger project. I am also grateful to Suzanne Guiod and Pamelia Dailey, who guided me throughout the publication process.

I also want to thank my friends and family, who have always encouraged me during my trek to complete this project. Finally, I am immensely grateful for my ever-supportive wife, Lori, and my dogs, who helped make this book a reality. Without Lori's love and advice, this book would never have been possible; without Trooper, Daisy, and Lobelia, my dutiful research assistants, my time writing this would have been very dreary.

NOTES

INTRODUCTION

1. Anonymous, *An Essay to Suppress Prophaness and Immorality, Pay the Nations Debts, Support the Government, and Maintain the Poor* (1699).
2. Roy Porter, "The Drinking Man's Disease: The 'Pre-History' of Alcoholism in Georgian Britain," *British Journal of Addiction* 80, no. 4 (1985): 390–391.
3. Harry G. Levine, "The Discovery of Addiction: Changing Concepts of Habitual Drunkenness in America," *Journal of Studies on Alcohol* 39, no. 1 (1978): 151.
4. Porter, "The Drinking Man's Disease," 385–396; Jessica Warner, "In Another City, in Another Time: Rhetoric and the Creation of a Drug Scare in Eighteenth-Century London," *Contemporary Drug Problems* 21, no. 3 (Fall 1994): 485–512; James Nicholls, *The Politics of Alcohol: A History of the Drink Question in England* (Manchester, UK: Manchester University Press, 2009), 58–71; and Jonathan White, "The 'Slow but Sure Poyson': The Representation of Gin and Its Drinkers, 1736–1751," *Journal of British Studies* 42, no. 1 (January 2003): 35–64.
5. Markman Ellis, Richard Coulton, and Matthew Mauger, *Empire of Tea: The Asian Leaf that Conquered the World* (London: Reaktion Books, 2015), 41.
6. Barbara M. Benedict, "Death and the Object: The Abuse of Things in The Rape of the Lock," in *Anniversary Essays on Alexander Pope's The Rape of the Lock*, ed. Donald W. Nichol (Toronto: Toronto University Press, 2016), 133.
7. Thomas Wilson, "Food, Drink and Identity in Europe: Consumption and the Construction of Local, National and Cosmopolitan Culture," in *Food, Drink and Identity in Europe* (Amsterdam: Brill Academic, 2006), 12.
8. Maxine Berg, *Luxury and Pleasure in Eighteenth-Century Britain* (Oxford University Press, 2005), 12.
9. Ann Bermingham, introduction to *The Consumption of Culture, 1600–1800: Image, Object, Text*, ed. Ann Bermingham and John Brewer (New York: Routledge, 1995), 12.
10. John Brewer, *The Pleasures of the Imagination: English Culture in the Eighteenth Century* (New York: Routledge, 2013), 342.

1 — "THE VICE OF THE TIME"

Material in this chapter previously appeared in another form as "'The Vice of the Time': Wine, Libertinism, and Commerce in the Age of Charles II," *Restoration: Studies in English Literary Culture, 1660–1700* 45, no. 1 (Spring 2021): 3–21.

1. John Evelyn, *The Diary of John Evelyn*, ed. Esmond Samuel De Beer (New York: Oxford University Press, 1959), 406.
2. Samuel Pepys, *The Diary of Samuel Pepys: A New and Complete Transcription*, ed. Robert Latham and William Matthews, 11 vols. (Berkeley: University of California Press, 1970), 2:85.
3. *Oxford English Dictionary Online*, "Frolic, n.," accessed July 30, 2023, https://doi.org/10.1093/OED/5616001740.

4. Susan J. Owen, "The Politics of Drink in Restoration Drama," in *A Babel of Bottles: Drink, Drinkers & Drinking Places in Literature*, ed. James Nicholls and Susan J. Owen (Sheffield, UK: Sheffield Academic, 2000), 47.
5. Charles II, *A Proclamation against Vicious, Debauch'd, and Prophane Persons* (1660), 1.
6. James Nicholls, *The Politics of Alcohol: A History of the Drink Question in England* (Manchester, UK: Manchester University Press, 2009), 27–28.
7. Rebecca Lemon, *Addiction and Devotion in Early Modern England* (Philadelphia: University of Pennsylvania Press, 2018), 137–164.
8. Daniel Defoe, *The Behaviour of Servants in England Inquired Into. With a Proposal Containing Such Heads or Constitutions as Would Effectually Answer This Great End, and Bring Servants of Every Class to a Just Regulation* (1726?), 59.
9. Jennifer L. Airey, *The Politics of Rape: Sexual Atrocity, Propaganda Wars, and the Restoration Stage* (Newark: University of Delaware Press, 2012), 35.
10. See, e.g., Bernard Capp, *England's Culture Wars: Puritan Reformation and Its Enemies in the Interregnum, 1649–1660* (Oxford: Oxford University Press, 2012).
11. Gregory A. Austin, *Alcohol in Western Society from Antiquity to 1800: A Chronological History* (Culver City: Southern California Research Institute, 1985), 234.
12. Charles Ludington, *The Politics of Wine in Britain: A New Cultural History* (Basingstoke, UK: Palgrave Macmillan, 2013), 19.
13. Ian S. Hornsey, *A History of Beer and Brewing* (Cambridge, UK: Royal Society of Chemistry, 2003), 380–382.
14. Marika Keblusek, "Wine for Comfort: Drinking and the Royalist Exile Experience, 1642–1660," in *A Pleasing Sinne: Drink and Conviviality in Seventeenth-Century England*, ed. Adam Smyth (Cambridge, UK: D. S. Brewer, 2004), 56.
15. Peter Clark, *The English Alehouse: A Social History, 1200–1830* (Boston: Longman, 1983), 45.
16. J. M. Sosin, *English America and the Restoration Monarchy of Charles II: Transatlantic Politics, Commerce, and Kinship* (Lincoln: University of Nebraska Press, 1980), 46.
17. Judith Hunter, "Legislation, Royal Proclamations, and Other National Directives Affecting Inns, Taverns, Alehouses, Brandy Shops and Punch, 1552–1757" (PhD diss., University of Reading, 1994), 187.
18. Dustin Griffin, *Authorship in the Long Eighteenth Century* (Newark: University of Delaware Press, 2013), 64–66.
19. As is the case with much of his work, there is some debate as to whether this poem was actually written by Rochester. Because of the stylistic choices, subject matter of the poem, and bitter self-mockery, I attribute the poem to the famous libertine. John Wilmot, *The Works of John Wilmot Earl of Rochester*, ed. Harold Love (Oxford: Oxford University Press, 1999), 274–275.
20. John D. Patterson, "Rochester's Second Bottle: Attitudes to Drink and Drinking in the Works of John Wilmot, Earl of Rochester," *Restoration: Studies in English Literary Culture, 1660–1700* 5, no. 1 (Spring 1981): 8.
21. William Wycherley, *The Gentleman Dancing-Master*, in *The Plays of William Wycherley*, ed. Arthur Friedman (Oxford, UK: Clarendon Press, 1979), 125–235.
22. J. Douglas Canfield, *Tricksters and Estates: On the Ideology of Restoration Comedy* (Lexington: University Press of Kentucky, 1997), 34.
23. W. Gerald Marshall, *The Restoration Mind* (Newark: University of Delaware Press, 1997), 5–6.
24. William R. Chadwick, *The Four Plays of William Wycherley: A Study in the Development of a Dramatist* (Paris: The Hague, 1975), 65.
25. Arthur Friedman, ed. in Wycherley, *The Gentleman-Dancing Master*, 147n1.
26. Susan Staves, "A Few Kind Words for the Fop," *Studies in English Literature, 1500–1900* 22, no. 3 (Summer 1982): 421.
27. Edward Ravenscroft, *The Careless Lovers*, in *The Broadview Anthology of Restoration & Early Eighteenth-Century Drama*, ed. J. Douglas Canfield (Ontario: Broadview, 2001), 987–1100.

28. In addition to *The Careless Lovers* and Wycherley's *The Gentleman Dancing-Master* discussed above, another exception is Sir Robert Howard's *The Committee* (1662), which features a short scene set in a tavern.
29. George Etherege, *The Man of Mode; Or, Sir Fopling Flutter*, in *The Broadview Anthology of Restoration & Early Eighteenth-Century Drama*, ed. J. Douglas Canfield (Ontario: Broadview, 2001), 526–589.
30. R. C. Richardson, *Household Servants in Early Modern England* (Manchester, UK: Manchester University Press, 2010), 175.
31. Charles H. Hinnant, "Pleasure and the Political Economy of Consumption in Restoration Comedy," *Restoration: Studies in English Literary Culture, 1660–1700* 19, no. 2 (Fall 1995): 80.
32. J. Douglas Canfield, ed. *The Broadview Anthology of Restoration & Early Eighteenth-Century Drama* (Toronto: Broadview Press, 2001), 527n2.
33. Aphra Behn, *The Rover: Or, the Banish'd Cavaliers*, in *Oroonoko, The Rover and Other Works*, ed. Janet Todd (London: Penguin, 2003), 73–141.
34. Richard Kroll, *Restoration Drama and "The Circle of Commerce": Tragicomedy, Politics, and Trade in the Seventeenth Century* (Cambridge: Cambridge University Press, 2007), 250.
35. Susan J. Owen, "Drink, Sex and Power in Restoration Comedy," in *A Pleasing Sinne: Drink and Conviviality in Seventeenth-Century England*, ed. Adam Smyth (Cambridge, UK: D. S. Brewer, 2004), 130–131.

2 — BOTTLING UP YOUR ANGER

1. Adam Smith, *An Inquiry into the Nature and Causes of the Wealth of Nations*, ed. Jonathan B. Wight (Petersfield, UK: Harriman House, 2007), 281.
2. Thomas A. Horne, *The Social Thought of Bernard Mandeville: Virtue and Commerce in Early Eighteenth-Century England* (New York: Columbia University Press, 1978), 64.
3. John Earle, *The Character of a Tavern* (1675); Charles Darby, *Bacchanalia, or a Description of a Drunken Club* (1680); and Anonymous, *The Paradice of Pleasure: Or, an Encomium upon Darby-Ale* (1700).
4. Michelle O'Callaghan, *The English Wits: Literature and Sociability in Early Modern England* (Cambridge: University of Cambridge Press, 2006), 63.
5. Adam Smyth, "'It were far better be a Toad, or a Serpant, then a Drunkard': Writing about Drunkenness," in *A Pleasing Sinne: Drink and Conviviality in Seventeenth-Century England*, ed. Adam Smyth (Cambridge, UK: D. S. Brewer, 2004), 201.
6. Charles Darby, *Bacchanalia, or a Description of a Drunken Club* (1680).
7. *Oxford English Dictionary Online*, "Condition, n.," accessed July 30, 2023, https://doi.org/10.1093/OED/7686499145.
8. Ashley Marshall, *The Practice of Satire in England, 1658–1770* (Baltimore: John Hopkins University Press, 2013), 103.
9. James Nicholls, *The Politics of Alcohol: A History of the Drink Question in England* (Manchester, UK: Manchester University Press, 2009), 31.
10. Charles Ludington, *The Politics of Wine in Britain: A New Cultural History* (Basingstoke, UK: Palgrave Macmillan, 2013), 25.
11. J. M. Sosin, *English America and the Restoration Monarchy of Charles II: Transatlantic Politics, Commerce, and Kinship* (Lincoln: University of Nebraska Press, 1980), 11.
12. Anonymous, *The Paradice of Pleasure: Or, an Encomium upon Darby-Ale* (1700).
13. Ned Ward, *Sot's Paradise, or, the Humours of a Derby-Ale-House with a Satyr upon the Ale* (1698).
14. Richard Ames, *The Search after Claret; Or, a Visitation of the Vintners, a Poem in Two Canto's* (1691).
15. Richard Ames, *The Bacchanalian Sessions; or the Contention of Liquors* (1693).

16. M. J. Daunton, *Progress and Poverty: An Economic and Social History of Britain 1700–1850* (Oxford: Oxford University Press, 1995), 507.
17. Benjamin Disraeli, *Sybil: Or, The Two Nations*, ed. Nicholas Shrimpton (Oxford: Oxford University Press, 2017), 21.
18. Jan de Vries and Ad van der Woude, *The First Modern Economy: Success, Failure, and Perseverance of the Dutch Economy, 1500–1815* (Cambridge: Cambridge University Press, 1997).
19. Judith Hunter, "Legislation, Royal Proclamations, and Other National Directives Affecting Inns, Taverns, Alehouses, Brandy Shops and Punch, 1552–1757" (PhD diss., University of Reading, 1994), 193.
20. John O'Brien, *Literature Incorporated: The Cultural Unconscious of the Business Corporation, 1650–1850* (Chicago: University of Chicago Press, 2016), 13–15.
21. John R. Krenzke, "Change Is Brewing: The Industrialization of the London Beer-Brewing Trade, 1400–1750" (PhD diss., Loyola University Chicago, 2014), 142–144.
22. Peter Clark, *The English Alehouse: A Social History, 1200–1830* (New York: Longman, 1983), 179.
23. Ian Hornsey, *A History of Beer and Brewing* (Cambridge, UK: Royal Society of Chemistry, 2003), 382.
24. Peter Parolin, "'The poor creature small beer': Princely Autonomy and Subjection in *2 Henry IV*," in *Culinary Shakespeare: Staging Food and Drink in Early Modern England*, ed. David B. Goldstein and Amy L. Tigner (Pittsburgh: Duquesne University Press, 2016), 26.
25. It is very possible that the poem was written by Ned Ward, as it uses his journalistic style as the speaker rambles around London, taking in the sights of the town. Anonymous, *The Tavern Hunter; Or, a Drunken Ramble from the Crown to the Devil* (1702).
26. Pope first mocked Ward in his 1718 poem, *Peri Bathous, or the Art of Sinking in Poetry*, but Ward responded directly to the more famous mockery of him, which comes in the 1728 *Dunciad*, Book I, lines 97–202. Alexander Pope, *The Dunciad* (1728) and *Peri Bathous, or the Art of Sinking in Poetry* (1718).
27. Fitz-Wilhelm Neumann, "Claret at a Premium: Ned Ward, The True Tory Defender of Fine Wines?" in *Drink in the Eighteenth and Nineteenth Centuries*, ed. Susanne Schmid and Barbara Schmidt-Haberkamp (New York: Routledge, 2015), 51.
28. Ned Ward, *The Hudibrastick Brewer; Or, a Prosperous Union between Malt and Meter* (1714).
29. Howard William Troyer, *Ned Ward of Grub Street: A Study of Sub-Literary London in the Eighteenth Century* (New York: Barnes & Noble Press, 1968), 170.

3 — SOT-WEED OR INDIAN WEED?

1. Stephen Coleman, "Background to Smoking: The Growth of a Social Habit," *History Today* 3, no. 6 (June 1953): 427.
2. Marcy Norton, *Sacred Gifts, Profane Pleasures: A History of Tobacco and Chocolate in the Atlantic World* (Ithaca, NY: Cornell University Press, 2008), 156.
3. Carole Shammas, "Changes in English and Anglo-American Consumption from 1550 to 1800," in *Consumption and the World of Goods*, ed. John Brewer and Roy Porter, 177–205 (London: Routledge, 1994).
4. Sara Pennell, "Material Culture in Seventeenth-Century 'Britain': The Matter of Domestic Consumption," in *The Oxford Handbook of the History of Consumption*, ed. Frank Trentmann (Oxford: Oxford University Press, 2012), 75.
5. Edmund Howe, *Annales, or a General Chronicle of England London* (1631), 1038; Angela McShane, "The New World of Tobacco," *History Today* 67, no. 4 (April 2017): 44.
6. Jordan Goodman, *Tobacco in History: The Culture of Dependence* (New York: Routledge, 1994), 62.
7. Matthew P. Romaniello, "Who Should Smoke? Tobacco and the Humoral Body in Early Modern England," *Social History of Alcohol and Drugs* 27, no. 2 (Summer 2013): 159.

8. Edward H. Cohen, *Ebenezer Cooke: The Sot-Weed Canon* (Athens: University of Georgia Press, 1975), 8; Janet Todd, *The Secret Life of Aphra Behn* (New Brunswick, NJ: Rutgers University Press, 1997), 56–66.
9. Thomas Harriot, *A Briefe and True Report of the New Found Land of Virginia* (1588).
10. Kelly Wisecup, *Medical Encounters: Knowledge and Identity in Early American Literatures* (Amherst: University of Massachusetts Press, 2013), 63.
11. James I, *Counterblaste to Tobacco* (1604).
12. Philaretes, *Work for Chimny-sweepers: Or a Warning for Tabacconists* (1602); John Deacon, *Tobacco Tortured, or, the Filthie Fume of Tobacco Refined* (1616).
13. David Harley, "The Beginnings of the Tobacco Controversy: Puritanism, James I, and the Royal Physicians," *Bulletin of the History of Medicine* 67, no. 1 (Spring 1993): 44.
14. Sabine Schülting, "'Indianized with the Intoxicating Filthie Fumes of Tobacco': English Encounters with the 'Indian Weed,'" *Hungarian Journal of English and American Studies* 11, no. 1 (Spring 2005): 99.
15. Iain Gately, *Tobacco: The Story of How Tobacco Seduced the World* (New York: Grove Press, 2001), 68–69.
16. Susan Campbell Anderson, "A Matter of Authority: James I and the Tobacco War," *Comitatus: A Journal of Medieval and Renaissance Studies* 29, no. 1 (October 1998): 136–137.
17. J. M. Sosin, *English America and the Restoration Monarchy of Charles II: Transatlantic Politics, Commerce, and Kinship* (Lincoln: University of Nebraska Press, 1980), 52.
18. Alan Taylor, *American Colonies: The Settling of North America* (New York: Penguin, 2001), 134.
19. Woodruff D. Smith, *Consumption and the Making of Respectability, 1600–1800* (New York: Routledge, 2012), 164.
20. Todd Butler, "Power in Smoke: The Language of Tobacco and Authority in Caroline England," *Studies in Philology* 106, no. 1 (2009): 102.
21. George Bate, *Elenchus motuum nuperorum in Anglia, or, a Short Historical Account of the Rise and Progress of the Late Troubles in England in Two Parts* (1685), 150.
22. Allan Kulikoff, *Tobacco and Slaves: The Development of Southern Cultures in the Chesapeake, 1680–1800*, 6th ed. (Chapel Hill: University of North Carolina Press, 1986), 37.
23. Aphra Behn, *Oroonoko; or, The Royal Slave*, in *Oroonoko, The Rover and Other Works*, ed. Janet Todd (London: Penguin, 2003), 140.
24. Susan B. Iwanisziw, "Behn's Novel Investment in 'Oroonoko': Kingship, Slavery and Tobacco in English Colonialism," *South Atlantic Review* 63, no. 2 (Spring 1998): 79–80.
25. James D. Rice, *Tales from a Revolution: Bacon's Rebellion and the Transformation of Early America* (Oxford: Oxford University Press, 2012), 16.
26. John Dryden, *The Indian Queen* (1664), and *The Indian Emperor, or the Conquest of Mexico by the Spaniards* (1665).
27. Robbie Richardson, *The Savage and Modern Self: North American Indians in Eighteenth-Century British Literature and Culture* (Toronto: University of Toronto Press, 2018), 7–8, 16–19.
28. Aphra Behn, *The Widow Ranter; Or, the History of Bacon in Virginia, A Tragicomedy*, in *Oroonoko, The Rover and Other Works*, ed. Janet Todd (London: Penguin, 2003), 269.
29. Tobacco played a pivotal role in the religious rites of American Indigenous groups, who by some accounts were cultivating tobacco as early as 8,000 years ago (*Sacred Gifts, Profane Pleasures*, p. 4).
30. Daniel Yu, "Crusoe's Ecstasies: Passivity, Resignation, and Tobacco Rites," in *Robinson Crusoe after 300 Years,* ed. Andreas K. E. Mueller and Glynis Ridley (Lewisburg, PA: Bucknell University Press, 2021), 103.
31. Daniel Defoe, *Moll Flanders* (1722).
32. James Davie Butler, "British Convicts Shipped to American Colonies," *The American Historical Review* 2, no. 1 (October 1896): 17.

33. Anita Pacheo, "Festive Comedy in *The Widdow Ranter*: Behn's Clown and Falstaff," *Restoration: Studies in English Literary Culture, 1660–1700* 38, no. 2 (Fall 2014): 52.
34. Heidi Hutner, "Aphra Behn's *The Widow Ranter*," in *Colonial Women: Race and Culture in Stuart Drama* (Oxford: Oxford University Press, 2001), 104.
35. See, e.g., Isaac Hawkins Browne, *A Pipe of Tobacco: In Imitation of Six Several Authors* (1736).
36. Ned Ward, *The London-Spy Compleat. In Eighteen Parts* (1700); Subsequent references to *The London-Spy* will be cited parenthetically by the original number of the monthly installment, followed by the relative page numbers.
37. Sandra Bell, "The Subject of Smoke: Tobacco and Early Modern England," in *The Mysterious and Foreign in Early Modern England*, ed. Helen Ostovich and Mary V. Silcox (Newark: University of Delaware Press, 2008), 161.
38. *Oxford English Dictionary Online*, "Sot-weed, n.," accessed December 15, 2023, https://doi.org/10.1093/OED/9184022247.
39. Ned Ward, *A Trip to New-England with a Character of the Country and People, both English and Indians.* (1699) and *The Secret History of Clubs: Particularly the Kit-Cat, Beef-Stake, Uertuosos, Quacks, Knights of the Golden-Fleece, Florists, Beaus, &c* (1709).
40. Ned Ward, *A Trip to Jamaica: With a True Character of the People and Island.* (1698).
41. Howard William Troyer, *Ned Ward of Grub Street: A Study of Sub-Literary London in the Eighteenth Century* (New York: Barnes & Noble Press, 1968), 21.
42. Ned Ward, *The Secret History of the Calves-Head Clubb, or, the Republican Unmasqu'd* (1703).
43. Unlike many of the clearly fictious clubs Ward describes, his version of the molly club was based on actual gatherings, which were being broken up by the Society for the Reformation of Manners. Randolph Trumbach cites Ward's description of molly-house rituals in his foundational text, *Sex and the Gender Revolution, Volume 1: Heterosexuality and the Third Gender in Enlightenment London* (Chicago: University of Chicago Press, 1998), 84.
44. Jonathan Swift, *Gulliver's Travels*, ed. Albert J. Rivero (New York: Norton, 2002), 243.
45. Lawrence Spooner, *A Looking-Glass for Smoakers* (1703).
46. Daniel Defoe, *The Life and Strange Surprizing Adventures of Robinson Crusoe (1719)*, in *The Novels of Daniel Defoe*, ed. W. R. Owens, vol. 1 (New York: Routledge, 2016), 126–127.
47. Lawrence Spooner, *Poetical Recreations: Or Pleasant Remarks on the Various Rumours upon the Publication of My Poem, Call'd, A Looking-Glass for Smoakers* (1705).
48. Kristen G. Brookes, "Inhaling the Alien: Race and Tobacco in Early Modern England," in *Global Traffic: Discourses and Practices of Trade in English Literature and Culture from 1550 to 1700*, ed. Barbara Sebek and Stephen Deng (New York: Palgrave Macmillan, 2008), 160.
49. *Oxford English Dictionary Online*, "Outlandish, adj. & n.," accessed July 30, 2023, https://doi.org/10.1093/OED/1591655318.
50. Catherine Molineux, "Pleasures of the Smoke: 'Black Virginians' in Georgian London's Tobacco Shops," *William and Mary Quarterly* 64, no. 2 (2007): 347.
51. *Oxford English Dictionary Online*, "Prank, n.2.," accessed July 30, 2023, https://doi.org/10.1093/OED/1136359602.
52. Craig Rustici, "Tobacco, Union, and the Indianized English," in *Indography: Writing the "Indian" in Early Modern England*, ed. Jonathan Gil Harris (New York: Palgrave Macmillan, 2012), 123–124.
53. Ebenezer Cooke, *The Sot-Weed Factor*, in *The English Literatures of America: 1500–1800*, ed. Myra Jehlen and Michael Warner (New York: Routledge, 1997).
54. Robert D. Arner, "Ebenezer Cooke's The Sot-Weed Factor: The Structure of Satire," *Southern Literary Journal* 4, no. 1 (1971): 33–47; J. A. Leo Lemay, *Men of Letters in Colonial Maryland* (Knoxville: University of Tennessee Press, 1972; Edward H. Cohen, *Ebenezer Cooke: The Sot-Weed Canon*, 26–27; Gregory A. Carey, "The Poem as Con Game: Dual Satire and the Three Levels of Narrative in Ebenezer Cooke's 'The Sot-Weed Factor,'" *Southern Literary Journal* 23, no. 1 (Fall 1990): 9–19; and Cy Charles League, "The Process of Americanization as Portrayed in Ebenezer Cooke's 'The Sot-Weed Factor,'" *Southern Literary Journal* 29, no. 1 (Fall 1996): 18–25.

55. Notably, the factor shows a great deal of respect to the wealthy gentleman planter, or "cockerouse" as he is referred to in the poem, recognizing the elevated position of the upper-class figure (*The Sot-Weed Factor*, pp. 1026–1027).
56. John F. Wing, "Shipping Productivity in Maryland's Tobacco Trade, 1689–1759," *International Journal of Maritime History* 20, no. 2 (December 2008): 232.
57. Jim Egan, "The Colonial English Body as Commodity in Ebenezer Cooke's 'The Sot-Weed Factor,'" *Criticism* 41, no. 3 (Summer 1999): 390.
58. Colin Kidd, *The Forging of Races: Race and Scripture in the Protestant Atlantic World, 1600–2000* (Cambridge: Cambridge University Press, 2006), 70–72.
59. Dror Wahrman, *The Making of the Modern Self: Identity and Culture in Eighteenth-Century England* (New Haven, CT: Yale University Press, 2004), 86–87.
60. Anna S. Agbe-Davies, *Tobacco, Pipes, and Race in Colonial Virginia: Little Tubes of Mighty Power* (Walnut Creek, CA: Left Coast Press, 2015), 39.
61. Al Luckenbach and Taft Kiser, "Seventeenth-Century Tobacco Pipe Manufacturing in the Chesapeake Region: A Preliminary Delineation of Makers and Their Styles," *Ceramics in America* (2006), accessed July 30, 2023, http://www.chipstone.org.
62. John L. Cotter, *Archeological Excavations at Jamestown, Virginia* (Washington, DC: National Park Service, U.S. Department of the Interior, 1958), 145.
63. For a map of this particular site, see *Tobacco, Pipes, and Race*, 120.
64. *Oxford English Dictionary Online*, "Truck, n.1.," accessed July 30, 2023, https://doi.org/10.1093/OED/6558999984.

4 — "THE CEREMONY OF THE SNUFF-BOX"

1. Joseph Addison, *The Spectator*, ed. Donald F. Bond, vol. 2, no. 275 (Oxford: Clarendon Press, 1987), 570–573. Subsequent references to *The Spectator* will rely on the Bond edition and will be cited parenthetically by the original issue number, followed by volume and page number.
2. Thomas Gordon, *The Humorist* (1720), 105. Gordon is best known for his *Cato's Letters* (1720–1723), which he cowrote with John Trenchard and which had a major impact on the thinkers of the American Revolution.
3. Emily C. Friedman, *Reading Smell in Eighteenth-Century Fiction* (Lewisburg, PA: Bucknell University Press, 2016).
4. Lauren Working, "Tobacco and the Social Life of Conquest in London, 1580–1625," *The Historical Journal* 65, no. 1 (2022): 16.
5. Stephen Coleman, "Background to Smoking: The Growth of a Social Habit," *History Today* 3, no. 6 (June 1953): 428.
6. Charles Lillie, *The British Perfumer, Snuff-Manufacturer, and Colourman's Guide* (1740).
7. Angela McShane, "The New World of Tobacco," *History Today* 67, no. 4 (April 2017): 41–47.
8. See Wetenhall Wilkes, *A Letter of Genteel and Moral Advice to a Young Lady* (1740), 123.
9. Richard Steele, *The Tatler*, ed. Donald F. Bond (Oxford, UK: Clarendon Press, 1987), 1:35, 255–260. Subsequent references to *The Tatler* will rely on the Bond edition and will be cited parenthetically by the original issue number, followed by volume and page number.
10. *Oxford English Dictionary Online*, "Dung, v.1.," accessed July 30, 2023, https://doi.org/10.1093/OED/1134722282; also, *Oxford English Dictionary Online*, "Mundungus, n.," accessed July 30, 2023, https://doi.org/10.1093/OED/2709976103.
11. Michael G. Ketcham, *Transparent Designs: Reading, Performance, and Form in the Spectator Papers* (Athens: University of Georgia Press, 1985).
12. *Oxford English Dictionary Online*, "Bauble, n.," accessed October 23, 2021, https://doi.org/10.1093/OED/6898056871.
13. Donald F. Bond, ed., footnote to *The Tatler*, no. 138, 2: 226nt; see also Alexander Pope, *The Rape of the Lock*, ed. Cynthia Wall (Boston: Bedford Books, 1998), 362–363.

14. Stephen Copley, "Commerce, Conversation and Politeness in the Early Eighteenth-Century Periodical," *The British Journal for Eighteenth-Century Studies* 18, no. 1 (1995): 66.
15. One outlier in Steele's discussion of snuff would be Steele's *The Spectator*, no. 222 in which he treats a pipe tobacco or snuff habit favorably in comparison to alcohol. *The Spectator*, no. 222, 2: 364.
16. Dwight Codr, "'Hairs less in sight': Meteors, Sneezes, and the Problem of Meaning in *The Rape of the Lock*," *Studies in Eighteenth-Century Culture* 45, no. 1 (2016): 175–196; and Richard Kroll, "Pope and Drugs: The Pharmacology of The Rape of the Lock," *English Literary History* 67, no. 1, (Spring 2000): 99–141.
17. Alexander Pope, *The Rape of the Lock*, ed. George Tillotson (New York: Routledge, 1989); Pope, *The Rape of the Lock*, ed. Wall; and Alexander Pope, *The Rape of the Locke (1712)*, in *The Poems of Alexander Pope: Volume One*, ed. Julian Ferraro and Paul Baine (New York: Routledge, 2019), 477–520.
18. Laura Brown, *Ends of Empire: Women and Ideology in Early Eighteenth-Century English Literature* (Ithaca, NY: Cornell University Press, 1993), 103–134; Stewart Crehan, "'The Rape of the Lock' and the Economy of 'Trivial Things,'" *Eighteenth-Century Studies* 31, no. 1 (Fall 1997): 45–68; and Colin Nicholson, *Writing and the Rise of Finance: Capital Satires of the Early Eighteenth Century* (New York: Cambridge University Press, 1994), 27–50.
19. Pope, *The Rape of the Lock*, ed. Wall, ll. 7–8.
20. One of the most famous representations of snuff-taking as foppery comes in *A Bold Stroke for a Wife* (1718), in which Colonel Fainwell easily gains the trust of Sir Philip Modelove, the beau guardian of Anne Lovely, simply by offering some fine French snuff from his French-made snuffbox. Susanna Centlivre, *A Bold Stroke for a Wife*, in *The Broadview Anthology of Restoration & Early Eighteenth-Century Drama*, ed. J. Douglas Canfield (Ontario: Broadview, 2001), 909.
21. Pope, *The Rape of the Lock*, ed. Wall, 362–363; Pope, *The Rape of the Locke (1712)*, ed. Ferraro and Baine, 495n85; and Pope, *The Rape of the Lock*, ed. Tillotson, 44–45n17.
22. Pope, *The Rape of the Locke (1712)*, ed. Ferraro and Baine, 506n48.
23. See Wall's footnote for lines 126–130, which also discuss Sir Plume's "fashionable" cursing. In the 1714 printing, there are three dashes used to omit the "oun" in "Zounds," which is an elision of the curse "God's wounds." These three dashes are also used for each of the punctuations I have discussed in this section. In this edition of the poem, Pope, or his publisher Bernard Lintot, may be using these similar punctuation styles to draw a parallel between cursing loudly and taking snuff to increase one's rhetorical power. However, in the 1717 edition, which constituted Pope's last round of major changes to the poem, these major pauses feature four dashes, rather than three.
24. Barbara M. Benedict, "Death and the Object: The Abuse of Things in The Rape of the Lock," in *Anniversary Essays on Alexander Pope's The Rape of the Lock*, ed. Donald W. Nichol (Toronto: University of Toronto Press, 2016), 133.
25. Jordan Goodman, *Tobacco in History: The Culture of Dependence* (New York: Routledge, 1994), 83–84.
26. Anonymous, *Whipping Tom: Or, a Rod for a Proud Lady* (1722).
27. Anonymous, *The Tryal, Examination and Conviction; of Thomas Wallis, Vulgarly Called Whipping Tom* (1740?). For more on these assaults, see, e.g., Sarah Toulalan, *Imagining Sex: Pornography and Bodies in Seventeenth-Century England* (Oxford: Oxford University Press, 2007), 108; and John Ashton, *Social Life in the Reign of Queen Anne* (London: Chatto & Windus, 1937).
28. Angela McShane, "Tobacco-Taking and Identity-Making in Early Modern Britain and North America," *The Historical Journal* 65, no. 1 (February 2022): 116.
29. *Oxford English Dictionary Online*, "Gall, n.3.," accessed July 30, 2023, https://doi.org/10.1093/OED/9296189901.
30. Jonathan Swift, *The Lady's Dressing Room*, in *The Writings of Jonathan Swift: Authoritative Texts, Backgrounds, Criticism*, ed. Robert A. Greenberg and William B. Piper (New York:

Norton, 1973); Anonymous, *The Gentleman's Study in Answer to the Lady's Dressing-Room* (1732). *The Gentleman's Study* was more widely published in Dublin as part of *The Dublin Magazine: Or, the Gentleman's New Miscellany* (1733); however, it is clear that the poem was in circulation by 1732, just months after Swift's poem appeared, as it is referenced in the short pamphlet, *Chloe Surpriz'd: Or, the Second Part of the Lady's Dressing-Room. To Which Are Added, Thoughts upon Reading the Lady's Dressing-Room and the Gentleman's Study. The Former Wrote by D—S—t, the Latter by Miss W—* (1732). As this pamphlet suggests, it is likely a woman wrote this harsh rebuke of Swift's infamous poem.

31. Marcy Norton, *Sacred Gifts, Profane Pleasures: A History of Tobacco and Chocolate in the Atlantic World* (Ithaca, NY: Cornell University Press, 2008), 192.
32. *Oxford English Dictionary Online*, "Fume, n.," accessed October 23, 2021, https://doi.org /10.1093/OED/3062429693.

5 — ENGLISH SATIRICAL WRITING IN THE AGE OF MOTHER GIN

1. Daniel Defoe, *Defoe's Review: Reproduced from the Original Editions, Facsimile Book 22, August 2, 1712, to June 11, 1713*, ed. Arthur Wellesley Secord (New York: Columbia University Press, 1938).
2. Daniel Defoe, *A Brief Case of the Distillers, and of the Distilling Trade in England, Shewing How Far It Is the Interest of England to Encourage the Said Trade* (1726).
3. Jessica Warner, *Craze: Gin and Debauchery in an Age of Reason* (New York: Four Walls Eight Windows Publishing, 2002), xiv.
4. Daniel Defoe, *Augusta Triumphans: Or, the Way to Make London the Most Flourishing City in the Universe* (1728), 45.
5. Daniel Defoe, *Colonel Jack*, ed. Gabriel Cerbantes and Geoffrey Sill (Ontario: Broadview Press, 2015).
6. *Oxford English Dictionary Online*, "Gin, n.3.," accessed July 30, 2023, https://doi.org/10 .1093/OED/9148892562.
7. Patrick Dillon, *Gin: The Much Lamented Death of Madam Geneva* (Boston: Justin, Charles & Co., 2003), 16.
8. Daniel Defoe, *Some Thoughts upon the Subject of Commerce with France* (1713).
9. Liz Bellamy, *Commerce, Morality and the Eighteenth-Century Novel* (Cambridge: Cambridge University Press, 1998), 13.
10. Warner notes that 1725 is the first year that people "started to worry publicly about gin" (85).
11. Jonathan White, "The 'Slow but Sure Poyson': The Representation of Gin and Its Drinkers, 1736–1751," *Journal of British Studies* 42, no. 1 (January 2003): 52.
12. Maxine Berg, *Luxury and Pleasure in Eighteenth-Century Britain* (Oxford: Oxford University Press, 2005), 28.
13. *Oxford English Dictionary Online*, "Luxury, n.," accessed October 23, 2021, https://doi.org /10.1093/OED/7949079244.
14. Joseph Addison, *The Spectator*, ed. Donald F. Bond (Oxford, UK: Clarendon Press, 1987), 232–236.
15. Edward Chandler, *A Sermon Preached to the Societies for Reformation of Manners, at St.Mary-le-Bow, on Monday January the 4th, 1724* (1724), 15.
16. According to an infamous contemporary advertisement for a gin shop, one could get drunk on gin at the shop by spending just one pence; whereas Judith Hunter notes that a single (cheaper) beer cost a pence by itself. See Hunter, "Legislation, Royal Proclamations, and Other National Directives Affecting Inns, Taverns, Alehouses, Brandy Shops and Punch, 1552–1757" (PhD diss., University of Reading, 1994), 254.
17. Bernard Mandeville, *The Grumbling Hive; or, Knaves Turn'd Honest* (1705).
18. I focus on these two editions in that they show perhaps the biggest changes to Mandeville's work regarding spirituous liquors. The 1714 edition has little to say about alcohol in

general, whereas in the 1723 edition, Mandeville directly discusses gin as a huge social problem. For the 1723 printing, Bernard Mandeville, *The Fable of the Bees*, ed. Phillip Harth (New York: Penguin, 1989).
19. Kathryn Sutherland, "The New Economics of the Enlightenment," in *The Enlightenment World*, ed. Martin Fitzpatrick, Peter Jones, Christa Knellwolf, and Ian McCalman (New York: Routledge, 2007), 475–476.
20. Roy Porter, *Flesh in the Age of Reason* (New York: Norton, 2003), 141.
21. Bernard Mandeville, *A Treatise of the Hypochondriack and Hysterick Passions, Vulgarly Call'd the Hypo in Men and Vapours in Women; In which the Symptoms, Causes, and Cure of those Diseases Are Set Forth after a Method Intirely New* (1711), 276.
22. See, e.g., Thomas Wilson, *Distilled Spirituous Liquors the Bane of the Nation: Being Some Considerations Humbly Offer'd to the Hon. the House of Commons* (1736), 55.
23. James Nicholls, *The Politics of Alcohol: A History of the Drink Question in England* (Manchester, UK: Manchester University Press, 2009), 38–39.
24. John Gay, *The Beggar's Opera and Polly*, ed. Hall Gladfelder (Oxford: Oxford University Press, 2013).
25. J. Douglas Canfield, "The Critique of Capitalism and the Retreat into Art in Gay's *Beggar's Opera* and Fielding's *Author's Farce*," in *Cutting Edges: Postmodern Critical Essays on Eighteenth-Century Satire*, ed. James E. Gill (Knoxville: University of Tennessee Press, 1995), 324; Pat Rogers, *Eighteenth-Century Encounters: Studies in Literature and Society in the Age of Walpole* (New Jersey: Barnes & Noble Press, 1985), 100–101; and David Nokes, *Raillery and Rage: A Study of Eighteenth Century Satire* (New York: St. Martin's Press, 1987), 145, 138.
26. One exception is William Empson's famous evaluation of the play, in his chapter, "The Beggar's Opera: Mock-Pastoral as the Cult of Independence," in which he provides an interesting close reading of the moments of betrayal, scenes that feature gin and wine. William Empson, *Some Versions of the Pastoral* (Norfolk, CT: New Directions Books, 1950), 229–230, 235–238.
27. Gay does not have a fixed classification in his usage of strong water, brandy, and gin, presenting the terms somewhat interchangeably. This lack of distinction between liquors is a common trait of the eighteenth century.
28. Judith Hunter, "Legislation, Royal Proclamations, and Other National Directives Affecting Inns, Taverns, Alehouses, Brandy Shops and Punch, 1552–1757" (PhD diss., University of Reading, 1994), 247–248.
29. In his diary entry for October 10, 1663, Samuel Pepys discusses taking gin ("a strong water made of juniper") for medicinal purposes, specifically to help his constipation and urinary problems. Samuel Pepys, *The Diary of Samuel Pepys: A New and Complete Transcription*, ed. Robert Latham and William Matthews (Berkeley: University of California Press, 1971), 4: 328–329.
30. Thomas Wilson, *Spirituous Liquors the Bane of the Nation* (1736); David Hall, *An Essay on Intemperance, Particularly Hard Drinking* (1742).
31. Colin Nicholson, *Writing and the Rise of Finance: Capital Satires of the Early Eighteenth Century* (Cambridge: Cambridge University Press, 1994), 131–132.
32. *Oxford English Dictionary Online*, "Curious, adj. & adv.," accessed July 30, 2023, https://doi.org/10.1093/OED/3381649003.
33. Many scholars (and contemporary audience members) see Peachum and Lockit as representing Walpole and Sir Charles Townsend. See, e.g., Isaac Kramnick, *Bolingbroke and His Circle: The Politics of Nostalgia in the Age of Walpole* (Cambridge, MA: Harvard University Press, 1968), 227.
34. Lesley Jacobs Solmonson, *Gin: A Global History* (London: Reaktion Books, 2019), 48.
35. Elias Bockett, *Blunt to Walpole: A Familiar Epistle on behalf of the British Distillery* (1730); Stephen Buck, *Geneva. A Poem in Blank Verse* (1734); and Anonymous, *The Informers Outwitted: A Tragi-Comical Farce* (1738).

36. Sir Daniel Dolins, *The Charge of Sr. Daniel Dolins, Kt. to the Grand-Jury, and Other Juries of the County of Middlesex; at the General Quarter-Sessions of the Peace* (1725), 33.
37. John Hervey, "Speech on 22 February, 1743," *The Gentleman's Magazine and Historical Chronicle* 13 (1743): 564–575.
38. Peter Clark, "The 'Mother Gin' Controversy in the Early Eighteenth Century," *Transactions of the Royal Historical Society* 38 (1988): 70.
39. Julian Hoppit, "Political Arithmetic in Eighteenth-Century England," *The Economic History Review* 49, no. 3 (1996): 517.
40. Peter Clark, "The 'Mother Gin' Controversy in the Early Eighteenth Century," *Transactions of the Royal Historical Society* 38 (1988): 74.
41. *Oxford English Dictionary*, "Prejudice, v.," accessed July 30, 2023, https://doi.org/10.1093/OED/7089303179.
42. *Distilled Spirituous Liquors*, 56.
43. Elias Bockett, *Geneva: A Poem* (1729).
44. Elias Bockett, *Blunt to Walpole: A Familiar Epistle on behalf of the British Distillery* (1730).
45. The most famous example of the squalor of gin shop came in 1736. The owner of the establishment posted the following three lines, advertising their gin: "Drunk for one pence. / Dead Drunk for two pence. / Clean Straw for nothing." Over the course of the following months, reformers used descriptions of the sign as political fuel, and it was eventually featured in William Hogarth's famous *Gin Lane* print of 1751.
46. Guy Routh, *The Origin of Economic Ideas*, 2nd ed. (Dobbs Ferry, NY: Sheridan House, 1989), 30.
47. Henry Fielding, *An Enquiry into the Causes of the Late Increase of Robbers and Related Writings*, ed. Malvin R. Zirker (Middletown: Wesleyan University Press, 2013).
48. Malvin R. Zirker Jr., "Fielding and Reform in the 1750's," *Studies in English Literature, 1500–1900* 7, no 3 (Restoration and Eighteenth Century, Summer 1967): 455.
49. Martin C. Battestin and Ruthe R. Battestin, *Henry Fielding: A Life* (New York: Routledge, 1989), 517.
50. Martin C. Battestin, "Fielding, Henry (1707–1754)," *Oxford Dictionary of National Biography*, accessed July 3, 2019, https://doi.org/10.1093/ref:odnb/9400.

EPILOGUE

1. James Boswell, *A Journey to the Western Islands of Scotland* and *The Journal of a Tour to the Hebrides*, ed. Peter Levi (New York: Penguin Books, 1984), 188.
2. In other texts, Johnson deliberates more heavily on snuff. Discussing the increase in manufacturing in England, Johnson alludes to the luxury of snuff: "others raising contributions upon those [developing new ways of enjoying tobacco], whose elegance disdains the grossness of smoky luxury, by grinding the same materials into a powder that may at once gratify and impair the smell." Despite referring to snuff in this way, it seems Johnson often enjoyed the powder himself. See Samuel Johnson, "The Adventurer (1753–1754), No. 67," in *Selected Essays*, ed. David Womersley (New York: Penguin, 2003), 344.
3. Iain Gately, *Tobacco: The Story of How Tobacco Seduced the World* (New York: Grove Press, 2001), 254.
4. Lesley Jacobs Solmonson, *Gin: A Global History* (London: Reaktion Books, 2019), 65.
5. William Bostwick, "How the India Pale Ale Got Its Name: A Look to the Hoppy Brew's Past Brings Us to the Revolution in Craft Beer Today," *Smithsonian Magazine*, April 7, 2015, https://www.smithsonianmag.com/history/how-india-pale-ale-got-its-name-180954891/.
6. Charles Ludington, *The Politics of Wine in Britain: A New Cultural History* (Basingstoke, UK: Palgrave MacMillan, 2013), 144–162.

BIBLIOGRAPHY

Addison, Joseph and Richard Steele. *The Spectator*. Edited by Donald F. Bond. 5 vols. Oxford, UK: Clarendon, 1987.
Agbe-Davies, Anna S. *Tobacco, Pipes, and Race in Colonial Virginia: Little Tubes of Mighty Power*. Walnut Creek, CA: Left Coast Press, 2015.
Airey, Jennifer L. *The Politics of Rape: Sexual Atrocity, Propaganda Wars, and the Restoration Stage*. Newark: University of Delaware Press, 2012.
Ames, Richard. *The Bacchanalian Sessions; or the Contention of Liquors*. (1693).
———. *The Search after Claret; Or, a Visitation of the Vintners, a Poem in Two Canto's*. (1691).
Anderson, Susan Campbell. "A Matter of Authority: James I and the Tobacco War." *Comitatus: A Journal of Medieval and Renaissance Studies* 29, no. 1 (October 1998): 136–163.
Anonymous. *Chloe Surpriz'd: Or, the Second Part of the Lady's Dressing-Room. To Which Are Added, Thoughts upon Reading the Lady's Dressing-Room and the Gentleman's Study. The Former Wrote by D—S—t, the Latter by Miss W—* (Dublin: 1732).
———. *The Dublin Magazine: Or, the Gentleman's New Miscellany* (Dublin: 1733).
———. *An Essay to Suppress Prophaness and Immorality, Pay the Nations Debts, Support the Government, and Maintain the Poor* (1699).
———. *The Gentleman's Study in Answer to the Lady's Dressing-Room* (1732).
———. *The Informers Outwitted: A Tragi-Comical Farce* (1738).
———. *The Paradice of Pleasure: Or, an Encomium upon Darby-Ale* (1700).
———. *The Tavern Hunter; Or, a Drunken Ramble from the Crown to the Devil* (1702).
———. *The Tryal, Examination and Conviction; of Thomas Wallis, Vulgarly Called Whipping Tom* (1740?).
———. *Whipping Tom: Or, a Rod for a Proud Lady* (1722).
Arner, Robert D. "Ebenezer Cooke's The Sot-Weed Factor: The Structure of Satire." *Southern Literary Journal* 4, no. 1 (1971): 33–47.
Ashton, John. *Social Life in the Reign of Queen Anne*. London: Chatto & Windus, 1937.
Austin, Gregory A. *Alcohol in Western Society from Antiquity to 1800: A Chronological History*. Culver City: Southern California Research Institute, 1985.
Bate, George. *Elenchus motuum nuperorum in Anglia, or, a Short Historical Account of the Rise and Progress of the Late Troubles in England in Two Parts* (1685).
Battestin, Martin C. "Fielding, Henry (1707–1754)." *Oxford Dictionary of National Biography*. Accessed July 3, 2019. https://doi.org/10.1093/ref:odnb/9400.
Battestin, Martin C., and Ruthe R. Battestin. *Henry Fielding: A Life*. New York: Routledge, 1989.
Behn, Aphra. "Oroonoko: Or, the Royal Slave." In *Oroonoko, The Rover and Other Works*, edited by Janet Todd, 73–141. London: Penguin, 2003.
———. "The Rover: Or, the Banish'd Cavaliers." In *Oroonoko, The Rover and Other Works*, edited by Janet Todd, 73–141. London: Penguin, 2003.
———. "The Widow Ranter; Or, the History of Bacon in Virginia, A Tragicomedy." In *Oroonoko, The Rover and Other Works*, edited by Janet Todd, 249–325. London: Penguin, 2003.
Bell, Sandra. "The Subject of Smoke: Tobacco and Early Modern England." In *The Mysterious and Foreign in Early Modern England*, edited by Helen Ostovich and Mary V. Silcox, 153–169. Newark: University of Delaware Press, 2008.

Bellamy, Liz. *Commerce, Morality and the Eighteenth-Century Novel*. Cambridge: Cambridge University Press, 1998.

Benedict, Barbara M. "Death and the Object: The Abuse of Things in The Rape of the Lock." In *Anniversary Essays on Alexander Pope's The Rape of the Lock*, edited by Donald W. Nichol, 131–149. Toronto: Toronto University Press, 2016.

Berg, Maxine. *Luxury and Pleasure in Eighteenth-Century Britain*. Oxford: Oxford University Press, 2005.

Bermingham, Ann. Introduction to *The Consumption of Culture, 1600–1800: Image, Object, Text*, edited by Ann Bermingham and John Brewer, 1–20. New York: Routledge, 1995.

Bockett, Elias. *Blunt to Walpole: A Familiar Epistle on behalf of the British Distillery* (1730).

———. *Geneva: A Poem* (1729).

Bostwick, William. "How the India Pale Ale Got Its Name: A Look to the Hoppy Brew's Past Brings Us to the Revolution in Craft Beer Today." *Smithsonian Magazine*, April 7, 2015. https://www.smithsonianmag.com/history/how-india-pale-ale-got-its-name-180954891/.

Boswell, James. *A Journey to the Western Islands of Scotland* and *The Journal of a Tour to the Hebrides*. Edited by Peter Levi. New York: Penguin Books, 1984.

Brewer, John. *The Pleasures of the Imagination: English Culture in the Eighteenth Century*. New York: Routledge, 2013.

Brookes, Kristen G. "Inhaling the Alien: Race and Tobacco in Early Modern England." In *Global Traffic: Discourses and Practices of Trade in English Literature and Culture from 1550 to 1700*, edited by Barbara Sebek and Stephen Deng, 157–178. New York: Palgrave Macmillan, 2008.

Brown, Laura. *Ends of Empire: Women and Ideology in Early Eighteenth-Century English Literature*. Ithaca, NY: Cornell University Press, 1993.

Browne, Isaac Hawkins. *A Pipe of Tobacco: In Imitation of Six Several Authors* (1736).

Buck, Stephen. *Geneva. A Poem in Blank Verse* (1734).

Butler, James Davie. "British Convicts Shipped to American Colonies." *The American Historical Review* 2, no. 1 (October 1896): 12–33.

Butler, Todd. "Power in Smoke: The Language of Tobacco and Authority in Caroline England." *Studies in Philology* 106, no. 1 (2009): 100–118.

Byron, George Gordon. *Don Juan* (1819–1824).

———. *The Island; or, The Adventures of Christian and his Comrades* (1824).

Canfield, J. Douglas, ed. *The Broadview Anthology of Restoration & Early Eighteenth-Century Drama*. Toronto: Broadview Press, 2001.

———. "The Critique of Capitalism and the Retreat into Art in Gay's *Beggar's Opera* and Fielding's *Author's Farce*." In *Cutting Edges: Postmodern Critical Essays on Eighteenth-Century Satire*, edited by James E. Gill, 320–334. Knoxville: University of Tennessee Press, 1995.

———. *Tricksters and Estates: On the Ideology of Restoration Comedy*. Lexington: University Press of Kentucky, 1997.

Capp, Bernard. *England's Culture Wars: Puritan Reformation and Its Enemies in the Interregnum, 1649–1660*. Oxford: Oxford University Press, 2012.

Carey, Gregory A. "The Poem as Con Game: Dual Satire and the Three Levels of Narrative in Ebenezer Cooke's 'The Sot-Weed Factor.'" *Southern Literary Journal* 23, no. 1 (Fall 1990): 9–19.

Centlivre, Susanna. "A Bold Stroke for a Wife." In *The Broadview Anthology of Restoration & Early Eighteenth-Century Drama*, edited by J. Douglas Canfield, 903–943. Ontario: Broadview, 2001.

Chadwick, William R. *The Four Plays of William Wycherley: A Study in the Development of a Dramatist*. Paris: Mouton & Company, 1975.

Chandler, Edward. *A Sermon Preached to the Societies for Reformation of Manners, at St. Mary-le-Bow, on Monday January the 4th, 1724* (1724).

Charles II. *A Proclamation against Vicious, Debauch'd, and Prophane Persons* (1660).

Clark, Peter. *The English Alehouse: A Social History, 1200–1830*. New York: Longman, 1983.

———. "The 'Mother Gin' Controversy in the Early Eighteenth Century." *Transactions of the Royal Historical Society* 38 (1988): 63–84.
Codr, Dwight. "'Hairs less in sight': Meteors, Sneezes, and the Problem of Meaning in *The Rape of the Lock*." *Studies in Eighteenth-Century Culture* 45, no. 1 (2016): 175–196.
Cohen, Edward H. *Ebenezer Cooke: The Sot-Weed Canon*. Athens: University of Georgia Press, 1975.
Coleman, Stephen. "Background to Smoking: The Growth of a Social Habit." *History Today* 3, no. 6 (June 1953): 423–430.
Cooke, Ebenezer. *The Sot-Weed Factor*. In *The English Literatures of America: 1500–1800*, edited by Myra Jehlen and Michael Warner, 1014–1031. New York: Routledge, 1997.
Copley, Stephen. "Commerce, Conversation and Politeness in the Early Eighteenth-Century Periodical." *The British Journal for Eighteenth-Century Studies* 18, no. 1 (1995): 63–77.
Cotter, John L. *Archeological Excavations at Jamestown, Virginia*. Washington, DC: National Park Service, U.S. Department of the Interior, 1958.
Crehan, Stewart. "'The Rape of the Lock' and the Economy of 'Trivial Things.'" *Eighteenth-Century Studies* 31, no. 1 (Fall 1997): 45–68.
Darby, Charles. *Bacchanalia, or a Description of a Drunken Club* (1680).
Daunton, M. J. *Progress and Poverty: An Economic and Social History of Britain 1700–1850*. Oxford: Oxford University Press, 1995.
de Vries, Jan, and Ad van der Woude. *The First Modern Economy: Success, Failure, and Perseverance of the Dutch Economy, 1500–1815*. Cambridge: Cambridge University Press, 1997.
Deacon, John. *Tobacco Tortured, or, the Filthie Fume of Tobacco Refined* (1616).
Defoe, Daniel. *Augusta Triumphans: Or, the Way to Make London the Most Flourishing City in the Universe* (1728).
———. *The Behaviour of Servants in England Inquired Into. With a Proposal Containing Such Heads or Constitutions as Would Effectually Answer This Great End, and Bring Servants of Every Class to a Just Regulation* (1726?).
———. *A Brief Case of the Distillers, and of the Distilling Trade in England, Shewing How Far It Is the Interest of England to Encourage the Said Trade* (1726).
———. *Colonel Jack*. Edited by Gabriel Cerbantes and Geoffrey Sill. Ontario: Broadview Press, 2015.
———. *Defoe's Review: Reproduced from the Original Editions, Facsimile Book 22, August 2, 1712, to June 11, 1713*. Edited by Arthur Wellesley Secord. New York: Columbia University Press, 1938.
———. *The Life and Strange Surprizing Adventures of Robinson Crusoe* (1719). In *The Novels of Daniel Defoe*. Edited by W. R. Owens, 10 vols. New York: Routledge, 2016.
———. *Moll Flanders* (1722).
———. *Some Thoughts upon the Subject of Commerce with France* (1713).
Dillon, Patrick. *Gin: The Much Lamented Death of Madam Geneva*. Boston: Justin, Charles & Co., 2003.
Disraeli, Benjamin. *Sybil: Or, The Two Nations*. Edited by Nicholas Shrimpton. Oxford: Oxford University Press, 2017.
Dolins, Daniel. *The Charge of Sr. Daniel Dolins, Kt. to the Grand-Jury, and Other Juries of the County of Middlesex; at the General Quarter-Sessions of the Peace* (1725).
Dryden, John. *The Indian Emperor, or the Conquest of Mexico by the Spaniards* (1665).
———. *The Indian Queen* (1664).
Earle, John. *The Character of a Tavern* (1675).
Egan, Jim. "The Colonial English Body as Commodity in Ebenezer Cooke's 'The Sot-Weed Factor.'" *Criticism* 41, no. 3 (Summer 1999): 385–400.
Ellis, Markman, Richard Coulton, and Matthew Mauger. *Empire of Tea: The Asian Leaf that Conquered the World*. London: Reaktion Books, 2015.
Empson, William. *Some Versions of the Pastoral*. Norfolk, CT: New Directions Books, 1950.

Etherege, George. "The Man of Mode; Or, Sir Fopling Flutter." In *The Broadview Anthology of Restoration & Early Eighteenth-Century Drama*, edited by J. Douglas Canfield, 526–589. Ontario: Broadview, 2001.

Evelyn, John. *The Diary of John Evelyn*. Edited by Esmond Samuel De Beer. New York: Oxford University Press, 1959.

Fielding, Henry. *An Enquiry into the Causes of the Late Increase of Robbers and Related Writings*. Edited by Malvin R. Zirker. Middletown: Wesleyan University Press, 2013.

Friedman, Emily C. *Reading Smell in Eighteenth-Century Fiction*. Lewisburg, PA: Bucknell University Press, 2016.

Gately, Iain. *Tobacco: The Story of How Tobacco Seduced the World*. New York: Grove Press, 2001.

Gay, John. *The Beggar's Opera and Polly*. Edited by Hall Gladfelder. Oxford: Oxford University Press, 2013.

Goodman, Jordan. *Tobacco in History: The Culture of Dependence*. New York: Routledge, 1994.

Gordon, Thomas. *The Humorist* (1720).

Griffin, Dustin. *Authorship in the Long Eighteenth Century*. Newark: University of Delaware Press, 2013.

Hall, David. *An Essay on Intemperance, Particularly Hard Drinking* (1742).

Harley, David. "The Beginnings of the Tobacco Controversy: Puritanism, James I, and the Royal Physicians." *Bulletin of the History of Medicine* 67, no. 1 (Spring 1993): 28–50.

Harriot, Thomas. *A Briefe and True Report of the New Found Land of Virginia* (1588).

Hervey, John. "Speech on 22 February, 1743." *The Gentleman's Magazine and Historical Chronicle* 13 (1743): 564–575.

Hinnant, Charles H. "Pleasure and the Political Economy of Consumption in Restoration Comedy." *Restoration: Studies in English Literary Culture, 1660–1700* 19, no. 2 (Fall 1995): 77–87.

Hoppit, Julian. "Political Arithmetic in Eighteenth-Century England." *The Economic History Review* 49, no. 3 (1996): 516–540.

Horne, Thomas A. *The Social Thought of Bernard Mandeville: Virtue and Commerce in Early Eighteenth-Century England*. New York: Columbia University Press, 1978.

Hornsey, Ian S. *A History of Beer and Brewing*. Cambridge, UK: Royal Society of Chemistry, 2003.

Howe, Edmund. *Annales, or a General Chronicle of England London* (1631).

Hunter, Judith. "Legislation, Royal Proclamations, and Other National Directives Affecting Inns, Taverns, Alehouses, Brandy Shops and Punch, 1552–1757." PhD diss., University of Reading, 1994.

Hutner, Heidi. "Aphra Behn's *The Widow Ranter*." In *Colonial Women: Race and Culture in Stuart Drama*, 89–106. Oxford: Oxford University Press, 2001.

Iwanisziw, Susan B. "Behn's Novel Investment in 'Oroonoko': Kingship, Slavery and Tobacco in English Colonialism." *South Atlantic Review* 63, no. 2 (Spring 1998): 75–98.

James I. *Counterblaste to Tobacco* (1604).

Johnson, Samuel. "The Adventurer (1753–1754), No. 67." In *Selected Essays*, edited by David Womersley, 342–347. New York: Penguin, 2003.

Keblusek, Marika. "Wine for Comfort: Drinking and the Royalist Exile Experience, 1642–1660." In *A Pleasing Sinne: Drink and Conviviality in Seventeenth-Century England*, edited by Adam Smyth, 55–68. Cambridge, UK: D. S. Brewer, 2004.

Ketcham, Michael G. *Transparent Designs: Reading, Performance, and Form in the Spectator Papers*. Athens: University of Georgia Press, 1985.

Kidd, Colin. *The Forging of Races: Race and Scripture in the Protestant Atlantic World, 1600–2000*. Cambridge: Cambridge University Press, 2006.

Kramnick, Isaac. *Bolingbroke and His Circle: The Politics of Nostalgia in the Age of Walpole*. Cambridge, MA: Harvard University Press, 1968.

Krenzke, John R. "Change Is Brewing: The Industrialization of the London Beer-Brewing Trade, 1400–1750." PhD diss., Loyola University Chicago, 2014.

Kroll, Richard. "Pope and Drugs: The Pharmacology of The Rape of the Lock." *English Literary History* 67, no. 1 (Spring 2000): 99–141.

———. *Restoration Drama and "The Circle of Commerce": Tragicomedy, Politics, and Trade in the Seventeenth Century*. Cambridge: Cambridge University Press, 2007.

Kulikoff, Allan. *Tobacco and Slaves: The Development of Southern Cultures in the Chesapeake, 1680–1800*. 6th ed. Chapel Hill: University of North Carolina Press, 1986.

League, Cy Charles. "The Process of Americanization as Portrayed in Ebenezer Cooke's 'The Sot-Weed Factor.'" *Southern Literary Journal* 29, no. 1 (Fall 1996): 18–25.

Lemay, J. A. Leo. *Men of Letters in Colonial Maryland*. Knoxville: University of Tennessee Press, 1972.

Lemon, Rebecca. *Addiction and Devotion in Early Modern England*. Philadelphia: University of Pennsylvania Press, 2018.

Levine, Harry G. "The Discovery of Addiction: Changing Concepts of Habitual Drunkenness in America." *Journal of Studies on Alcohol* 39, no. 1 (1978): 143–174.

Lillie, Charles. *The British Perfumer, Snuff-Manufacturer, and Colourman's Guide* (1740).

Luckenbach, Al, and Taft Kiser. "Seventeenth-Century Tobacco Pipe Manufacturing in the Chesapeake Region: A Preliminary Delineation of Makers and Their Styles." *Ceramics in America* (2006). Accessed July 31, 2023. http://www.chipstone.org.

Ludington, Charles. *The Politics of Wine in Britain: A New Cultural History*. Basingstoke, UK: Palgrave Macmillan, 2013.

Mandeville, Bernard. *The Fable of the Bees*. Edited by Phillip Harth. New York: Penguin, 1989.

———. *The Grumbling Hive; or, Knaves Turn'd Honest* (1705).

———. *A Treatise of the Hypochondriack and Hysterick Passions, Vulgarly Call'd the Hypo in Men and Vapours in Women; In which the Symptoms, Causes, and Cure of those Diseases Are Set Forth after a Method Intirely New* (1711).

Marshall, Ashley. *The Practice of Satire in England, 1658–1770*. Baltimore: John Hopkins University Press, 2013.

Marshall, W. Gerald. *The Restoration Mind*. Newark: University of Delaware Press, 1997.

McShane, Angela. "The New World of Tobacco." *History Today* 67, no. 4 (April 2017): 41–47.

———. "Tobacco-Taking and Identity-Making in Early Modern Britain and North America." *The Historical Journal* 65, no. 1 (February 2022): 108–129.

Molineux, Catherine. "Pleasures of the Smoke: 'Black Virginians' in Georgian London's Tobacco Shops." *William and Mary Quarterly* 64, no. 2 (2007): 327–376.

Neumann, Fitz-Wilhelm. "Claret at a Premium: Ned Ward, The True Tory Defender of Fine Wines?" In *Drink in the Eighteenth and Nineteenth Centuries*, edited by Susanne Schmid and Barbara Schmidt-Haberkamp, 47–57. New York: Routledge, 2015.

Nicholls, James. *The Politics of Alcohol: A History of the Drink Question in England*. Manchester, UK: Manchester University Press, 2009.

Nicholson, Colin. *Writing and the Rise of Finance: Capital Satires of the Early Eighteenth Century*. New York: Cambridge University Press, 1994.

Nokes, David. *Raillery and Rage: A Study of Eighteenth Century Satire*. New York: St. Martin's Press, 1987.

Norton, Marcy. *Sacred Gifts, Profane Pleasures: A History of Tobacco and Chocolate in the Atlantic World*. Ithaca, NY: Cornell University Press, 2008.

O'Brien, John. *Literature Incorporated: The Cultural Unconscious of the Business Corporation, 1650–1850*. Chicago: University of Chicago Press, 2016.

O'Callaghan, Michelle. *The English Wits: Literature and Sociability in Early Modern England*. Cambridge: University of Cambridge Press, 2006.

Owen, Susan J. "Drink, Sex and Power in Restoration Comedy." In *A Pleasing Sinne: Drink and Conviviality in Seventeenth-Century England*, edited by Adam Smyth, 127–139. Cambridge, UK: D. S. Brewer, 2004.

———. "The Politics of Drink in Restoration Drama." In *A Babel of Bottles: Drink, Drinkers & Drinking Places in Literature*, edited by James Nicholls and Susan J. Owen, 41–51. Sheffield, UK: Sheffield Academic, 2000.

Oxford English Dictionary Online. "Bauble, n." Accessed October 23, 2021. https://doi.org/10.1093/OED/6898056871.

———. "Condition, n." Accessed July 30, 2023. https://doi.org/10.1093/OED/7686499145.

———. "Curious, adj. & adv." Accessed July 30, 2023. https://doi.org/10.1093/OED/3381649003.

———. "Dung, v.1." Accessed July 30, 2023. https://doi.org/10.1093/OED/1134722282.

———. "Frolic, n." Accessed July 30, 2023. https://doi.org/10.1093/OED/5616001740.

———. "Fume, n." Accessed October 23, 2021. https://doi.org/10.1093/OED/3062429693.

———. "Gall, n.3." Accessed July 30, 2023. https://doi.org/10.1093/OED/9296189901.

———. "Gin, n.3." Accessed July 30, 2023. https://doi.org/10.1093/OED/9148892562.

———. "Luxury, n." Accessed October 23, 2021. https://doi.org/10.1093/OED/7949079244.

———. "Mundungus, n." Accessed July 30, 2023. https://doi.org/10.1093/OED/2709976103.

———. "Outlandish, adj. & n." Accessed July 30, 2023. https://doi.org/10.1093/OED/1591655318.

———. "Prank, n.2." Accessed July 30, 2023. https://doi.org/10.1093/OED/1136359602.

———. "Prejudice, v." Accessed July 30, 2023. https://doi.org/10.1093/OED/7089303179.

———. "Sot-weed, n." Accessed December 15, 2023. https://doi.org/10.1093/OED/9184022247.

———. "Truck, n.1." Accessed July 30, 2023. https://doi.org/10.1093/OED/6558999984.

Pacheo, Anita. "Festive Comedy in *The Widdow Ranter*: Behn's Clown and Falstaff." *Restoration: Studies in English Literary Culture, 1660–1700* 38, no. 2 (Fall 2014): 43–61.

Parolin, Peter. "'The poor creature small beer': Princely Autonomy and Subjection in *2 Henry IV*." In *Culinary Shakespeare: Staging Food and Drink in Early Modern England*, edited by David B. Goldstein and Amy L. Tigner, 21–40. Pittsburgh: Duquesne University Press, 2016.

Patterson, John D. "Rochester's Second Bottle: Attitudes to Drink and Drinking in the Works of John Wilmot, Earl of Rochester." *Restoration: Studies in English Literary Culture, 1660–1700* 5, no. 1 (Spring 1981): 6–15.

Pennell, Sara. "Material Culture in Seventeenth-Century 'Britain': The Matter of Domestic Consumption." In *The Oxford Handbook of the History of Consumption*, edited by Frank Trentmann, 64–84. Oxford: Oxford University Press, 2012.

Pepys, Samuel. *The Diary of Samuel Pepys: A New and Complete Transcription*. Edited by Robert Latham and William Matthews. 11 vols. Berkeley: University of California Press, 1970.

Philaretes. *Work for Chimny-sweepers: Or a Warning for Tabacconists* (1602).

Pope, Alexander. *The Dunciad* (1728).

———. *Peri Bathous, or the Art of Sinking in Poetry* (1718).

———. *The Rape of the Lock*. Edited by Geoffrey Tillotson. New York: Routledge, 1989.

———. *The Rape of the Lock*. Edited by Cynthia Wall. Boston: Bedford Books, 1998.

———. *The Rape of the Locke (1712)*. In *The Poems of Alexander Pope: Volume One*, edited by Julian Ferraro and Paul Baine, 477–520. New York: Routledge, 2019.

Porter, Roy. "The Drinking Man's Disease: The 'Pre-History' of Alcoholism in Georgian Britain." *British Journal of Addiction* 80, no. 4 (1985): 385–396.

———. *Flesh in the Age of Reason*. New York: Norton, 2003.

Ravenscroft, Edward. "The Careless Lovers." In *The Broadview Anthology of Restoration & Early Eighteenth-Century Drama*, edited by J. Douglas Canfield, 987–1100. Ontario: Broadview, 2001.

Rice, James D. *Tales from a Revolution: Bacon's Rebellion and the Transformation of Early America*. Oxford: Oxford University Press, 2012.

Richardson, R. C. *Household Servants in Early Modern England*. Manchester, UK: Manchester University Press, 2010.

Richardson, Robbie. *The Savage and Modern Self: North American Indians in Eighteenth-Century British Literature and Culture.* Toronto: University of Toronto Press, 2018.

Rogers, Pat. *Eighteenth-Century Encounters: Studies in Literature and Society in the Age of Walpole.* New Jersey: Barnes & Noble Press, 1985.

Romaniello, Matthew P. "Who Should Smoke? Tobacco and the Humoral Body in Early Modern England." *Social History of Alcohol and Drugs* 27, no. 2 (Summer 2013): 156–173.

Routh, Guy. *The Origin of Economic Ideas.* 2nd ed. Dobbs Ferry, NY: Sheridan House, 1989.

Rustici, Craig. "Tobacco, Union, and the Indianized English." In *Indography: Writing the "Indian."* In *Early Modern England*, edited by Jonathan Gil Harris, 117–131. New York: Palgrave Macmillan, 2012.

Schülting, Sabine. "'Indianized with the Intoxicating Filthie Fumes of Tobacco': English Encounters with the 'Indian Weed.'" *Hungarian Journal of English and American Studies* 11, no. 1 (Spring 2005): 93–116.

Shammas, Carole. "Changes in English and Anglo-American Consumption from 1550 to 1800." In *Consumption and the World of Goods*, edited by John Brewer and Roy Porter, 177–205. London: Routledge, 1994.

Smith, Adam. *An Inquiry into the Nature and Causes of the Wealth of Nations.* Edited by Jonathan B. Wight. Petersfield, UK: Harriman House, 2007.

Smith, Woodruff D. *Consumption and the Making of Respectability, 1600–1800.* New York: Routledge, 2012.

Smyth, Adam. "'It were far better be a Toad, or a Serpant, then a Drunkard': Writing about Drunkenness." In *A Pleasing Sinne: Drink and Conviviality in Seventeenth-Century England*, edited by Adam Smyth, 127–139. Cambridge, UK: D. S. Brewer, 2004.

Solmonson, Lesley Jacobs. *Gin: A Global History.* London: Reaktion Books, 2019.

Sosin, J. M. *English America and the Restoration Monarchy of Charles II: Transatlantic Politics, Commerce, and Kinship.* Lincoln: University of Nebraska Press, 1980.

Spooner, Lawrence. *A Looking-Glass for Smoakers* (1703).

———. *Poetical Recreations: Or Pleasant Remarks on the Various Rumours upon the Publication of My Poem, Call'd, A Looking-Glass for Smoakers* (1705).

Staves, Susan. "A Few Kind Words for the Fop." *Studies in English Literature, 1500–1900* 22, no. 3 (Summer 1982): 413–428.

Steele, Richard. *The Spectator.* Edited by Donald F. Bond. 5 vols. Oxford, UK: Clarendon, 1987.

———. *The Tatler.* Edited by Donald F. Bond. 3 vols. Oxford, UK: Clarendon Press, 1987.

Sutherland, Kathryn. "The New Economics of the Enlightenment." In *The Enlightenment World*, edited by Martin Fitzpatrick, Peter Jones, Christa Knellwolf, and Ian McCalman, 473–485. New York: Routledge, 2007.

Swift, Jonathan. *Gulliver's Travels.* Edited by Albert J. Rivero. New York: Norton, 2002.

———. *The Writings of Jonathan Swift: Authoritative Texts, Backgrounds, Criticism*, edited by Robert A. Greenberg and William B. Piper, 535–538. New York: Norton, 1973.

Taylor, Alan. *American Colonies: The Settling of North America.* New York: Penguin, 2001.

Todd, Janet. *The Secret Life of Aphra Behn.* New Brunswick, NJ: Rutgers University Press, 1997.

Toulalan, Sarah. *Imagining Sex: Pornography and Bodies in Seventeenth-Century England.* Oxford: Oxford University Press, 2007.

Troyer, Howard William. *Ned Ward of Grub Street: A Study of Sub-Literary London in the Eighteenth Century.* New York: Barnes & Noble Press, 1968.

Trumbach, Randolph. *Sex and the Gender Revolution, Volume 1: Heterosexuality and the Third Gender in Enlightenment London.* Chicago: University of Chicago Press, 1998.

Wahrman, Dror. *The Making of the Modern Self: Identity and Culture in Eighteenth-Century England.* New Haven, CT: Yale University Press, 2004.

Ward, Ned. *The Hudibrastick Brewer; Or, a Prosperous Union between Malt and Meter* (1714).

———. *The London-Spy Compleat. In Eighteen Parts* (1700).

———. *The Secret History of the Calves-Head Clubb, Or, the Republican Unmasqu'd* (1703).

———. *The Secret History of Clubs: Particularly the Kit-Cat, Beef-Stake, Uertuosos, Quacks, Knights of the Golden-Fleece, Florists, Beaus, &c* (1709).
———. *Sot's Paradise, or, the Humours of a Derby-Ale-House with a Satyr upon the Ale* (1698).
———. *A Trip to Jamaica: With a True Character of the People and Island*. (1698).
———. *A Trip to New-England with a Character of the Country and People, both English and Indians* (1699).
Warner, Jessica. *Craze: Gin and Debauchery in an Age of Reason*. New York: Four Walls Eight Windows Publishing, 2002.
———. "In Another City, in Another Time: Rhetoric and the Creation of a Drug Scare in Eighteenth-Century London." *Contemporary Drug Problems* 21, no. 3 (Fall 1994): 485–512.
White, Jonathan. "The 'Slow but Sure Poyson': The Representation of Gin and Its Drinkers, 1736–1751." *Journal of British Studies* 42, no. 1 (January 2003): 35–64.
Wilkes, Wetenhall. *A Letter of Genteel and Moral Advice to a Young Lady* (Dublin: 1740).
Wilmot, John. *The Works of John Wilmot Earl of Rochester*. Edited by Harold Love. Oxford: Oxford University Press, 1999.
Wilson, Thomas. *Distilled Spirituous Liquors the Bane of the Nation: Being Some Considerations Humbly Offer'd to the Hon. the House of Commons* (1736).
———. "Food, Drink and Identity in Europe: Consumption and the Construction of Local, National and Cosmopolitan Culture." In *Food, Drink and Identity in Europe*. Amsterdam: Brill Academic, 2006.
Wing, John F. "Shipping Productivity in Maryland's Tobacco Trade, 1689–1759." *International Journal of Maritime History* 20, no. 2 (December 2008): 223–239.
Wisecup, Kelly. *Medical Encounters: Knowledge and Identity in Early American Literatures*. Amherst: University of Massachusetts Press, 2013.
Working, Lauren. "Tobacco and the Social Life of Conquest in London, 1580–1625." *The Historical Journal* 65, no. 1 (2022): 30–48.
Wycherley, William. *The Gentleman Dancing-Master*. In *The Plays of William Wycherley*, edited by Arthur Friedman, 125–235. Oxford, UK: Clarendon Press, 1979.
Yu, Daniel. "Crusoe's Ecstasies: Passivity, Resignation, and Tobacco Rites." In *Robinson Crusoe after 300 Years,* edited by Andreas K. E. Mueller and Glynis Ridley, 99–114. Lewisburg, PA: Bucknell University Press, 2021.
Zirker, Malvin R., Jr. "Fielding and Reform in the 1750's." *Studies in English Literature, 1500–1900* 7, no 3 (Restoration and Eighteenth Century, Summer 1967): 453–465.

INDEX

Page numbers in italics refer to illustrations.

Acts of Navigation of 1651, the, 16, 70–71
addiction, disease model of, 4–6, 175–176
Addison, Joesph, *The Spectator*, 109–111, 115, 188–119, 122, 126, 128, 130, 135, 140
adulterating alcohol, 32, 40
advertisement: African and Native Americans portrayed in tobacco advertising, 93–94; in *The Spectator*, 117–120, 122; through alehouse verses, 46–47; through tavern verses, 59, 62
Africans: as enslaved pickers of tobacco, 67, 72, 100; equated to Native Americans, 93–94; as exoticized bodies, 75; and sugar processing, 73, 75. *See also* skin color difference
ale and beer: associations with Whigs, 43; association with parliamentarians, 15–16; differences between the two, 53; importance as domestic product, 13, 46–47, 51, 55–56, 63, 171–172; as lower-class beverages, 28, 53, 149; materiality of, 7, 50, 61; middle-class promotion of, 9–10, 37–38, 55–56, 58, 62–63, 171–172; as possible export, 47–48, 51; price and cheapness of, 25, 62–63, 162; taxation of, 17, 53–54, 153. *See also* brewing; India pale ale; porter beer
alehouses and inns: amenities provided in, 7, 14, 39; Charles II proclamation against, 28; closures during Interregnum, 15–16; keepers of, 47–48, 55, 60–63; lower-class environment of alehouse, 26
Ames, Richard, *The Bacchanalian Sessions; or the Contention of Liquors*, 10, 37–38, 46, 48–54, 60; *A Search after Claret*, 48
Anglo-Dutch War, the, 32
Anne I, 9, 38, 59, 65, 68, 72, 122–123
anti-gin narratives: gin as destabilizing gender roles, 158–160, 168, 172–174; gin as disruptor of social hierarchy, 157–158, 165–166; gin as poison, 154–155, 174

anti-tobacconist thinking, 69–70, 90, 75, 88–90, 93, 95–96, 103. *See also* racialized bigotry against Native Americans
anxieties: about class and gender lines, 13, 157–158; about luxury and consumerism, 7, 10–11; definition of, 2. *See also* loss of aristocratic power
apothecaries, 155, 157, 165, 167

Bacon's Rebellion (historical), 73–74
balance of trade, the, 138. *See also* trade deficit
balderdashing. *See* adulterating alcohol
Bank of England, the, 3
Behn, Aphra, 96–98, 100, 107–108; *Oroonoko: or, the Royal Slave*, 10, 72–73; *The Rover, Part I*, 9, 13, 25, 30–35, 75; *The Widow Ranter; Or, the History of Bacon in Virginia, A Tragicomedy*, 10, 67, 72–84
Benedict, Barbara M., 125
Berg, Maxine, 7, 140
Berkeley, William, 73–74
Bermingham, Anne, 8
Bockett, Elias, 141, 164–166, 168–170, 173; *Blunt to Walpole: A Familiar Epistle in behalf of the British Distillery*, 156, 160–163; *Geneva: A Poem*, 153, 160
Bordeaux. *See* claret
Boswell, James, *The Journal of a Tour to the Hebrides with Samuel Johnson*, 177–178
bourgeois power, 7, 24, 148–149, 152–153. *See also* loss of aristocratic power; middle class
Bow Street Runners, 174
brandy: compared to gin, 142; as expensive beverage, 148–152; as a French import, 37, 137–138, 143, 148, 163; interchangeability of liquor names, 192n27; personification of, 51; popularity in American colonies, 78. *See also* punch

[203]

INDEX

Brewer, John, 8
breweries, large scale, 7, 52; taxation of, 16. *See also under* licensing
brewing: compared to writing satirical verse, 55–56, 60–62; first India pale ale, 178–179; for private consumption, 1; on private estates, 15, 22
Brummell, Beau, 178
Buck, Stephen, 141, 168–170, 173; *Geneva. A Poem in Blank Verse*, 164–166
Byron, Gordon George, *Don Juan*, 178; *The Island; or, The Adventures of Christian and his Comrades*, 178

canary wine, 10, 19–20, 23–26, 29–30, 32–33, 40–41, 50, 56
Canfield, J. Douglas, 19, 21, 147
capitalism, as a system, 4, 146, 169; early capitalism, 139; proto-capitalism, 5, 10, 51, 54, 140, 147–148, 155–156, 176. *See also* laissez-faire; Smith, Adam
cash crop, tobacco as, 65, 67, 69, 73, 84, 94, 98
Catherine of Braganza, 6
Catholicism, 15–16, 43
Centlivre, Susanna, *A Bold Stroke for a Wife*, 190n20
Chandler, Edward, *A Sermon Preached to the Societies for Reformation of Manners*, 141
Charles I, 32, 70–71, 87, 89
Charles II: court, 3, 34–35, 113; financial policies regarding alcohol, 9, 16–17, 30; financial policies regarding tobacco, 71; later reign and political turmoil, 38, 42–43; *A Proclamation against Vicious, Debauch'd, and Prophane Persons*, 14–15, 28; return to England and coronation, 12–13
Chaucer, Geoffrey, *The Canterbury Tales*, 82
chewing tobacco, 133
chocolate, 6–7, 17
cigars, 178
claret: comparison to Spanish canary, 24, 32; drinkers equated to, 41, 44; expensiveness, 25, 45, 58, 179; as an import, 13, 29–30, 38, 43, 46, 50–51, 97; popularity among middle class, 10, 26; popularity with tavern poets, 48, 53, 60, 63, 85; as an upper-class drink, 27, 77–78, 134
Clark, Peter, 52, 158, 165
class interactions, inappropriate, 42, 133–135

clay pipes, 7, 57, 65–66; colonial pipes, 102–*104*, 105; traditional English pipes, 102–*103*
coffee, 6–7, 17, 125
coffeehouses, 65, 85, 103, 118–119, 129
Colbert, Jean-Baptiste, 43
Coleridge, Samuel Taylor, 178
consumable material, 3, 7–8, 176; gin as, 144, 148, 175; plant and pipe tobacco as, 74–76, 85, 102, 108; snuff as, 116, 129; wine as, 13. *See also* clay pipes; drinking vessels; materiality; shippable containers; snuffboxes
consumerism, 3, 7, 110, 134–135, 139–143
conversation, 10, 40–41, 79–80, 83, 110–119, 122–126
Cooke, Ebenezer, *The Sot-Weed Factor*, 10, 67–68, 72, 86, 96–108
cordials, 46, 148, 154–155. *See also* medicinal uses of alcohol
Cromwell, Oliver, 15, 16, 53, 61, 71
customs duties, 3, 13, 24, 30, 49, 71, 143. *See also* excise duties; licensing

Darby, Charles, 10, 47, 58–59, 63; *Bacchanalia, or a Description of a Drunken Club*, 37–38, 41–45
Davenant, Charles, 159
Deacon, John, *Tobacco Tortured, or, the Filthie Fume of Tobacco Refined*, 69
Defoe, Daniel, 4, 60, 139–140, 147–149, 153–154, 175; *Augusta Triumphans*, 137; *The Behaviour of Servants in England Inquired Into*, 15; *A Brief Case of the Distillers, and of the Distilling Trade in England*, 137; *Colonel Jack*, 137; *Moll Flanders*, 78; *The Review*, 137; *Robinson Crusoe*, 76, 89
de Riqueti, Victor, 139
de Vries, Jan, and Ad van der Woude, 49
distilling, 1, 137–138, 145, 153, 157, 160–163, 167–170
Dolins, Daniel, 156–157, 161
domestic commerce, 3, 9–10, 17, 28, 37–40, 49, 54, 117; disruption of, 163; domestic products, 29, 37, 45–46, 51–52, 145, 153; internal shipping and, 53; sites of, 54, 63; taxation and, 16. *See also* ale and beer
dram shop. *See* gin shops
drawers, 25–27, 40, 57. *See also* alehouses and inns; publicans; taverns
drinking, sinful pride in, 2, 5, 15, 42, 47

[204]

INDEX

drinking vessels: bottles, 25, 28–29; glasses, 15, 28–29, 144, 155, 160; glass flasks, 56; mugs, beer pots, bumpers, 7, 50; pints of beer, 16, 47–48; pints of wine, 40, 57; recognition by British citizens, 7

Dryden, John, 13; *The Indian Emperor, or the Conquest of Mexico by the Spaniards*, 75; *The Indian Queen*, 75

Dutch trade ships, 16, 51, 71

Dymock, Edward, 12

Earle, John, 10, 37; *The Character of a Tavern*, 38–39, 44–45, 55, 59, 63

Earl of Rochester. *See* John Wilmot

Earl of Shaftesbury. *See* Ashley-Cooper, Anthony

Elizabeth I, 57, 68–70

Ellis, Markman, Richard Coulton, and Matthew Mauger, 6

embargoes, 37, 43, 51, 56, 60. *See also* tariffs; trade deficit; trade wars

Empson, William, 149, 192n26

English Civil Wars, 13, 16, 71

English merchant: facilitator of luxury, 143; interactions with upper-class, 42; poetic treatments, 39, 45, 98, 107; treatment in drama, 19, 23–24, 81–82; treatments in periodicals, 119

English military: drunken disobedience, 159; funding via alcohol, 49–50; political arithmetic, 174–176; positive effects of alcohol use, 145, 165; treatment of Charles I, 71. *See also* cigars; India pale ale

Essay to Suppress Prophaness and Immorality, Pay the Nations Debts, Support the Government, and Maintain the Poor, and Immorality, Pay the Nations Debts, Support the Government, and Maintain the Poor, An, 1–2, 5

Etherege, George, *The Man of Mode; or, Sir Fopling Flutter*, 9, 13, 17, 27–30, 33, 45, 53, 97

Evelyn, John, 12

excise duties, 3, 10, 156; during Charles II's reign, 16–17; during the Interregnum, 16, 53; during William III's reign, 49, 52, 138; on gin, 153, 156, 170. *See also* Excise Office, the

Excise Office, the, 3–4; officers of, 53, 78

Exclusion Crisis, the, 42–43

exports: beer as potential export, 45–47, 51; specializations for, 36–37; tobacco as English export, 81; wool as primary English, 43

factor system, 67, 96, 98, 101

female libertine, 25, 30

femininity, lack of traditional, 77, 82–84, 87, 120–121, 130–131, 158, 168. *See also* women consuming alcohol; women gin sellers; women snuff takers; women tobacco smokers

fetal alcohol syndrome, 158–160, 171–175. *See also* motherhood

Fielding, Henry, 4; *An Enquiry into the Late Increase in Robbers*, 11, 139–141, 159, 170–176

food, 2, 4, 14, 39–40, 58–59, 61, 120, 155. *See also* meals

foppishness: antipathy to pipe tobacco, 85; critiques of French-imported luxury, 9, 21, 29; inability to drink, 22, 30; lack of libertine masculinity, 19–20; overindulgence of snuff, 109, 118, 120, 122, 124, 129–130, 178, 190n20

foreignness of wine: in anti-tavern poetry, 38–41, 46–48; availability in middle-class taverns, 26–30, 39–41; and capitalism, 36–37; connected to Catholicism, 15–16; elision of, 9–10, 17, 28–30; as an example in *The Wealth of Nations*, 36–37; mockery of, 15–16, 32, 39–41, 46–48; in tavern-friendly poetry, 55–56, 63–64. *See also* claret; imported wine

foreign snuff, 109–110, 112–114, 118, 121, 124, 129, 190n20; effect on pricing, 7–8

free market, 36, 54. *See also* capitalism; laissez-faire

French wine. *See* claret

Galenic theory, 4, 16, 66, 68–69, 89, 95

Gay, John, *The Beggar's Opera*, 8–9, 11, 140–141, 147–155, 192nn26–27

Gentleman's Study in Answer to the Lady's Dressing-Room, The, 11, 111, 131–135

George IV, 178

German wine. *See* Rhenish wine

Gin Acts, the, 139, 141, 153, 156–157, 161–164, 167–170, 175, 193n45

gin informers, 157, 164, 166–170. *See also* Gin Acts

gin shops, 54, 141, 164–165, 191n16, 193n45

gluttony: addiction represented as, 5–6; and alcohol consumption, 16, 142; and tobacco smoking, 10, 67, 72, 85, 89, 96

[205]

INDEX

Gordon, Thomas, *The Humorist*, 111, 189n2
Graunt, John, 4, 159
gross domestic product, 139
Grub Street, 8, 48, 60

Hall, David, *An Essay on Intemperance, Particularly Hard Drinking*, 150
Harriot, Thomas, *A Briefe and True Report of the New Found Land of Virginia*, 68–70, 89
health drinking, 12–13, 14–15, 26–27, 101
Hervey, John, 157–158, 166
Hogarth, William, 170, *171*, *172*, 173
homosexuality, 18, 41–42, 87
homosocial bonding, 29, 38–39, 42, 47, 54–55, 64. *See also* male clubs
hops, 53, 62, 179
Horatian satire, 130. *See also* Juvenalian satire
Hume, David, 139
humoralism. *See* Galenic theory
hybridity, English fears of Indigenous and colonist, 92–95; of tobacco pipes, 104–105

idleness, as a sin, 2, 5; among lower-class laborers, 146, 173; racialized treatments of Native American regarding, 85–86; tobacco smoking as, 6, 10, 85, 89, 96, 101, 105. *See also* gluttony; lust; drinking, sinful pride in
importation, 3, 9, 28, 50, 68, 91; balance of trade and, 138; of clay pipes, 102–104; of French brandy, 137, 148, 152, 163; limiting of, 37; merchants and, 143; of pipe tobacco, 65, 70, 72, 85, 148; of snuff, 110, 113–114, 121; taxes on, 16, 138
imported wine, 13, 16, 26, 27–30, 32, 34, 39, 45–46, 56, 58, 148. *See also* foreignness of wine
indentured servants, 72, 75, 77–78, 82, 98, 100
India pale ale, 179
Informers Outwitted: A Tragi-Comical Farce, The, 141, 156, 166–170, 173
Interregnum, 15–16, 53, 71. *See also* Cromwell, Oliver; Parliament
invasion, metaphorical, 111; of Native behavior via tobacco, 91, 94; of snuff, 122, 127–128

James I, 4, 67, 86; *Counterblaste to Tobacco*, 69–70, 75, 88–90, 95–96, 103. *See also* under licensing
James II, 49, 72
Johnson, Samuel, 177–178, 193n2

juniper berries, gin ingredient of, 137–138, 144, 192n29
Juvenalian satire, 41, 50, 97–98, 107, 110, 128, 130. *See also* Horatian satire

King, George, 59

laissez-faire, 36, 146. *See also* capitalism; free market; physiocracy
landed gentry, 22–23, 82, 153, 157. *See also* loss of aristocratic power
libertine: characters, 13, 19, 21–22, 28, 34, 148–149; court life, 14, 17, 32; ethos, 24, 27, 34, 148–149; masculinity, 17, 20–21, 23–24, 31, 35; sexuality, 31; sexual violence, 34–35; wine drinking, 28–30, 34; writers, 9, 13, 17–19, 31. *See also* female libertine; upper-class male privilege
licensing: of breweries, 52–53; of gin, 157–158, 161–162, 170. *See also* Gin Acts
Lillie, Charles, 111, 117–119, 124, 127, 129; *The British Perfumer, Snuff-Manufacturer, and Colourman's Guide*, 113–114
Lintot, Bernard, 190n23
liquor. *See* brandy; gin; rum
loss of aristocratic power, 81–82, 84, 149, 155, 157–158
lower-class luxury, gin as, 140, 144–147, 149–150, 152–153, 157, 173–175
Ludington, Charles, 15–16, 28, 32, 43, 60
lust, sin of, 5, 142; tobacco as infused with Indigenous desires of, 6, 10, 67, 70, 72, 89–91, 94
luxuriousness, 2, 5–6; as consumer pride, 2, 5–6, 19, 121, 129, 140, 163, 173. *See also* vanity
luxury, 3, 6, 122, 128–130, 133; early modern concept of, 139–140; as economically beneficial, 142–143, 173; wine as, 9–10, 13, 16, 39, 43, 56. *See also* lower-class luxury

male clubs, 41–47, 87–88, 188n43
Mandeville, Bernard, 4, 11, 153–157, 165, 173, 175, 191n18; *The Fable of the Bees*, 139–150; *The Grumbling Hive; or, Knaves Turn'd Honest*, 142; *A Treatise of the Hypochondriack and Hysterick Passions*, 144
manhood. *See* masculinity
manufacturing, 43, 113–114, 137, 193n2
market women, 160–161, 164–168, 171
marriage market, 19–21, 74, 77, 82–84, 94–95, 108

[206]

INDEX

Mary II, 49, 59, 72
masculinity: alehouse impact on, 47; deviation from heteronormative, 29–30, 41–42; libertine, 17, 19–24, 27, 35; lower-class, 164–165; middle-class, 38–39, 41; upper-class, 10, 24, 110, 122, 126; wine's negative effect on, 54, 58. *See also* libertine
materiality, 3, 7–8, 67–68, 152
meals, 4, 7, 40, 102. *See also* food
medical discourse, 109, 110, 131, 144. *See also* medicinal uses of alcohol; medicinal uses of tobacco
medicinal uses of alcohol, 144, 150, 154–155, 162, 167, 175, 192n29. *See also* medical discourse
medicinal uses of tobacco, 66, 68–69, 88–90, 92, 131–132. *See also* Harriot, Thomas; medical discourse
mercantilism, tenets of, 4, 11, 37, 139, 146
mercantilist thinking: class issues associated with, 146; imagery of gold bullion, 46; mercantilist policies, 43; nontraditional views in Mandeville, 139–143; rejection of imported wine, 38–41, 48, 64. *See also* balance of trade; trade deficit
middle class: consumerism, 10, 39; wealth, 14, 38, 45, 56, 63–64, 148
Middlesex Quarter Sessions of 1725, The, 156, 161
Millar, John, 139
money, imagery, 27–28, 31–34, 46
monopoly, 52–53
motherhood, 158–160, 171–175. *See also* fetal alcohol syndrome
mouth tobacco. *See* chewing tobacco

Native American origins, theories of, 95, 99–100
Native American tobacco rituals, treated as demonic, 2, 67, 69, 88, 91–93, 102–103
necessities: gin for lower-class productivity, 160, 163, 166–167, 170; wine for aristocratic masculinity, 19, 27, 30, 35
Nicholls, James, 5, 14, 43, 146
nineteenth-century prohibitionists, 16
Nine-Years War, the, 49, 56, 60, 72, 137
Nokes, David, 147

Oates, Titus, 42–43
ordinary. *See* alehouses and inns
Owen, Susan J., 13, 34

Paradice of Pleasure: Or, an Encomium upon Darby-Ale, The, 38, 45–48, 55
Parliament: acts combating gin, 139, 153, 156–157, 161–164, 167, 170, 175, 193n45; alcohol policies during Interregnum, 15–16; alcohol taxation to fund monarchs, 17, 49; and Charles I, 71; members of landed gentry, 138; trade deficit with France, 13, 28, 43–44. *See also* Acts of Navigation of 1651, The
Pepys, Samuel, 12–15, 192n29
Petty, William, 159
Philaretes, *Work for Chimny-sweepers: Or a Warning for Tabacconists*, 69, 90, 93
physiocracy, 139
policing, 157, 161, 164, 167, 170, 174–175. *See also* Bow Street Runners; Gin Acts; gin informers
political arithmetic, 146, 158–160, 173–174
Pope, Alexander, 9, 63; *The Dunciad*, 59, 186n26; *Peri Bathous, or the Art of Sinking in Poetry*, 186n26; *The Rape of the Lock*, 6, 10, 110–111, 118, 122–128, 130, 190n23
Popish Plot, The, 42–44
Porter, Roy, 4–5, 144
porter beer, 25, 179
port wine, 10, 16, 25, 51, 54, 56, 60, 179
pro-gin narratives, 145–146, 160–168. *See also* anti-gin narratives; Gin Acts
prostitution: in *The Beggar's Opera*, 149–152; in libertine poetry, 17–19; in Restoration comedies, 25–27, 31–34; tobacco personified as foreign prostitute, 90–91
publicans, 54, 157, 167–170. *See also* alehouses and inns; licensing; taverns
punch, 51, 75, 77–78, 80–82, 101, 151, 168. *See also* brandy; gin; rum

Queen Anne's War, 72
Quesnay, François, 139

racialized bigotry against Native Americans, 2, 67, 86, 88–91, 93–95. *See also* lust; skin color difference
Raleigh, Walter, 65, 68
rape, threats of: connected to libertine wine drinking, 33–34; in parliamentary propaganda, 15; in racially-bigoted writing, 91–92, 94–95. *See also* libertine; upper-class male privilege
Ravenscroft, Edward, 17; *The Careless Lovers*, 9, 13, 24–27

[207]

INDEX

Regency period, the, 178
Rhenish wine, 10, 29, 41
riots: related to tobacco policy, 71; response to gin informers, 157
Rogers, Pat, 147
Rolfe, John, 65, 70
Romanticism Movement, The, 178
Royal College of Physicians, 153
royalism: associations with sexual violence, 15, 34; associations with wine, 15–16, 30–31, 43, 148, 151
Royal Society, the, 109, 118
rum, 75, 77–78, 82, 89, 101, 151

sack. *See* canary wine
savagery, of Native Americans, 2, 67, 92, 94; of Africans, 93; of American colonists, 10, 67, 95–97, 99–100, 105–107; of tobacco pipe, 104–105. *See also* hybridity; lust; Native American tobacco rituals; racialized bigotry against Native Americans
scatological imagery, 44, 58, 87, 131–134
Scroope, Car, 29
sexually transmitted diseases, 25, 87; compared to Indigenous tobacco use, 90, 92
Shakespeare, William, *Othello*, 93
shippable containers: barrels, 23–24, 50, 113, 171; canisters of snuff, 113; casks, 24–25, 105, 113; hogsheads, 50; puncheons, kilderkins, firkins, 50; quarts, 50; tuns, 7, 23, 50
shop keeping, 85, 117–119, 149, 164–168, 191n16, 193n45. *See also* alehouses and inns; publicans; taverns; vintners
sinking fund, the, 3, 153
skin color difference, theories of, 67, 91–95, 98–10. *See also* Africans; Native American origins
small beer, 55, 58
Smith, Adam, *Wealth of Nations*, 4, 36–37, 54, 139, 173
smuggling, 71, 138, 148, 168
sneezing, 109, 122, 126–127
snuffboxes: conversational usage, 111, 114, 118–119, 121, 123–125; featuring pornographic images, 135; foppishness associated with, 118, 190n20; luxuriousness of, 111–*112*, 114, 123, 190n20
social distinctions, lack of, 6, 129–130, 142, 145–147. *See also* class interactions; loss of aristocratic power; upper-class male privilege

Society for the Reformation of Manners, the, 1–2, 5–6, 141, 147, 188n43
South Sea Event, the, 147, 153
Spanish wine. *See* canary wine
Spooner, Lawrence, 10, 67, 72, 86, 98, 100, 107; *A Looking-Glass for Smoakers*, 89; *Poetical Recreations: Or Pleasant Remarks on the Various Rumours*, 89–96
Steele, Richard, 113, 123–126, 128, 135; *The Spectator*, 10, 110–111, 118–122, 130, 190n15; *The Tatler*, 10, 110–111, 114–120, 130
sugar, 73, 75
Swift, Jonathan, 9, 128; *Gulliver's Travels*, 88; *The Lady's Dressing Room*, 11, 111, 131–135, 191n30

tariffs, 37, 43. *See also* trade wars; embargoes; balance of trade
Tavern Hunter; Or, a Drunken Ramble from the Crown to the Devil, The, 38, 54–60, 63, 186n25
taverns: amenities provided in, 7, 14, 39; differences from alehouses and inns, 14; diversity of spirits in, 150; keepers of, 40, 56–60, 78, 157, 168; as sites of business dealings, 7, 14, 37, 54, 56, 80–81; as sites of homosocial bonding, 54
tea, 6, 123
tobacco cultivation, 73, 79, 81, 101–102
Tories, 13, 43, 60–61, 81
Townsend, Charles, 192n33
trade deficit, 28, 138. *See also* balance of trade
trade wars, 36. *See also* embargoes; tariffs
Turgot, Anne-Robert-Jacques, 139

upper-class male privilege, 9, 17–19, 28, 30, 34–35; middle-class desire for, 24. *See also* libertine; loss of aristocratic power

vanity, 6, 29, 110, 131; associated with commercial luxuries, 129, 142–143, 156; excessive upper-class spending styled as, 173
vintners: as greedy, 2, 39–40, 50; as lower-level merchants, 23; as tavern owners, 48, 60; as wine makers, 16. *See also* publicans; taverns

Wall, Cynthia, 118, 122, 124, 190n23
Walpole, Robert, 4, 11, 163; critiques on his corruption and proto-capitalistic methods, 141, 152–155, 169–170,

192n33; position on gin, 9, 153, 156–157, 160–161; rise to power, 147
Ward, Ned, 10, 37, 67, 72, 96–98, 101, 107, 186nn25–26, 188n43; *The Hudibrastick Brewer; Or, a Prosperous Union between Malt and Meter*, 38, 55, 59–63; *The London-Spy*, 84–85; *The Secret History of the Calves-Head Clubb, or, the Republican Unmasqu'd*, 87; *The Secret History of Clubs*, 85, 87–89; *Sot's Paradise, or, the Humours of a Derby-Ale-House with a Satyr upon the Ale*, 45, 48; *A Trip to Jamaica: With a True Character of the People and Island*, 86; *A Trip to New-England with a Character of the Country and People*, 85–87
Warner, Jessica, 5, 6, 137–139, 153, 158, 167, 170, 191n10
War of the Austrian Succession, The, 170
Whigs, 60–61
Whipping Tom attacks, the, 128–129, 190n27
Whipping Tom: Or, a Rod for a Proud Lady, 11, 110, 128–132, 135
Whiston, William, *An Exposition of the Curse upon Cain and Lamech: Shewing that the Present Africans and Indians Are Their Posterity*, 99–100

widowhood, 77, 82–84. *See also* femininity
Wilkes, Wetenhall. *A Letter of Genteel and Moral Advice to a Young Lady*, 114
William III, 1, 53, 59, 96, 137–138; gin's introduction to England, 137–138; involvement in war, 9, 49–50, 72
Wilmot, John, 9, 13–14, 17–20, 24, 27, 31, 34, 45, 53, 56, 184n19
Wilson, Thomas, *Spirituous Liquors the Bane of the Nation*, 150, 158–160, 173–175, 192n22
women consuming alcohol: communally with other women, 151, 161, 164–166; with their husbands, 12–13; Mrs. Trapes with her male counterparts, 152, 154; prostitutes with men, 25–27, 149–151
women gin sellers, 158, 168. *See also* femininity; women consuming alcohol
women snuff takers, 114, 116–117, 120–121, 130–131
women tobacco smokers, 66, 82–84, 87, 94–95
Wordsworth, William, 178
Wycherley, William, 17; *The Country Wife*, 19; *The Gentleman Dancing-Master*, 9, 13, 17, 19–24, 27, 185n28; *The Plain-Dealer*, 19

ABOUT THE AUTHOR

DAYNE C. RILEY is assistant director of the Oklahoma Center for the Humanities at the University of Tulsa, where he organizes public humanities exhibitions and events. He lives in Tulsa with his wife and dogs.